"*Warrior* is a powerful remir
daily encounter with the Cro
spiritual war."

Chris Hodges

Lead Pastor, Church of th

"This book is what I'm screaming for men to hear, but even more importantly, challenging them to do something about!"

Rick Burgess

Co-Host, Rick & Bubba Show

"*Warrior* is an intense and timely rallying cry for men to return to the fundamentals of fighting for what matters."

Gus Malzahn

Head Football Coach, Auburn University

"Whether we admit it not, there is an unrelenting spiritual battle taking place around us. It is critical to align every part of ourselves with the truth of God's Word so that we can succeed and lead as husbands and fathers. In *Warrior*, Lance provides powerful and practical tools that I can easily understand and apply to my life. If you want to be better equipped for the battle, this book is a powerful and valuable resource."

Wes Hampton

Vocalist, Gaither Vocal Band

"*Warrior* is an excellent resource for men looking to find real peace and purpose. It is strategically structured to deliver a thorough, Biblical checkup of every area in a man's life to ensure spiritual victory."

Layne Schranz

Associate Pastor, Church of the Highlands; 2016 Pikes Peak International Hill Climb Champion

"Now more than ever before, our society needs men of God who will rise up in the face of the status quo. Men who will fight for their faith, their families, and for the culture around them. Men who answer the call to live for more than what is just handed to them. *Warrior* is an honest and empowering road map to becoming that man. I am thrilled to see this timely book change the hearts and minds of men at such a crucial moment in history!"

John Larson
Worship Pastor, Church of the Highlands

"Timing is everything, and *Warrior* is coming at a time when men need to be challenged in a new way. The challenge is here in this book! This message will grip men in a way that motivates them to lead their families, lead their communities, and lead a life that God has called them to live as men of God. After reading *Warrior*, you will be inspired and enlightened on practical ways to combat everyday hardships that you never thought you could overcome. You can and you will! Read this book!"

CJ Blount
Worship Pastor, Church of the Highlands

"I am living proof of how buying into these *Warrior* principles can transform a man. After 31 years of drifting through life, I finally surrendered every area of my life to Jesus, allowing Him to purify me both spiritually and physically. Now here I am with an indescribable peace, having lost over 100 pounds in under a year, with the woman of my dreams soon to be my wife. It is undoubtedly the result of fighting to align my life with God's purpose!"

Drew Wright
Physician, Birmingham, Alabama

WARRIOR

Equipping Men for Spiritual Victory

LANCE INGRAM

Warrior Publishing

Warrior: Equipping Men for Spiritual Victory

First edition, fourth print published by Warrior United, a part of Ingram Image. Visit us online at warriorunited.com.

Edited by Kristie Garner and Burr Ingram

Cover design by Warrior United.

Library of Congress Control Number: 2017901839

ISBN: 978-1-63587453-2

AUTHOR

"I just want men to encounter Jesus."
- Lance Ingram

Lance Ingram has served as a core musician at one of the largest churches in the country, Church of the Highlands in Birmingham, Alabama, leading tens of thousands into the presence of God behind Pastor Chris Hodges and Highlands Worship on a weekly basis since 2009. These supernatural encounters behind the drum kit have inspired Lance's dynamic passion for men to know Jesus and obey Jesus so they can experience true peace and purpose in every area of their lives.

"Those who listen to our show know Lance Ingram has a very clever sense of humor, as evidenced by his 'Dr. Lou' character. But what people might not know is Lance is a man of God who knows and lives the Scriptures."

- RICK BURGESS

Many may recognize Lance as radio personality "Dr. Lou" from the nationally syndicated *Rick & Bubba Show*, which reaches more than a million listeners daily. He has been featured on *Sports Illustrated's si.com* for his clever college football satire on the wildly popular comedy program based in Birmingham, Alabama.

Lance is a successful entrepreneur, operating his marketing and web technologies small business since 2008. He is a communications graduate from Auburn University having followed in the footsteps of his grandfather, Bob Ingram, a well-known political editor and newspaper columnist in the state of Alabama.

Lance and his wife, Brooke, have two children.

CONTENTS

FOREWORD

I was standing on the stage of my home church in Birmingham, Alabama, minutes after burying my youngest son's body at a graveside service. I wasn't even sure I was going to be able to speak at all for this memorial service for a little boy who had only lived two and a half years on earth, but I was already being used by God to impact many for His Kingdom. I had nothing planned to say; I just knew God was going to say something. As my eyes scanned the audience, I looked at my beautiful, Godly wife so powerful as she sat there praising God and obedient to His will over her will. Then, I looked at my four children, and these words came out of my mouth as they were inspired by the Holy Spirit: "We will no longer judge whether we are successful by the world's standards. I just want you all to be warriors for Christ. That's it. If you will commit to being warriors for Christ, then your life will be successful regardless of how the world may judge your success. That's the goal of this family as we go forward – to just be warriors for Christ."

I think if you have taken the time to pick up this book, then you have taken the first step. You desire to be a warrior for Christ. The good news is this book has been inspired by the Holy Spirit, and it will give you the instructions on how this looks in your everyday life. Survey after survey has been done by all sorts of resources, and the conclusion has been the same every time. God designed men and women equally, but not the same. As my wife would say looking back on that horrible night in the Children's Hospital emergency room when everyone was trying to comfort her, our family, our friends, and even members of the church staff, including our pastor, "They all knew that they could not be my husband. They all knew that they could not be our children's father. We waited on Rick to arrive because no one could replace him."

I think one of the lies that the adversary has perpetuated throughout this fallen creation is that someone else can do the job of spiritual leadership in the church, the home, and society – the lie that men are disposable and are no more important than any other force. The only problem with this logic is that it's a lie. All research points to the man as being the most influential force in all three of these areas, and he cannot be replaced. I began to share this truth every time I was honored to speak at a church, and I would ask the pastor about the health of the men's ministry of their church. Almost every time their countenance would change, their eyes would go downcast, and they would shake their heads. Why?

I asked many of them if they were taught that as men you cater to women and children, and then you plan on just being part of the family that joins? Unofficially, they all felt they had been taught that strategy. The only problem with this approach is that it isn't Biblical! If you want a man to solidify himself in the church, you speak to a man in his language. You intentionally plan on discipling him, and then he will bring his family in solidifying the family and himself in the church.

Lance Ingram has taken the time and effort to seek God's voice for the men of our society, and to speak to men in our language. He has, in great detail, mapped out a game plan to be a warrior for Christ. And not just in some areas of your life, but in all areas of your life. I challenge you to dive in seeking God's will for your life. God has always and will always call on the men He created to become the men He says you should be. He has never been silent on this topic. Let's get started.

Rick Burgess
Co-Host of the Rick and Bubba Show

FROM THE AUTHOR

APPROACH

Go into the Warrior experience wanting to be challenged.

This entire study is just a conversation. It's me challenging me. It's me reminding me. It's me gut-checking me. It's me trying to safeguard me from me. And that's the way every one of us needs to approach this: as a personalized call to action to align our habits with our purpose. Let's not go into this looking to be offended. Instead, let's go into this wanting to be challenged.

Pray first.

If we want to experience something supernatural, we need supernatural intervention. And whether we are reading this study by ourselves or meeting with other men to unite in our purpose, the results will be infinitely greater if we just ask God to supernaturally move and reveal to us how we can be more like Him.

Add worship music.

Whether we are reading this by ourselves or discussing it among a group of men, this collection of words immediately becomes more powerful if we add worship music as a background palette. Worship music changes the atmosphere, softens our hearts, and opens our eyes. So, if we want to get the most out of this study, let's set the tone of worship with music that quietly allows us to reflect. We need a setting that brings more *motivation*, not just more *information*. If anyone needs great worship music to supplement this reading experience, check out our Warrior playlists and resources at warriorunited.com.

INTRODUCTION

It's time to unite and fight.

Authentic Christian manhood has become increasingly rare in our world today. It seems many men have lost the fighting spirit for the things of God, which is the very purpose for which we were created. We've become all things to all people and have made our own comfort and pleasure our gods. *Warrior* is a 10-chapter study that is intended to help us recapture who and what God intended us to be: Warriors for Christ and for the things of God. This study is aimed at helping us reconnect with Jesus in every aspect and detail of our lives and discover how He wants to be a part of every little thing we do.

Being a true man of God has never been easy...and it wasn't intended to be that way. It's a daily fight. Whether we like it or not, we are in a war every day, and to ignore that fact is the path to certain defeat. So the question is: how do we set ourselves up for victory in this spiritual war? How do we experience Christ's fulfillment, His abundance, and His victory on a daily basis? It starts with a power that is supernatural, unexplainable, and incomprehensible – the Holy Spirit – given to us through a relationship with Jesus. It continues with a war that we must fight every day, and that's where the rubber meets the road. Jesus spelled it out simply for us in John 14:15 (ESV) when He said, "If you love Me, you will keep My commandments."

We are in a war every day, and to ignore that fact is the path to certain defeat.

The goal of this study is to prepare us for battle, to give us the tools to win the daily fights – which ultimately are the difference between victory and defeat in our spiritual lives. Fighting to be close to Jesus is the example we want to set for our families, our friends, and our world. In that fight, we find our highest purpose, and we experience peace with God and the peace of God. This is the man who leaves a Warrior's legacy.

It's time for us to step up and be the Warriors that God has called us to be!

CHAPTER 1

PREPARING FOR WAR

Victory in the spiritual war begins with knowing how God wired us for war.

Money. Power. Fame. Attention. Sex. Food. Vacations. Parties. Sports. Music. Games. Fashion. Vehicles. We've tried 'em all. And yet here we are again... searching. We really are not even sure what it is we're searching *for*, but there sure as heck must be something better than whatever *these* things have given us. But what if we were created with a purpose in mind? A purpose that gave us true peace? A purpose that brought us contentment? A purpose that kept us motivated? A purpose that inspired us to fight every day? That purpose exists; it's just not found where we've been spending all our time and energy. That purpose is found in a place where we stop feeding our desires and start following God's desires.

We were made for a relationship.

Psalm 107:9 "For He satisfies the longing soul, and the hungry soul He fills with good things." (ESV)

We can search for peace and purpose all we want, but the search will fail until we land in a relationship with Jesus, because it is *the* only thing that will ever satisfy our spirit. We will *never* be truly satisfied outside of the supernatural peace of Jesus. Never. That's because God designed us that way!

A relationship with Jesus provides our peace and reveals our purpose.

Try to fill a diesel engine up with chocolate syrup and see if it will crank. It's not gonna happen. That's because it was designed to run on diesel fuel only. Now what if someone asked us to get that engine running efficiently? What would our first step be? Would we sit there all day and deny that diesel fuel is the only thing that can start that engine? Would we test other substances by pouring them into the engine to see if it might turn over? Or would we follow the instructions that the engineer included and use diesel fuel?

Whether we *believe* Jesus is the only thing that can satisfy our spirit doesn't change the fact that Jesus *is* the only thing that can satisfy our spirit. Our Engineer, God the Father, said so in Psalm 107:9 (ESV) telling us that only *He* "satisfies the longing soul!" God engineered us to be satisfied only by connecting to Him. Then and only then will our engines turn over and function according to our Inventor's intent.

But how in the world do we connect to God and discover this satisfaction? What is the path to experiencing that optimal performance? John 14:6 gives us the answer as God's one and only Son Jesus tells us, "No one can come to the Father except through *Me*." We discover satisfaction when we connect to God, and we connect to God by beginning a relationship with Jesus! That relationship with Jesus – it's our diesel fuel, guys. And when we start operating according to our designer's intention, we will realize He knows what He's talking about. It makes no sense to us until we've seen it in action, but there is an unexplainable, unfathomable power that comes from Jesus' death and resurrection, and it can only be experienced through a relationship with Him. God designed us to run only on that relationship. And when it fuels us, we'll see the purpose in our design!

A lot of us right now are completely miserable. We're tired of searching. We're tired of mediocrity. We're tired of emptiness. And we're tired of not knowing what we're even doing in this life. But it wasn't meant to be this way. There *is* something more, and that something is a relationship with a man named Jesus, who endured the most gruesome killing in the history of the world, and not even *that* could keep Him in the grave!

See, guys – this isn't about religion. It's about a relationship with *the* most remarkable human being that ever walked the face of the Earth. Religion is stale and repulsive, but this relationship is satisfying and refreshing! I used to be the most skeptical of religious cynics, but now I'm the most passionate of relational fanatics...because I've experienced more than church. I've experienced Christ. And I've grasped the enormity of what our Creator did by sending His one and only Son, Jesus, to pay for our nastiest mistakes.

And that's what this entire Warrior study is about – knowing and following this real, living person who is Jesus! I know now with 100% confidence that a relationship with Jesus is *the* one element in my lifetime that has given me an indisputable, indescribable contentment. And don't miss this – that relationship with Jesus has brought peace and purpose to everything *else* in my daily life – family, friends, career, money, passions, possessions. Knowing Jesus unlocks the understanding to everything's purpose.

So how do we begin this relationship with Jesus and discover that peace and purpose? Thankfully, it's incredibly simple. Romans 10:9 says if we just confess with our mouths that "Jesus is Lord" and believe in our hearts that God raised Jesus from the dead, we will be saved! And *that* is step one of this journey to becoming the Warriors that God has called us to be. When we begin a relationship with Jesus, we acknowledge that the Creator knows the most about His creation. And with that admission, we discover the truth – that we are *satisfied* only through a relationship with Jesus, and we are *fueled* to fulfill our purpose only through a relationship with Jesus.

Let's follow our Creator's instructions and go on this Warrior journey together. I'm *guaranteeing* it will be the most rewarding decision of your life.

A relationship with Jesus is our motivation in the fight for obedience.

A relationship with Jesus brings the peace and purpose that our Creator intended, but that's just the beginning. Once we cultivate that relationship, we find out that Jesus only asks one thing of us. Just one thing – to do things *His* way! In John 14:15 (ESV), Jesus said, "If you love Me, you will keep My commandments." Jesus spells it out clearly and leaves little room for misunderstanding, guys. A real love for Him results in obedience! And this is what *Warrior* is all about – fighting to know Jesus and fighting to intentionally align every meticulous detail to His manual. And it is indeed a fight! Galatians 5:17 talks about this war and how "the sinful nature wants to do evil, which is just the opposite of what the Spirit wants." It goes on to say that "these two forces are constantly fighting against each other so that [we] are not free to carry out [our] good intentions." The war exists, and every approach will lead to defeat...except for knowing Jesus.

Men – a relationship with Jesus is the source of our emergence as Warriors, generating both the *desire* and the *power* to fight for Biblical obedience. Without that relationship fueling us, we'll have zero motivation to do what God engineered us to do. That's where far too many of us are right now… we have no relationship, so we have no desire to fight! And we can't win a war without having a motivation to fight.

In order for us to get that motivation, we must go to the ultimate Motivator – a *man's man* who died a brutal death for each one of us. A man who is such a beast that He delivered the ultimate smack down on the enemy and straight up dominated death in the process! A man who Revelation 1:18 tells us robbed the tomb of its power and now "hold[s] the keys of death and the grave!" His name is Jesus! And He decisively won the most crucial war in history even while He was dead! There is nothing more motivating than that. Jesus is a man who is stronger *dead* than Satan is *alive!* It satisfies my soul as a man when I think of how ridiculously tough and powerful our Savior is! Warriors – we serve the greatest superhero of all time! And *that* is some motivation to fight for obedience!

We need the Holy Spirit.

Micah 3:8 "But as for me, I am filled with power – with the Spirit of the Lord."

This relationship with Jesus…it's not boring, guys. Or at least it shouldn't be! And if it invokes no emotion, no gratefulness, no excitement, no energy, then we haven't tapped into the most powerful gift that God gave us for life here on Earth – His Holy Spirit! Everybody freak out now because we just mentioned the phrase "Holy Spirit!" Sadly, it's a term that carries a negative, and oftentimes strange, stigma in culture. We've disregarded this part of God's Trinity – the Father, the Son, and the Holy Spirit – because it's the part we can't wrap our minds around. We can talk about the Father and the Son, but we don't want anything to do with some mysterious spirit that we can't envision! Unfortunately, we're eliminating the most enjoyable part of our everyday relationship with Jesus!

The Holy Spirit empowers our spirit.

Guys – the Holy Spirit is the vehicle that allows us to *feel* Jesus' supernatural power here on Earth. It isn't a creepy ghost who follows us or some fist to the head that knocks us down during church services. The Holy Spirit is a peaceful presence who empowers us! Let's just be real for a moment and say what we're all thinking: "The Holy Spirit logically makes no sense to us!" We can try to comprehend or describe it all we want, but it's something that can only be experienced! And in order to experience the indescribable peace and power of the Holy Spirit, all we have to do is have faith that it's real and ask God to show us! It's that simple.

But a fair warning: Warriors – once we experience it, we'll have an epiphany. Everything clicks...in a good way. It defies logic and surpasses human comprehension. Philippians 4:7 confirms my experience with the Holy Spirit saying, "God's peace...exceeds anything we can understand." It's pointless trying to put it into words, so I will stop. When we ask God for His Holy Spirit, it is far from creepy, strange, or off-putting. In fact, there's no greater feeling than when God's presence is around us. I'm just going to tell it like it is: We all want to feel the way the Holy Spirit makes us feel. Period. I guarantee that if you could have one day when you experience what it feels like to have the Holy Spirit's peace and presence over you, it would trump any other thrill or emotional satisfaction you've experienced.

The Holy Spirit is our fuel in the fight for obedience.

Guys – it is impossible and exhausting to obey God's Word through pure human effort. There is zero chance we will win the war and experience the peace we're all looking for if we don't have the Holy Spirit to give us the power to obey. In fact, God specifically gave us His Holy Spirit so it would be possible for us *to* obey. If we were relating it to watching a football game, the Holy Spirit is our coach, star player, helmet, pads, playbook, and hydration wrapped into one! He is the presence that leads, inspires, empowers, protects, directs, energizes, and ultimately dominates our spiritual opponent! And guys – we can't win without His presence.

We were wired for war.

Ephesians 6:13 "Therefore, put on every piece of God's armor so you will be able to resist the enemy in the time of evil. Then after the battle you will be standing firm."

We can try to ignore any truth we choose, but it won't make it untrue. And the truth is there's a spiritual war going on at this very moment for your thoughts as well as mine. We already read about that war in Galatians 5:17 and how those two forces – the flesh and the spirit – are constantly battling each other to control our minds. Ignoring this reality inevitably means our spirit is already defeated.

A war exists that challenges our spirit every moment of every day.

In the context of our football analogy, if a game has been scheduled between our team and our toughest opponent, and we choose not to show up, that's a guaranteed loss for our team. It's called a forfeit, and unfortunately that's where a lot of men are today spiritually. Our opponent is deceptively smart and intimidatingly strong. The environment on the battlefield is uncomfortably hot and humid. Not to mention, things can get challenging, even painful at times, when we get up and fight for our team. We elect to sit out instead. After all, it's just easier to ignore the battle entirely! And that's inherently the problem...here we are in the only war that matters, and we're sitting out because it's hard to fight. It's inconvenient to fight. Meanwhile, God has given us the assignment in Colossians 3:2 (NIV) urging us to "set [our] minds on things above, not on earthly things." But we aren't concerned with that. We'd rather forfeit.

Let's be real. It is a brutal challenge for us to set our minds on things that are unseen, because there are so many things that we *can* see that are *distracting* us! Those are "earthly things," and it takes a relentlessly dedicated effort to be steadily focused on the "things above." We're talking incessant monitoring and filtration. And this isn't for the faint of heart. That's *exactly* why there are so few Warriors on the field of spiritual battle. The assignment is waiting. And that assignment might be overwhelming at times, but God made us for this war! Luke 10:19 says, "Look, I have given you authority over all the power of the enemy, and you can walk among snakes and scorpions and crush them. Nothing will injure you." That pumps me up! It makes me want to let out my manliest roar and go rough somebody up! The Creator of the Universe, who holds all power and truth in His words, just said, "Men – I'm giving you authority to *crush* the enemy, and by the way – *nothing* can hurt you." That is some *serious* authority!

Men – it's time to quit relaxing and be alert. It's time to unite and engage in violent, spiritual combat to take back the identity of the Warriors we were created to be! It's time for us to raise the banner of victory over the enemy and stop living for our selfish cravings and addictions! It's time to start shouting the motto of 2 Corinthians 10:5 and skewer every thought as it enters our minds to make sure it pleases God! It's time to quit settling for worldly comfort and embrace the discomfort our flesh feels when we deny ourselves of earthly pleasures! This is what we are wired to do, and when we do it, we come alive in a way we never thought possible!

The war demands our commitment to fight for obedience.

Fighting this war for obedience is anything but easy. It takes an unyielding, unrelenting commitment. And that commitment is unwavering and immovable. It is unaffected by circumstances. It is unselfish. It is unglamorous. It is the epitome of loyalty. It is consistent and unwilling to compromise under pressure. And it is the vessel by which God makes us Warriors. Commitment is absent from Christian manhood today. And soon it will be extinct if we don't make a concrete decision that we will stand firm in the fight for obedience as Ephesians 6:13 says! Warriors – let's bring commitment back to the front lines of battle.

We were created for excellence.

Daniel 6:3 "Daniel was preferred...because an excellent spirit was in him." (KJV)

Our world has redefined what a man is, portraying us as lazy, lukewarm, dishonest, inconsistent, apathetic, feminine, filthy...you fill in the blank. Society has reduced us to these animalistic beings that exist only for our own hedonistic pleasures. And sadly, we've bought into this pathetic lie of mere existence and mediocrity. If given the choice between excellence and comfort, we'll choose comfort any day of the week. Comfort is why we exist, and that's why excellence has become extinct...because God forbid we experience some discomfort!

Excellence is painful, but it maximizes our potential.

Excellence requires discipline, and discipline brings pain. The Bible says so. Hebrews 12:11 acknowledges that "no discipline is enjoyable while it's happening," and that "it's painful." We're going to reference this verse frequently in our journey to become Warriors because there's pain on the path to excellence! And there's no shortcut! Warriors – excellence is marked by attention to even the finest detail, and it's achieved through a painful discipline that will often exhaust 100% of our effort. And this is woefully uncommon among men because most of us dread discipline and fear pain when God intended for us to embrace them. Relating this to our football analogy – excellence emerges in the last round of sprints during two-a-day practices during the most unbearably hot summer day. During the moment when no one is watching, our legs are burning, our breathing is labored, and we feel like the circumstances are so overwhelming that we can't possibly give another ounce of effort, we find a way to set ourselves apart from the others and do what we are asked to do. It is mentally the toughest thing we do, but it's the introductory point for God's abundance.

Excellence is our focus in the fight for obedience.

Excellence is defined by *complete* alignment with God's way. It isn't partial. It isn't most. It is whole, and it is thorough. And excellence allows God to utilize us to the fullest. And when we minimize our attachment to "earthly things," we maximize our purpose for the "things above." Excellence optimizes potential. We see that in Daniel 6:3 (KJV) where Daniel was "preferred above the presidents and princes, because an excellent spirit was in him." Warriors – God wants to escalate us to greater places, positions, and purposes, but He's waiting on our complete alignment. In essence, our excellence is the permission God needs before He will enlarge our territory and increase our impact.

When we hold onto any thought, habit, or pleasure that is even the slightest bit out of line with God's Word, we relinquish the ability to be used to our greatest potential. God knows how detrimental sin is to our usefulness, and that's why He tells us to flee it. Not just some of it...but all of it. And this difference between "some" and "all" defines the toughest part of being a Warrior. When the "all" becomes our fixation, we become true Warriors. Because even if we have an intimate relationship with Jesus, are filled by the Holy Spirit's power, and are committed to the fight – there will *still* be times when it is hard to make the right choices...because the world is enticingly overwhelming at times. But those moments are when our willful focus on excellence helps us make the right choice and follow the Holy Spirit's lead to flee temptation.

We are encouraged throughout God's Word to be proactive about excellence. In Hebrews 12:1, we are urged to "strip off" *every* sin that trips us up. Then in Galatians 5:16, we are instructed to "let" the Holy Spirit guide our lives so that we won't do what our sinful nature craves. Notice how these verses use verbs that require *our* action, not God's. Only we have the power to "strip off" every sin, and only we have the ability to "let" the Holy Spirit guide our lives. God can do everything for us except make the choice. That's what free will is. And without excellence as our focus and knowing that our choices have impact, we will inevitably use our free will to choose the comfortable option that satisfies self. We need to be reminded that our choices matter, and it's with right choice after right choice that we cultivate excellence. That's when we will experience victory in the spiritual war and a tangible increase of peace and purpose. And to be honest, I'm just tired of giving up true peace and purpose for momentary pleasures that leave me miserable the rest of the time. I'm tired of floating through life and blending in with culture. I'm tired of watching our generation of men put one hand in earthly things and the other hand in the things above. I'm ready to transcend the status quo, and if it requires some pain, so be it!

SUMMARY

+ God made us to be satisfied only by a relationship with Jesus, which is our motivation to fight the spiritual battle.

+ God designed us to be empowered only by the Holy Spirit, which serves as our fuel to fight the spiritual battle.

+ God wired us for war, but the war demands our commitment to be victorious in the fight.

+ God wired us for excellence, and excellence must be our focus to be victorious in the fight.

RESPONSE

God, thank You for wiring me the way that You did. I may try to find satisfaction in the world, but I recognize that You didn't design me to be fulfilled by earthly things. And only through a relationship with Your Son, Jesus, can I experience the peace and the purpose You uniquely placed on my life.

I may not completely understand what a real relationship with You looks like yet, but I choose to believe that Your Holy Spirit is real and it gives me access to a supernatural peace and power that leads me to be a Warrior and fight for Your purpose.

And Lord, although I might not fully comprehend the concept of a spiritual war, I do acknowledge that there are countless choices every day that have massive impact on my life and the lives of others. God, I need Your unmatchable, unexplainable power to fulfill me so I can position myself for daily victory in the spiritual war.

I want to get to a place of commitment and excellence, but I need Your help. Jesus, begin moving my spirit right now so I can become the Warrior You created me to be.

CHAPTER 2

THE WARRIOR MENTALITY

Assuming a Warrior's mentality is critical to victory in the spiritual war.

We're in a cutthroat spiritual war, and we don't win that war on accident. It takes planning and strategy. And it takes an uncommon mentality. But if we win the battle in between our ears, the victory on the battlefield will certainly ensue. And vice versa. If we lose the battle in our minds, we'll get destroyed on the battlefield.

Men – let's begin to *think* like Warriors as we prepare for victory!

This world cannot satisfy me.

1 John 2:15 "Do not love this world nor the things it offers you, for when you love the world, you do not have the love of the Father in you."

A Warrior mentality takes doing what isn't easy and coming to grips with a reality that many of us just don't want to face – the reality that this world will *never* satisfy us. It takes remarkable maturity to say, "Hey, I'm okay with the fact that nothing on this Earth will truly satisfy me," because it forces us to live for something we haven't ever actually seen with our eyes. It's a depressing reality for most men, and probably the main reason we avoid talking about it altogether! We'd rather just make the most of our time here on Earth moving from one pleasure to the next rather than cope with the truth. Guys – it's uncomfortable to deal with the fact that our spirit can only be satisfied by Jesus. In fact, our flesh hates it. And the declaration alone demands a funeral for our selfish desires forcing us to grieve its death. That's something that most men have zero desire to do...which explains the desolation on the battlefield.

We're still loving the world in hopes that one day it will give us some lasting contentment. And it won't. Ever.

Then why is it that we continuously try to find identity and satisfaction through worldly things? Why is it always the next event, the next milestone, the next purchase, or the next thrill that gets us through every day? It's always what's "next" that gives us reason to be excited. 1 John 2:15 warns us about falling in love with the world and tells us that love for God and love for the world can't coexist: "When you love the world, you do not have the love of the Father in you." I'm convinced that a lot of us are there. We get up thinking about worldly things. We go to bed thinking about worldly things. Worldly things motivate our existence. They have surpassed sources of enjoyment. They're now *obsessions*. Let's just call it like it is. They're now *gods*.

It's time for us to stop flippantly writing these gods off as "passions." Look, there's absolutely nothing wrong with enjoying the slices of life...the relationships, the hobbies, even the possessions. But there's a point at which our enjoyment becomes worship, and those worldly things, slowly but surely, *consume* our thoughts, our time, and our energy. Then one day we take a step back and realize Jesus isn't even *on* our radar. This isn't new news. It has actually happened for thousands of years. In 2 Kings 17:15, the Israelites dealt with this same issue. It says they "worshiped worthless idols, so they became worthless themselves." Guys – what we think will satisfy us steals from us, and when we worship worthless things, it makes *us* worthless.

And the irony is – these idols are not giving us any lasting satisfaction anyway! Seriously. What are we even doing? We invest so much into our sports, social lives, jobs, money, cars, houses, food, and comforts...and yet we're so unhappy. And if we're not unhappy, we will be soon. Hebrews 11:25 reminds us that sin is only enjoyable for a season! Let's stop settling for mediocrity, guys. Don't we want the best there is even in this life? It's like we're filling up our stomachs with dog food thinking, "This is as good as it gets." Meanwhile, God's got a delicious filet mignon cooked to perfection that He's ready to serve us. The problem is we don't want to give up our doggie bowl to try it out.

Only Jesus can satisfy me.

Knowing Jesus gives me a more abundant life now.

John 10:10 "...I came that they may have life and have it abundantly." (ESV)

A Warrior knows that worldly things are not for him. And a Warrior knows that true satisfaction is only experienced through a relationship with Jesus. This mindset is what leads us to the "abundant life" described in John 10:10. Jesus didn't just come to give us a more secure later. He came to give us a more satisfying now! When we know Jesus, we experience supernatural peace and purpose that is marked by passion, direction, order, energy, excitement, clarity, motivation, and meaning in every area of our lives. Simply said – when we know Jesus, our lives make sense. He is truly the source of unexplainable contentment.

Now I know that some of us are probably confused and even deterred by the church phrase "knowing Jesus." And I'm totally with you! What does that even mean? Well, we're going to talk specifics of what "knowing Jesus" actually looks like a little bit later, but for now, let's keep pounding the truth in our heads – that only Jesus can bring lasting, substantial satisfaction in this life.

Knowing Jesus gives me an eternal life in Heaven later.

John 17:3 "And this is the way to have eternal life – to know You, the only true God, and Jesus Christ, the one You sent to earth."

As great as it is to focus on the benefits here on Earth, let's not miss the greatest gift and miracle of all – the eternal life that Jesus gave us through His life, death, and resurrection! Even the abundance of *this* life pales in comparison to the assurance of eternal life in Heaven. Unfortunately, most Christians have this inaccurate, unappealing stigma tied to the phrase "eternal life" as if Heaven will involve robes and ritualistic liturgy...and that's not even close! Our misperception of Heaven is the very reason why we rarely look forward to getting there! So many of us *say* that we look forward to Heaven, but seriously – *do* we? It's time to start treating Heaven like the truly luxurious, enjoyable lifestyle that it's going to be!

I don't think we've grasped the vision of Heaven. Just think about this. Crystal clear water. Solid gold streets. Sapphire and emerald walls. Just let that sink in for a minute. It is luxury redefined! And it will outdo even the most pristine Caribbean vacation destination we've seen or experienced! But that's not even the best part. How about unlimited VIP access to the greatest superhero of all time – a real man who faced all the overwhelming temptations we face, but never sinned. And even though He was sinless, He still took the worst beating in history because He didn't want us to have to endure being bloodied and beaten to a pulp like He was.

But there's even more! This Man named Jesus then emasculated death as an incomprehensible superpower from Heaven; like something out of a Hollywood movie, He visited Earth and obliterated death. Talk about ridiculous! Here we are as men, so compelled with these movies that involve completely made-up superheroes like the Hulk, Superman, and Captain America...while this real-life version that upstages them all – Jesus – didn't need computer generated animations to pull off the greatest feat of all time! And what's crazy is that it happened on the same planet and the same ground that we walk on today. It's all real!

And how about another baffling reality – one day we will get to be around the One who invented each one of us. Think about that – does it get any better than being around our Creator? I will be indescribably honored and absolutely star-struck when I meet both my Savior and Creator face-to-face one day. There's so much excitement in Jesus. And that excitement doesn't have to be forced when we have an accurate perspective on His realness and on His power. And Warriors – the more time we spend with Him, the more accurate our perspective of Him will become.

Making time daily to read the Word, pray, and worship Jesus is my foundation for victory in the spiritual war.

Preparation is pivotal to win the spiritual war. Without preparation, we'll get absolutely annihilated on the battlefield by a highly intelligent opponent. And that preparation must happen daily. We win today's battle through today's preparation! So how do we prepare for the high-stakes battle that awaits us every morning when we wake up? Well, as we discussed in chapter one, it all boils down to knowing Jesus. And knowing Jesus starts with getting familiar with the instruction manual that He gave us, because as odd as it sounds, Jesus *is* that instruction manual!

The Word – I know Jesus by knowing the Word, because Jesus is the Word.

John 1:1 "...The Word was God." (NIV)

John 1:14 "The Word became flesh..." (NIV)

Seriously though? The Bible is Jesus? Absolutely. God tells us in John 1 that "the Word was God" and that "the Word became flesh" through His Son, Jesus! Knowing the Word is literally knowing Jesus. If we don't know the Word, we don't know Jesus! Let that marinate, guys. A whole lot of us *claim* we have a deep relationship with Jesus, but our knowledge of the Word is as shallow as a kiddie pool. It's impossible to know Jesus intimately and not know the Bible thoroughly, because the two are one in the same!

Warriors – let's stop treating the Bible like it is stale and outdated! That kind of pathetic, world-watered-down perspective is what has led our generation of men to its embarrassing state! Progressive culture can roll its eyes at the power of the Word, but Warriors know that it is *the* most vibrant, effective weapon we possess in spiritual combat! Hebrews 4:12 says, "The Word of God is alive and powerful...sharper than the sharpest two-edged sword, cutting between soul and spirit," and it, "exposes our innermost thoughts and desires."

Men – the Bible is *alive!* And it is *relevant* to our today and our tomorrow! It diagnoses our spiritual health exposing the beautifully packaged lies and temptations that dampen and darken our days. And in doing so, the Word improves our days! Truthfully, we miss out on the most abundant version of each day when we don't take advantage of reading the Word. So why *wouldn't* we want to know the Bible forwards and backwards? Not knowing and applying the Word is like deliberately choosing lower quality days. It's unreasonable if you think about it!

But how does this fit into our practical daily structure? Well, we can't read the Word without making time in our daily routine to read the Word.

The key is making time...no matter what. Look, every schedule is completely different, but let's all begin to think of a 3-, 5-, 10-, or 15-minute time in our day that we can consistently feed ourselves with who Jesus is by reading at least a verse or even a chapter a day. There are tons of ways to insert the Word of God into our daily lives – reading plans, devotions, studies – but are we *doing* it? And are we doing it *consistently?* It's time to start, Warriors.

Prayer – I know Jesus' peace and direction when I have a continuous conversation with Him about everything on my mind.

Jeremiah 29:12 "Then you will call on Me and come and pray to Me, and I will listen to you." (NIV)

1 Thessalonians 5:17 "Never stop praying."

We know Jesus by knowing the Word, but we also know Jesus by carrying on a conversation with Him. And just like a relationship with a spouse, family member, or friend, our relationship with Jesus thrives off of communication. God wants to be involved with every detail of our lives – even the seemingly mundane, daily activities that we think have *nothing* to do with our relationship with God. No matter where we are, He wants to hear our thoughts, and He wants us to hear His thoughts on even the tiniest, most insignificant decisions we make. God wants to be included at the ballpark, on the vacation, at the grocery store, in the office, and at the hunting lodge.

But inclusion requires conversation. God tells us in 1 Thessalonians 5:17 that He wants to be in the conversation...all the time. God knows this is the most useful navigational tool in battle, and if we'll stay connected to Him, He's going to keep us from straying off course. That's why it says, "Never stop praying." It only takes a split second for us to do something stupid that costs us monumentally. Praying *all* the time is a signature Warrior attribute. Reality check – are we in a constant conversation with God? Are we literally talking to God, either audibly with our mouths or silently in our spirit, about every encounter we have with people? With our money? With our jobs? With our wives? With our possessions? It takes a rare discipline to sharpen this habit. But once we go there, we're going to quickly realize that the enjoyment we reap from staying connected to God's direction will fuel our desire to remain there!

Prayer takes discipline at times, but an overall perspective change on prayer wouldn't hurt either. And honestly, many of us need to change our attitudes from "we've *got* to pray" to "we *get* to pray!" Guys – we have unprecedented access to the universe's most supreme superpower, and yet we act like it's an inconvenience to take advantage of it. Men – it is a *privilege* to pray, and that's how a Warrior approaches it. If we had VIP access to a prestigious leader, athlete, or musician, we would all treat it as a privilege. So why in the world would that not apply to the most distinguished authority of all time?

What's even crazier is that we not only have access to God, but we have anticipation from God! It says in Jeremiah 29:12 when we *do* call on Him, He "will listen!" It's ridiculous...we have a friend that is interested in *everything* we do and is on call to help us in every situation we face. It should pump us up that God, who spoke oceans and mountain ranges into existence, is eagerly waiting to hear from us! It makes no sense...I mean, if someone cost me *my* son's life, I probably wouldn't ever want to hear from that person again. The sheer fact that God wants anything to do with us is reason enough for us to occasionally shut our mouths and listen to what He has to say! There's a decent chance our Creator might have some wisdom for us!

Serious business – if we believe Jesus is real and that He has the power to conquer anything we need, then why aren't we talking to Him about everything all the time? Y'all – we have *the* unrivaled Warrior with us...all the time...and we aren't talking to Him? Either it's time to stop *claiming* that God is all-powerful, or start *conversing* with Him like He is! Let's believe that God is who He says He is, and start talking to Him continuously! Warriors are prayers.

Worship – I experience true excitement and passion that is rooted in Jesus when I invest time reflecting on who He is and what He did for me.

Psalm 95:6 "Come, let us bow down in worship, let us kneel before the Lord our Maker." (NIV)

There's the Word, there's prayer, and then there's my favorite – worship! This is where knowing Jesus gets fun, because worship refreshes us in dramatic fashion. It tangibly transforms our perspective and gives us an undeniable feeling of wind in our sails.

I cannot boast about the power of worship enough. Hands down, the most powerfully peaceful moments that I've ever experienced have come while listening to a worship song, reflecting on who God is, considering what He did for us through His Son Jesus, and envisioning the unmatchable power of the cross and resurrection of Jesus. It's during these moments of worship when God's presence comes to us and gives us peace through the power of His Holy Spirit. When we intentionally concentrate our efforts on imagining and comprehending the greatness of our God through music, its effects are indisputable and indescribable. It's an experience that cannot be put into words when we utilize music in our efforts to grasp His greatness.

It's like a breathtaking mountaintop moment that we try to capture through photography. Every time we show someone that impressive image, we always pair it with a disclaimer: "This picture just doesn't do it justice." The description just doesn't do worship justice. We have to get our own mountaintop experience before we can understand, but that requires going to the mountain. And going to that mountain requires planning, climbing, and occasionally waiting while the clouds blow over. But when we "bow down in worship" and our perspective is just right, the breathtaking moment commences (see Psalm 95:6). And that's the moment that ultimately sparks the supernatural motivation to fight the spiritual battle.

The Word, prayer, and worship – these are the three heavy hitters in our arsenal, guys. The key to victory on the spiritual battlefield is simple: use them every day. Not some days. Not most days. Every day. It's the Bible, the conversation, and the adoration that fulfill, empower, encourage, and enable us to accomplish every challenge and call to action in this entire study. We will go into the details of what it looks like to practically use these three weapons in chapter three when we discuss the daily regimen of a Warrior. But for now, let's understand that we lose without 'em.

Only the Holy Spirit can provide the power that I need to win the spiritual war.

Romans 8:26 "And the Holy Spirit helps us in our weakness."

It is impossible for us to win the fight for obedience without the supernatural presence of God. It's only by the power of the Holy Spirit that we are able to withstand the burdens of battle to emerge victoriously. We need to remind ourselves daily that without God's supernatural power, we are certainly going to live for the world and what it has to offer. Our opponent will make sure of it. He is ferocious and clever. And he doesn't give up, especially when we lack the Holy Spirit's protection. He will come after us again and again until we eventually wear down and fall in a brief moment of vulnerability. And if we don't fall, we'll live in endless exhaustion trying to meet God's desires. When we try to obey solely on our efforts, we will inevitably be defeated. God didn't intend for us to go into battle without the proper protection. That protection comes through the companion of the Holy Spirit.

Recently, a snake came out of the woods behind our backyard and tried to make *our* home *his* home. Obviously, we weren't fond of his idea, so we prepared to foil his plot as he slithered into a nook on our back patio. I walked out quickly to take care of business, but little did I know that this snake was going to come at me as if I had invaded his property. I grabbed him with my bare hands and slung him around in the air like a lasso, slamming his head against the concrete! Yeah right.

You know what I did to take care of that snake? I immediately armed myself with a tool that would make my mission monumentally easier. And I took that shovel and utilized the dramatic reach advantage that it gave me over my opponent. I extended that shovel and sliced its torso, completing the mission without any trouble at all! Take that shovel away from this scenario, and watch me try to eliminate that snake. It would not have happened. On top of that, it would have been dangerous, exhausting, and senseless to try to win that battle on my own. Acquiring that shovel was second nature, because it compensated for my weakness. Enter Romans 8:26, where it says the Holy Spirit powers us in our weakness. Guys – the Holy Spirit is our companion who will always get the job done. But we must utilize Him. Otherwise, the enemy will expose our weaknesses in a split second, because he is quick, smart, and aggressive.

We just can't do this on our own, guys. We have to remind ourselves of that daily. We have got to pick up that shovel *every* day. We can't miss even one day, because that's when the enemy will strike at our weakest point. This goes against all of the stereotypes of being a man. We are fixers and doers, always possessing the "I've-got-this" mentality. Well, I have some bad news... we *don't* have this one. We need to humble ourselves enough to ask for that unexplainable, incomparable, peaceful presence to power us, alert us, and steer us in the right direction...or else we're gasless and headed for exhaustion and failure.

I get the skepticism and oddity of the Holy Spirit. This supernatural power doesn't make logical sense to any of us. But that's a *good* thing...I sure hope we serve a God that transcends the intellect of this pea-brain! We don't need to understand it, guys. We just need to *choose* to trust that it's real, *receive* His power, and *ask* for His guidance so that we can win those battles on the patio! We will talk more practical details of how to experience the Holy Spirit's guidance in the next chapter, but building on what we discussed last chapter – the Holy Spirit is an essential fuel for our daily battle, and we have to embrace His companionship to be a victorious Warrior.

A commitment to fight means consistently taking every thought and prayerfully comparing it to God's Word.

2 Corinthians 10:5 "...take captive every thought to make it obedient to Christ." (NIV)

Living for Jesus demands an uncommon commitment and an unbroken alertness. There is no break in any day where we can relax our minds, because that will become the breach in our obedience. God wants us to violently confront *every* thought to win the war in our minds. The bad news? We think thousands of thoughts every day, and they can get away from us in a fraction of a second if we aren't careful. The good news? God doesn't expect us to be the filter for what's right and wrong. Rather, He wants us continually talking to Him so *He* can tell us the moment when our thoughts get out of line.

Don't miss this. This is huge: A commitment to fight really means a commitment to constant prayer. That commitment to constant prayer keeps us connected to the Holy Spirit, and then *He* does the brunt of the work by alerting us when we need to combat a thought. But let's not even pretend that this Warrior habit is always a walk in the park! It ain't for the weak! It is a commitment that demands profound effort and tenacious mental toughness. Yes, some moments, days, and seasons, it is easier to remain engaged in prayer. But write this down – there *will* be moments, days, and seasons when the prospect of having a conversation with God feels like the *last* thing we want to do. Warriors are prepared for this reality though, and we are trained to execute unwavering commitment to prayer-led, Word-filled living in these challenging moments.

Excellence is achieved in the painful moments that exhaust 100% of my effort to make the right choice.

Hebrews 12:1 "Let us strip off every weight that slows us down, especially the sin that so easily trips us up. And let us run with endurance the race God has set before us."

Are we "walking the walk" or just "talking the talk" when it comes to obeying God completely? Can we honestly say that we are as committed to excellence in our obedience of God's Word as we are in our careers, passions, hobbies, appearance, or plans for the future? Do we measure each day based on how our choices align with God's Word, or do we measure each day based on how our feelings align with our comfort? If we truly believe that eternity *is* all that matters, then it's time to step up and make sure that every tiny detail of our lives is in line with His Word.

I would venture to say that almost every one of us has at least one area that we know deep down is not in line with God's Word. Whatever that area is, or that habit that we just call our "struggle," *that* is what God wants. And *that* is what brings us to excellence. It isn't the other 99% where we're kicking tail and taking names. God wants that pesky 1% that's been giving us fits and costing us abundance!

Men – God desires our best in every area of our lives. And it's time to give God control of the one missing part, and starve it until the habit is dead. It might be sports, money, materialism, vanity, fashion, sexual pleasure, pornography, anger, video games, social media, language, humor, eating, laziness... it might even be a combination of several of these. Whatever the case, God wants to take the place of these struggles and indulgences. This all starts with our identifying that area and preparing our minds, hearts, and bodies to withstand a little pain as we starve them to death. The question is: who's willing to go through a little pain in the flesh to experience a lot of fulfillment in the spirit? That's the path to excellence, and we have got to remind ourselves every day when we wake up!

Every thing I have, activity I do, place I go, and circumstance I am in are opportunities to love people and look like Jesus.

Matthew 5:16 "Let your good deeds shine out for all to see, so that everyone will praise your heavenly Father."

We are compartmentalizers. We tend to separate every part of life into categories, and rarely do we ever see these categories overlap or integrate with one another. We like division and organization, which is why we compartmentalize not only *categorically*, but also *seasonally*. We have our religion over here. Work over there. Sports are here, while family is there. Saturdays here. Sunday mornings there. Fall for hunting and football. Summer for vacationing and relaxing. January for dieting and exercise. November and December for food and family. Our perspectives and priorities adjust based on the hats we are wearing and the seasons we are in. But the fact of the matter is there are no compartments in God's eyes. All of life's compartments are interwoven together, and all of them exist for one unified purpose: to love people and look like Jesus!

Guys – God intended everything to be used for His purpose. Every item, every activity, every environment, every day, every season – they are all just *opportunities* to leverage His agenda first! God wants us to use every one of those situations to find a way to demonstrate Jesus' love to people and to act like Jesus in our conversations and actions. Just like Sunday morning worship with the family is all about Jesus, so is the Friday night hangout at the local Mexican restaurant with my school friends. And just like my Bible study on Tuesday nights is all about Jesus, so is my sales meeting at work on Thursday afternoon. Every situation is an opportunity to look like Jesus and draw others to God with our obedience.

Warriors have the mentality of Matthew 6:33 branded in our minds. We seek *first* the Kingdom of God in everything. We seek *God's* purpose with every dollar, every platform, every possession, every situation...because they all exist as vehicles to testify to who He is and bless others in the process. But here's where principle meets practical: Are we using our Christmas bonuses, our tickets to Alabama's big game versus LSU, our Wednesday morning workout at the gym, and our picturesque hunting land to look like Jesus and bless someone in the process? Or are we doing just what the enemy wants and using these opportunities to indulge and satisfy our own desires?

It's time for us to stop subconsciously thinking to ourselves, "How can I enjoy this?" and start consciously asking God, "How can I use this for You?" A Warrior sees that *everything* is relevant to eternity! It's time for us to start using it all for God's glory and as Matthew 5:16 says, "Let [our] good deeds shine...so that everyone will praise [our] Heavenly Father!"

SUMMARY

Declarations of a Warrior's Identity:

+ This world cannot satisfy me.

+ Only Jesus can satisfy me.

+ Making time daily to read the Word, pray, and worship Jesus is my foundation for victory in the spiritual war.

+ Only the Holy Spirit can provide the power that I need to win the spiritual war.

+ A commitment to fight means consistently taking every thought and prayerfully comparing it to God's Word.

+ Excellence is achieved in the painful moments that exhaust 100% of my effort to make the right choice.

+ Every thing I have, activity I do, place I go, and circumstance I am in are opportunities to love people and look like Jesus.

RESPONSE

Jesus, even if I don't feel like it sometimes, I know that only You satisfy me. Although there are so many things in this world that my flesh desires and so many things that I have passion for, I boldly confess that I know there's nothing in this world that will give me more than a brief moment of satisfaction. I know that true satisfaction can only be found in You, and there's nothing on this Earth that compares to the love, power, and peace of Your cross and resurrection.

Jesus, give me the desire and discipline to read Your Word daily and invest time in worship, reflecting on the magnitude of what You did for me in Your life, death, and resurrection. Lord, I need the unexplainable power of Your Holy Spirit to be with me every moment of every day, to equip me, alert me, and guide me in Your direction. Jesus, I know that constant conversation with You is the key to living the committed life that You called me to, and through that constant conversation, I'm able to take every thought captive and compare it with Your Word.

God, I know that living for You is the most peace-filled, satisfying path for my life, but I also know that there will be moments where it requires me to make the uncomfortable choice for my flesh. Lord, help me to start embracing challenges and enjoying painful moments knowing that You are strengthening and maturing me. Motivate me like never before to give 100% of my effort to pursue excellence as I set the example of a Warrior.

Lord, my entire life is about You. No matter how irrelevant my daily activities, possessions, and environments may seem, You've provided them for an eternal purpose. God, help me to begin seeing every part of my life as an opportunity to glorify You and bless other people.

CHAPTER 3

THE DAILY REGIMEN

Our daily regimen ultimately determines whether we win the spiritual war.

Up to this point, our focus has been strictly on understanding the existing spiritual war and assuming the mentality necessary to emerge victoriously. But now it's time to put that knowledge to use and examine the real-life, everyday details of our routine and adopt a Warrior's regimen. Men – this chapter holds the *keys* to winning the war. Period. And if we don't take action here, there is *no* point *whatsoever* in proceeding to the final seven chapters. Serious business – if we aren't intentionally taking steps to *know Jesus* and let Him live through us, this entire journey will be a bust. We absolutely cannot sustain long-term obedience and purity without supernatural motivation and empowerment. If we're propelled by human effort, we'll eventually run out of fuel. Plus, we'll realize that it's exhausting to try to live a spirit-led life without the spirit actually leading! Now let's get ready to go to war!

TIME - Make time in our daily routine to connect with God.

Ephesians 5:15-17 "Look carefully then how you walk, not as unwise but as wise, making the best use of the time, because the days are evil. Therefore do not be foolish, but understand what the will of the Lord is." (ESV)

Time paves the pathway to progress, and progress won't ever take place until we set aside *the time* in which it can take place. If I want to become a professional athlete, it starts by *making time* to train in the gym. If I want to become a world-class chef, it starts by *making time* to cook in the kitchen. By the same token, if I want to become a spiritual Warrior, it starts by *making time* to know the greatest Warrior to ever fight battle. Before there's action, there has to be *time* for that action to take place.

We've all heard that "practice makes perfect," but the question is are we making time for practice? Without the time to practice, we'll never make it to the perfect. So before we get too fixated on the end goal of perfection, let's start by making sure we have the *time* set up to practice! It's planning *time* for "practice" that precedes making "perfect" possible. And that's our choice. We have the life of the specimen Warrior already written out for us, but our days are so saturated with meaningless clutter that we don't spend any time investing in the relationship that matters most! Whether we realize it or not, neglecting this all-important relationship with Jesus has a detrimental effect on every other part of our lives.

Investment creates desire.

There might be some guys right now saying, "I have zero desire to do this," and I completely understand, because we've all been there. However, I dare you to invest the time *first*...maybe 10 minutes a day for a week or so. And in that time, pray that God will change your heart and give you the desire to know Him more. Then just watch. I would almost guarantee that God will change something in your spirit to ignite a desire.

Too many of us want the desire before the investment, and we've got it all backwards. We don't get to enjoy something until we have a vested interest in it. Hear this important truth: *investment* creates *desire*. As my Pastor, Chris Hodges at Church of the Highlands, often says, "Choices lead. Feelings follow." Indeed, it is choices that lead every day. And God doesn't make choices for us. He can *lead* us to make the right choices, but the choices are always *ours* to make. And making time is not a convenient thing...it takes effort and flexibility in certain seasons. However, the mark of a mature Warrior is consistently doing whatever is necessary to make the time to make it happen. That's our responsibility as Warriors – to do *whatever it takes* to make the time.

God doesn't want our time. He wants our hearts.

As men, whenever we receive an assignment or a challenge, we immediately assume a checklist mentality. And while a systematic approach is a necessity in establishing a winning Warrior routine, this mentality can turn into a legalistic, religious gold star in a split second. We will do what we have to do just to check it off the list. Guys – our relationship with Jesus isn't a ritual or measurable task that we can check off our list every day. It may require us to tackle tasks like reading the Word, praying, and worshipping. But the *tasks* themselves are not what God wants. He wants our hearts. It's critical to understand that God wants our time, but only as a vehicle to get our hearts. That's why giving God 15 minutes a day doesn't do a thing for us *or* for God. He doesn't want the minutes – He wants the sincere focus and acknowledgement that we need Him *during* those minutes. And our time with God, in and of itself, is useless to us *and* to God if He doesn't get genuine passion from our hearts during that time.

Stay the course on the mundane days.

There will likely be days when we don't *feel* like reading God's Word, when it *feels* like we are going through the motions. On those days, it's critical that we stay the course and feed our spirit, because those feelings are indications that the flesh is picking up momentum and trying to call the shots. Once we get in a healthy, heart-focused routine with God, Satan wants more than anything for us to tire from the routine of seeking Jesus and step back into a worldly way of living for just a *moment*. Satan is the *master* of deception, and he'll lie to us and try to convince us that the daily grind is not having impact in our lives or the lives of others. We know better. Let's stay the course even when we aren't "feeling" it!

We're all busy. Make the time.

Let's ask ourselves: "Where are the 3, 5, 10, 15, 30 minutes of my day when I can consistently invest time and sincere focus on my relationship with Jesus?" This might be a decision that we need to discuss with our wives taking into consideration the kids' schedules, work schedules, and all of the daily activities that make our routines one of a kind. It's critical that we have the conversations and organize the chaos to make this time a reality.

Let's be real – this is a challenge for every one of us. Hey – we're *all* busy, but *making* time is where the rubber meets the road. It's time to *make* the time. And when we do, we'll experience the difference instantly. Do we want to experience overwhelming blessing in our marriage? Our families? Our career? Our finances? Our dreams? Then let's put our time where our mouths are and begin to think about where that investment might work in our unique routines.

THE WORD – Read and reflect on something from God's Word.

Hebrews 4:12 "For the Word of God is alive and powerful. It is sharper than the sharpest two-edged sword, cutting between soul and spirit, between joint and marrow. It exposes our innermost thoughts and desires."

Making time in our daily routine sets the stage for us to focus on getting to know Jesus, but the question then becomes – what does this look like? We've set aside the time to invest in our relationship with Jesus, but now *how* do we invest? What does it *literally* look like in our daily schedule to utilize the three primary weapons of battle – the Word, prayer, and worship – so that we can know Jesus? Since God told us in John chapter one that Jesus *is* the Word, I would say that *reading* the Word is a great place to start. Men – reading the Bible *is* getting to know Jesus, and it is where *spiritual progress* requires *literal action.*

Are we reading it? Are we consistently consuming its truth? When we do, we'll see firsthand how it is indeed "alive and powerful" (Hebrews 4:12). And as Pastor Chris Hodges often says, when we read the Word, we find out the Word actually reads us! The Bible is genius, but we have got to open it up to find that out.

Pick a time and place that work with our schedules.

Reading the Word daily is a discipline. It begins by solidifying a time and place, knitting this habit into the fabric of our daily routines. This will look drastically different for all of us, but let's determine what our Bible-reading time is going to look like so we can stick with it! It might mean waking up, immediately grabbing our phones or iPads, and using a Bible app to pull up a verse or a chapter to read while we're lying in bed. Or maybe it means keeping a Bible in our nightstand and flipping to a Psalm with our wives 10 minutes before bedtime to discuss just how great God has been to us. Perhaps it means setting our alarms 20 minutes earlier, getting the family around the breakfast table, and reading a handful of verses and discussing them for a couple of minutes before everyone heads their separate ways.

Whatever the case, these Bible-reading sessions don't just magically happen. They take preparation. We don't just *happen* to end up with a Bible in our hands with our families gathered around the table 20 minutes earlier than normal. It takes *intentional* planning and communication to change the culture of a household schedule. So where does the Bible fit into our schedules?

Have the uncomfortable conversation.

This entire Bible-reading scenario might be *so* far from normal or comfortable for us that we're almost embarrassed to even start doing something like this. We might not even know how to start making this a reality, and it's *totally* normal to feel that way. But after we *step* out and *set* this new example, we'll reap the supernatural benefits of leading our families to their purpose. Let's have that uncomfortable conversation with our wives and our kids. Let's tell them that we want to start *leading* our households by reading the Word every day. It might feel awkward to us for a brief moment, but once we step out in obedience, the awkwardness will quickly subside as we unlock a new level of blessing over our lives and our families' lives.

Start with our favorite.

If we're going to start reading the Bible daily, where do we begin? What do we even read? First of all, we don't need to be worried about *what* to read, but just be sure *that* we read. Let's find a book of the Bible that we enjoy, and stick with it for a season. For me, it's the Psalms. I connect almost instantaneously to God's love for me and to His power over all my circumstances when I read out of the Psalms.

I'm gonna be blatantly honest and tell you that parts of the Bible sometimes confuse me, and, frankly, make me tired in trying to follow along! Stories that involve kings and nations and tribes that I can't pronounce – the "Whatever-ites from Whatever-onia" – a lot of times these stories make me want to take a nap when I try to follow them! But even those stories hold supernatural wisdom. 2 Timothy 3:16 tells us that *every* story in the Word is "inspired by God, and is useful to teach us what is true, [and] make us realize what is wrong." It also "corrects us when we are wrong and teaches us to do what is right."

So let's not get lost in the clutter of the characters involved. Let's realize that God doesn't want us to know these stories for knowledge sake. He wants us to know these stories so we get a glimpse of the power that is available for us! God didn't give us the story of David and Goliath because it was a feel-good story about an underdog who killed a giant. No...God wanted to show us that He can use *anyone* to do *anything*, because His power is greater than any human power. That's as relevant today as it was thousands of years ago. Warriors – the Bible is filled with countless genius, timeless truths!

Just read something.

Let's not get concerned with *how much* to read either, guys. "Christian" culture might tell us there's a certain amount of Scripture or time that is required each day to be obedient, but that's legalistic nonsense! There is no quota that we need to meet each day. We just need to make sure we are feeding ourselves with *something* from God's Word every day. Even if it is just one verse that we read and a minute or two of reflection on what God is telling us, that might have the power to change our day or even our week! And you never know – God might give us something that could change someone *else's* life. We can't predict when and how the Word of God might come alive!

Speak it over every circumstance, good or bad.

Reading and reflecting on God's Word – be it a verse, a chapter, or several chapters – holds incredible promise when we speak it over our circumstances, too. As I write this, I'm battling discouragement and worry over a family member's ominous medical prognosis, and I've armed myself with Psalm 30:2 during this season claiming, "Oh Lord my God, I called to You for help, and You restored my health." That verse is bringing me encouragement, faith, trust, and peace as I look to God as the ultimate Healer! And when the enemy casts fear in my mind, no way will I doubt God's abilities! In Matthew 8, Jesus healed a man with leprosy, and I'm confidently anticipating that same kind of medical miracle in *my* situation! I'm claiming the promise of Isaiah 53:5 (NIV) that "by [Jesus'] wounds, we are healed!" Men – *no* attack can stand up to the Word of God!

Warriors know God's Word. We are armed with a promise for every pain. We attach a truth to every trial. We speak Scripture over every situation whether good or bad. Because guys – if we don't know the Word and don't claim it over our circumstances, we will be *completely* decimated by the lies of fear, death, destruction, and depression that accompany the enemy's initiative.

Speak it over every thought and temptation.

The Scripture literally comes alive inside of us when we recall it even in the most silent moments when no one but us knows we are being tempted. This battle in our minds is where the brutality of war rears its ugly head, and we've got to be armed to fight it. It might be at the local mall when we walk by a seductive ad for a lingerie store or in the electronics store when we get the urge to buy that new gadget that we *know* we don't have the money to buy. These quietly chaotic moments reach DEFCON 5 on the spiritual front, and without a supply of Scripture, we're sitting ducks. It is only by recalling God's Truth softly in our minds, and sometimes even *loudly* with our *mouths*, that we can destroy the thoughts and temptations that try to lure us off the path of obedience.

Warriors – God's Word safeguards our spirit from stupidity. And when our "natural desires" and "feelings" are enticing us to satisfy the flesh, we *must* be equipped with the Word in order to save us from stupid! Let's know the Word, guys. Let's have the conversation with the family, pull out the iPad, dust off the Bible, set the alarm half an hour earlier, get everyone ready for bed 15 minutes sooner – whatever it takes. Our families, friends, coworkers, and even strangers need Warriors leading by reading.

PRAYER – Communicate with Jesus constantly.

Colossians 4:2 "Devote yourselves to prayer with an alert mind and a thankful heart."

Every great Warrior is a great pray-er. Warriors pray about everything. And we pray all the time. We "*devote* [ourselves] to prayer with an alert mind and a thankful heart" as Colossians 4:2 says, because we know that the very *moment* we disconnect from the Holy Spirit's power, we will be targeted by an opportunistic opponent who wants to steal our peace and sabotage our purpose. Men – it only takes a second for us to be neck-deep in disobedience. News flash: the enemy doesn't fear us. He fears the Holy Spirit *in* us. And when we abandon that companionship by cutting off communication with our supernatural power source, we are destined for disobedience and destruction.

Warriors – prayer is the most valuable moment-to-moment asset in our arsenal of weaponry because of *Who* is on the other end of the line! As Acts 1:8 describes it, "[We] will receive *power* when the Holy Spirit comes upon [us]!" That power is what keeps us attuned to God's purpose every moment of every day. And when that power is present, its impact is substantial. Our manpower and willpower are *laughable* compared to this supernatural power. That is precisely why the conversation with Jesus can't subside, men. We're too vulnerable. And our survival depends on that unbroken, unyielding camaraderie with our Paraclete – our Advocate – on the battlefield! The more we communicate, the more we dominate!

See prayer as an honor.

The right perspective of prayer will transform our prayer life. We talked about it in chapter two, but prayer is a privilege. And we as Warriors deliberately declare that every day because we realize how ridiculous it is for God to give us the time of day after *we* cost Him His Son's life. *We* nailed Jesus to the cross, guys. Yet His Dad is our biggest fan! Just look at 1 Peter 5:7, which tells us to "give all [our] worries and cares to God" because "He *cares* for [us]." I don't know why He cares, but I sure as heck am glad He does. God's love for us is unprecedented, and it is one that has never been seen. Warriors – let's not lose perspective of just how undeserving we are of God's attention. We *get* to pray, guys! And that's what we testify to everyone – that it's an *honor* to pray.

Make it about Jesus.

So often we act like it's putting coins in a vending machine, but prayer isn't about us, guys. God definitely wants to hear about our needs and desires, but He is concerned most about His will. 1 John 5:14 gives us a glimpse at God's priority when it comes to prayer, saying, "He hears us whenever we ask for anything that pleases *Him!"* God is listening to the heart *behind* the request more than He is the request itself. James 4:3 is proof. It tells us "even when

[we] ask, [we] don't get it because [our] motives are all wrong – [we] want only what will give [us] pleasure." God's plan, not our pleasure, is a Warrior's primary focus in prayer. A Warrior starts his prayers by *worshipping*, not asking. Let's be men who seek *God's* list first. There's nothing wrong with asking God for the things we desire, but the priority of our heart is all that matters. It's another textbook example of applying the principle of Matthew 6:33 (ESV): "Seek *first* the kingdom of God...and all these things will be added." Oh, the power of first!

Be real, honest, and passionate.

It's frustrating how prayer is depicted in the majority of mainstream media, and sadly it has even spilled over into some church environments. Inaccurate as it may be, prayer is portrayed as a taxing, ritualistic, rehearsed, robotic task that relieves us of our religious duties. It is a reflection of the stale, repetitive nature of denominational practices that have plagued our churches depriving us of the enjoyment that a true relationship with Jesus brings! This is the polar opposite of God's intent. Our prayer life was meant to be enjoyable! And when we abandon religious buzzwords and just *talk* to God like we would a great friend, we'll get a taste of how *refreshing* conversation with Him can be. We don't need to speak in King James Version language when we pray adding -est to every word we voice! God just wants our honesty and passion.

Countless stories throughout the Bible demonstrate to us that God wants our passionate, transparent, unrehearsed, heart-led conversation. He didn't intend for us to memorize prayers and recite them to Him every day. He just wants to hear our thoughts! God *wants* to hear about that disdain for our coworker, that struggle to remain pure on date nights, and that frustration with our finances – because then He can help us align those thoughts with His will! Let's drop the pretend perfection, and give God the impressionable imperfection that He desires! Let's be real, honest, and passionate in our prayers!

Pray about every situation.

"Pray about everything" is hard to misinterpret. That's why I love Philippians 4:6. It doesn't matter how spiritual or unspiritual we may consider something, or how major or minor a decision may seem. *Everything* is worth praying about. Prayer preps us for God's purpose, and we've got to be connected to Him at all times, because we never know *when* God might use us to draw someone to Himself. God has a track record of using the most unlikely people in the most unexpected moments, and that's exactly why Warriors cover every moment, every thought, every decision, every environment, and every person in prayer.

Woke up tired: "Hey God – I need You today. It's gonna be crazy busy, and I'm stressed and tired, but I wanna live like You. Jesus, give me patience and the discipline to pray today if I get discouraged. Just let my day at work glorify You, and give me supernatural joy in every conversation that I have today!"

The MRI that we're worried sick over: "Lord, I'm so nervous about this MRI being done for this spot on my brain today, but I know that You're greater than any fear that I have, and that Your Word tells me to be anxious over nothing! Jesus, I trust You and know that You're in control. I pray that the report comes back completely clear, and I ask that You'd give me peace during this challenging time!"

That hunting trip that has us excited: "Jesus, thank You for the opportunity to go and spend some time relaxing and enjoying the beauty of nature. God give me safety, and refresh my energy, but most importantly – let me be an example to my buddies who need You. Let my words, my jokes, and my attitude be in line with Your Word, and give me an opportunity to testify to Your greatness and power in my life today!"

Pray in every situation.

Even more critical than praying *about* every situation is praying *in* every situation. Guys – we are terrible about getting sidetracked from our purpose in the blink of an eye. We can have our game faces on, our weapons drawn, our destination pinpointed – and then an attractive girl walks by. Or we find out that our friend has been gossiping about us. Or we see that the number in our bank account is getting lower than we realized. And just like that, our path has been diverted, and we're chasing a rabbit that the enemy released just for us. We are awfully gullible without the uninterrupted navigation of the Holy Spirit.

As Warriors, the Holy Spirit helps us see beyond the allure of those rabbits, and we are ready for these moments because no matter where we are, we're already praying! That rabbit might grab our attention for a split second, but not for long, because we're in constant connection with our personalized GPS, and He keeps us on track to our destination. The more times we experience the reliability of His navigation and the fulfillment of the intended destination, the more we'll want to utilize His direction in future outings! But we must start talking to Jesus at some point. We as men are great at talking about what we should do, but our follow-through is marginal at best. Let's actually try this today or tomorrow. Let's include Jesus conversationally in every situation, in every environment. Either silently in our heads, or audibly from our mouths – "God, is this glorifying to You?" and, "God, what do You want me to do?" Time to put up and not shut up!

Take every thought captive and use the name of Jesus.

Prayer connects us to God's discernment, but ultimately *we* have to take action! And mastering this fight against temptation is what separates the Warriors from the boys! Let's be real – it ain't easy at all, because temptation takes no timeout. The good news is – God promises us in 1 Corinthians 10:13 that "He will not allow temptation to be more than [we] can stand," and "He will show [us] a way out so that [we] can endure!" There's a way out of every temptation, guys. But that way out requires us to initiate confrontation! And 2 Corinthians 10:5 defines that confrontation when it tells us to "take every thought captive." The problem is, this is where most of us are losing. In fact, we're not just losing. We're getting demolished.

"Taking our thoughts captive" has become church speak for many of us. Yes, we're great at saying "amen" when the Pastor talks about it, but most of our thoughts are storming through the gates of our minds in droves with no resistance whatsoever. The ultimate result? Negligible impact for Jesus, discontentment with life, mediocrity in our marriages, frustration in our households – all because sin has received unimpeded access to our thoughts and habits, and it's the polar opposite of what the word "captive" means. In fact, the Greek etymology of the word "captive" is "aichmalotizo," which literally means "to be captured" or "brought into subjection" by using "a spear."

I'm no theology expert, but the translation seems pretty cut and dried! Taking a thought captive means we set up an armed security checkpoint at the front gate of our minds. And when any thought approaches the entrance, it is aggressively confronted and paused for examination before it goes any further. Then we stick the point of a spear up to that thought's neck and lead it immediately over to the Judge's seat before it is permitted to infiltrate our intellect. And if the Holy Spirit reveals to us that He doesn't like it, we instantaneously execute that thought by piercing it with the razor-sharp head of that spear! Now *that* is how we win war, men!

But what does this look like in real life? Well, it starts with being alert at all times. It means being skeptical of every worldly object that crosses our radars, understanding that *if* something is appetizing to our flesh, it's likely cancerous to our spirit! And this might happen *hundreds* of times a day. Welcome to the Warrior life! When we feel our flesh's interest being piqued, that's when we avoid a security breach by going into high alert. We confront that thought and take it to the Holy Spirit for examination, while deliberately telling Jesus that we want Him to keep our minds *off* of impurities and *on* His cross.

There is no greater way to capture and slaughter a temptation or impure thought than by audibly saying the name "Jesus!" Look at Acts 3:6 when Peter heals a lame beggar by telling the man, "In the name of Jesus Christ, get up and walk," and sure enough – he does! Guys – Jesus' name holds just as much power today as it did when this physical, Biblical miracle happened thousands of years ago! Yet, for some reason, we don't sincerely believe that or else we would be dropping the name of Jesus all the time to overcome the temptations and trials we face!

A practical example of how this meets real-life temptation: Let's say we are out at a restaurant, and an attractive girl walks by us. Our attention is automatically drawn to her for literally half a second. Now at this point, we've been tempted in several ways. First, if we're married, even a second glance is investing passion or a thrill into another woman. And even if we *aren't* married, the temptation to either visualize or fantasize lustfully about that girl is waiting to be dealt with. *This* is the moment. *This* is the point where we find out where our priority is – our pleasure or God's purpose. Because in the blink of an eye, we will have won or lost the battle. It's *this* moment where a Warrior's preparation meets its purpose. But what do we do?

Warriors – let's not fall for these tricks. We're trained to know that Satan uses beauty to mask destruction, and we call him out for it! We aggressively confront him saying, "Get behind me!" We utilize the power that comes from vocalizing the name "Jesus" saying it again and again until the devil flees like James 4:7 promises us! Lastly, we finish the battle by quoting truth from God's Word while physically and intentionally turning our eyes away from the girl who is luring our flesh. Warriors – let's get comfortable being uncomfortable, and let's start living by principles and not by feelings. It's time to fight the war by confronting every thought with the most powerful weapon we have – the name of Jesus!

Have dedicated, daily prayer time.

Constantly remaining in a prayerful state as we go about our days is an attribute of every great Warrior. But it is also crucial for us to set aside daily time in which prayer is our *only* focus. Luke 5:15-16 tells us that even though Jesus became popular and busy as word about His ministry spread, He would often get away from everyone specifically to pray. Guys – Satan is winning the daily battles because we aren't "getting away" often enough. We're fighting the enemy *one* day a week, but he's working all seven of them! It's no wonder we are getting destroyed. We aren't spending dedicated time in prayer over the specific situations and struggles that surround our unique circumstances.

Not only have we become susceptible to the enemy's attacks and all the junk the world throws in our paths every day, but our families and friends are vulnerable as well because we are no longer pray-ers. Hey, if *we* aren't praying, no one is. So let's stop acting like we don't know why our world is going down a completely self-centered, destructive path, and call it like it is: Satan is winning the overall war because he is winning the daily battles! We aren't spending any time fervently praying for our families, our health, our jobs, our friends, our challenges, our attitudes, our struggles, our fears, our passions. Warriors – prayer absolutely works, but we've got to *pray* for it to work!

Daily prayer will look different for every person. My wife and I usually wake up 15 minutes before we need to get moving, and we will read a verse or chapter from the Word with our sons. And after discussing the piece of Scripture that stands out the most, we will spend around 10 minutes praying about every little thing on our minds. Yes, we have morning breath. Yes, we are sometimes half asleep. And yes, my throat will be so dry some mornings that I can barely talk. But starting our days with Jesus as our focus – placing Him above all of the day's activities and challenges – *that* is what covers us with peace, protection, and perspective. It's a no-brainer when considering the return on investment. Those 15 minutes are *well* worth it to see a drastic improvement in the quality of the other 23 hours and 45 minutes!

Be still and listen.

The tendency in prayer is to spend a lot of time talking, and that's why a huge obstacle I wrestle with in prayer is just being quiet to listen to what God is trying to tell me. Shutting up is often hard for us as men to do, but it is the only way to receive God's direction! We've probably all heard Psalm 46:10 where God tells us to "be still and know that I am God." But how many of us actually do this? Occasionally, we need to practice being still and silent while we listen to what God is telling us in our spirit. He will speak to us by putting Scripture in our minds, putting people on our hearts, and putting perspective in our circumstances. But the key is eliminating all the noise and interference that consumes our time and attention. Warriors make a habit of shutting off everything and listening to God for direction.

Ask for the Holy Spirit.

There is no component of prayer more crucial to spiritual victory than receiving the power of the Holy Spirit. That tangible, indescribable presence is a surefire source of divine direction equipping us with the energy, focus, and wisdom needed to win the daily battles. And that's why, if we had time for just *one* prayer every day, this would be the prayer: "God – give me Your Holy Spirit fulfillment, power, guidance, and conviction during every moment of today!"

Some men might still be sitting there right now saying, "I don't quite understand or know about this Holy Spirit stuff." And all I can say is we've all been there. But at some point, we have to abandon "understanding," and just choose to believe that God's presence through His Holy Spirit is real. It's guaranteed that once we experience it, we'll stop trying to figure it out! So, the question becomes: what do we do to experience the Holy Spirit? It's not rocket science...it's just a matter of having faith:

CHOOSE TO TRUST that God and His Holy Spirit are real.
Micah 3:8 – "But as for me, I am filled with power – with the Spirit of the Lord."

> "God, my mind may not fully understand this, but I have faith that You're real and that Your Holy Spirit lives in me!"

RECEIVE HIS POWER that will fuel us for obedience.
Acts 1:8 – "But you will receive power when the Holy Spirit comes upon you."

> "God, I need Your power to enable me to live the life You've called me to live, and to make the right choices in all that I do!"

ASK FOR GUIDANCE to direct our steps.
John 16:13 – "However, when He, the Spirit of truth, has come, He will guide you into all truth." (NIV)

> "God, in literally every thought that I think, I need You to reveal truth, and guide me to fight against my sinful desires!"

EXPERIENCE PEACE that is truly unexplainable.
Philippians 4:7 – "And the peace of God, which transcends all understanding, will guard your hearts and your minds in Christ Jesus." (NIV)

> "God, I invite You to fill me with Your presence. Now let me experience the peace that transcends all understanding."

Identify with others' situations and actually pray for them.

We live in an overwhelmingly, increasingly self-centered, narcissistic world. And it's easy to get caught up in our lives, our schedules, our kids, our obligations, our vacations, and our treasures here on Earth. But God's true treasures are people, and He wants us interceding on their behalf! Job 42:10 is confirmation as it says, "When Job prayed for his friends, the Lord restored his fortunes. In fact, the Lord gave him twice as much as before!" This is a perfect picture of God's heart. He desires our hearts to be all about His heart. And *His* heart is all about others! Guys – when we intentionally identify with others' situations and purposefully meditate on their difficulties as if they were ours, it triggers God's favor and transforms our compassion!

There is power in empathy. I've gotta say – when a friend's five-year-old son has a massive brain tumor, and I spend some time identifying with that and putting myself in their shoes – it sure does make my prayers for them more pointed and passionate. How often do we let our hearts and emotions truly connect with others' unimaginable situations? It'll change our hearts to be more like Jesus! Let's not be the Christian who says, "I will pray for you," but doesn't pray at all. Instead, let's be men who go out of our way to identify with others and actually pray for their situations.

Focus on prayer for the first 21 days of every year.

I cannot testify enough to the power that accompanies giving God the first of everything we have. I've personally seen irrefutable evidence and unexplainable blessing in every area where our family has given our first to Him! That's because the best for God is the first from us, and when we give God our best, He'll bless the rest (see Proverbs 3:9-10). And this applies to more than just money, guys. It applies to our time and focus, too. When we align our focus with God's focus at the beginning of each year, the results are nothing short of supernatural. Try it. Give God the first three weeks of your year with 30 - 45 minutes of daily, specific prayer. Focus on intentionally allowing *His* agenda to drown out *your* agenda, and watch what happens. I no longer need to be convinced of its importance. I've seen the proof in the prayer pudding too many times to count!

Let's challenge ourselves at some point this next year to give God sincere, extended prayer time for three weeks, and let's allow Him the opportunity to prove to us that it works. I think we'll all make it a tradition if we do it once. And if we are looking to take it up a notch, let's fast from something that we're used to living with – whether it is media, food, or something else – so that there are no distractions from immersing ourselves in His plan! Men – there's inconceivable power in deliberately and simultaneously connecting to God while disconnecting from the world.

WORSHIP – Connect with God's presence.

2 Kings 3:15 "'Now bring me someone who can play the harp.' While the harp was being played, the power of the Lord came upon Elisha."

Whether we are discouraged, empty, or apathetic, there is *nothing* that can transform our demeanor or our days more instantaneously than reflecting on how great our God is. That is what worship is. It is taking our thoughts off of our issues and placing them on God's identity! We may not realize it, but a *huge* part of why we are losing spiritual battles is because we are lacking the effects of worship. Our tanks are empty. We are apathetic about living for Jesus. Biblical obedience has become exhausting and bothersome. And it's because we are in desperate need of God's presence. We are in desperate need of *worship!*

Worship is the channel that connects us to the supernatural. It reveals false realities, reinstates divine perspective, rebuilds complete confidence, and refills genuine desire for obedience. And all of these benefits are just a worship song away from becoming a reality if we'll just go there! Sometimes we need to just turn on some worship music and reflect on God's greatness – especially in the midst of trials.

2 Kings 3:15 describes this exact scenario when King Jehoshaphat, while facing ominous circumstances amid a time of war, brings in the Prophet Elisha to hear from God before going into battle. And what is Elisha's first course of action in this urgent situation? Setting the right mood with music! He turns *immediately* to worship as the *first* line of defense summoning a musician to play so he could receive a word from God. And unsurprisingly "while

the harp was being played, the power of the Lord came upon Elisha." It was a bold move to turn first to worship in this tense time of uncertainty, but it was indeed the right move. It should come as no surprise that God showed up and showed out to protect King Jehoshaphat's people throughout the ensuing battle!

Men – worship has to be our go-to...our *first* line of defense. Music has to be one of our *first* weapons drawn when we're fatigued or frustrated on the field of battle. And just how the Lord's presence came to Elisha, it will come to us, too! We already know from Elisha's example that when we prepare for God's presence, He will pour out His power! So let's find some great worship music, crank up the volume in the house or the car, and just wait for God. He *will* show up! But we've got to set favorable conditions for His presence to reside!

Every one of us should be spending *daily* time envisioning ourselves at the foot of the cross of Jesus with His blood dripping down on us – intentionally immersing ourselves in the reality of the crucifixion and resurrection! It will transform our worship time. I try to reflect and *visualize* these powerful provisions every day...because they simultaneously humble me and pump me up:

- God's inconceivably loving gift
- Jesus' perfectly sinless life
- Jesus' voluntarily selfless sacrifice
- Jesus' completely bloody cross
- Jesus' incomprehensibly brutal crucifixion
- Jesus' incomparably powerful resurrection
- God's ultimately untouchable victory

Use music as a vehicle to enter God's presence.

No matter who we are, the power of music when combined with the meditation of who Jesus is will transform our attitudes, our feelings, and our perspectives. When we get in a funk and are discontent, depressed, or discouraged, it's because God has become too small in our minds while our problems have become too big in our minds. Worship eliminates that false reality and allows us to have an accurate perspective on our circumstances. It usually takes just seconds for even the most depressing thoughts to dissolve when we turn on worship music and reflect on Jesus. The hard part is – turning off the other junk that we listen to and choosing to let our music be music that will draw us closer to God. There's no way to measure the difference it makes in our lives when we use music the way God intended.

But what does this look like in the context of our day? Well, when we enter God's presence through worship, it might look different every day for every person! For some, once the music is playing, it might mean walking around and raising their hands. For others, it might mean bowing on their knees and whispering prayers to God. For me, it differs every day. Sometimes it involves couch sitting and crying. Other days it involves jogging and shouting! There's no right or wrong way, but let's just make sure that Jesus is getting more passionate worship than our hunting trips and football teams! Does our worship depict this? One thing is for sure – even our most intense passions for worldly things *all* became strangely secondary once we experience the authentic presence of God in worship! Worship precisely puts worldly things into perspective.

Get some great worship music and decide where, when, and how we can use it.

Because of the power that music has, there is *nothing* that the enemy wants to keep us from doing more than using it to worship Jesus. When worship is absent, our perspective is wrong, and our emotions lead us to worldly medication…and that's exactly where Satan wants us. That's why we have to set ourselves up with the right tools to fight the enemy in this area. This all starts with having access to some great, Christian worship music. There is no shortage of great, Christian music out there, and although it hasn't always been this way, the musical quality in Christian music is now as excellent as its secular counterparts! So that's no excuse for opting out of a Christian musical catalog. No matter the genre, there are some solid options available.

Great Christian music is readily available, but it can't be effective until we make it easily accessible. That means actually downloading it and having it handy on our various devices. Otherwise, worship music won't practically integrate with our daily routine. So whether it's streaming on our computer at work, playing on our iPod or iPhone during our workout, or blasting on the surround sound in our den – let's all start thinking practically about how this can happen if it isn't already! It seems like common sense, but Warriors must figure out ways to fill our hearts and our households with music that glorifies Jesus so that we aren't blinded and misguided by the world's opinions and perspectives on the situations we face every day.

When we want to worship least, we need to worship most.

One thing we need to be aware of when it comes to worship is that it will sometimes be the *last* thing that our flesh wants to participate in, and that's because Satan knows that he will lose the spiritual battle if we *do* go there. So, let's be on guard for those times when we find ourselves wanting to avoid worship or even prayer, Bible reading, or fellowship with other believers – because that's likely the place where our hearts will be healed. One moment in the presence of Jesus will change *everything*, so let's set ourselves up to be consistently connected to God's presence in daily worship!

ACCOUNTABILITY – Initiate transparency and accountability with other Warriors.

James 5:16 "Confess your sins to each other and pray for each other so that you may be healed. The earnest prayer of a righteous person has great power and produces wonderful results."

It sounds cliché, but war isn't won alone. We need other Warriors who have our backs and protect us from blind spots. We need other strong men of God who know what's going on with us, can cover us in prayer, and can call us out when we're getting off track. That's what accountability is, and it's crucial in our daily regimen to do *whatever it takes* to force this accountability on ourselves. Self-initiated accountability is a trait of a true Warrior.

It is my responsibility to keep myself accountable.

It's safe to say self-initiated accountability is something that most of us lack on a daily basis. That's because sharing our mistakes is inconvenient and uncomfortable. We'd rather just remain quiet about our missteps and let time heal our wounds and regrets. By doing so, we've settled *yet again* for less than God's best because we think we know better than Him. After all – dealing with the pain and emptiness of our slipups sure beats the embarrassment we would suffer in admitting our wrongdoing! Right? Wrong. When we find the kind of accountability God intended, it brings us help, not harm. Proverbs 27:17 describes this partnership that pushes us saying that "a friend sharpens a friend" like "iron sharpens iron." Biblical accountability isn't punishment; it's progress! And the enemy will use everything to withdraw us from accountability so he can prey on us while we're isolated from the pack.

There's absolutely nothing wrong with letting someone else initiate the accountability and ask us the hard questions. But we can't depend on that. Warriors initiate our *own* accountability. We're grown men, not little babies. And we don't need someone to follow up with us regarding our spiritual successes or failures all day, every day. Besides, we shouldn't have to be pestered by a friend to fess up to our flaws. Real Warriors *initiate* the accountability without being badgered. We *report* our vulnerabilities to someone else because that's how we prevent annihilation in the spiritual war! Who cares if we bother another man of God for a few minutes each week? We've got to have another Warrior that knows what we're facing.

It's a question worth asking – how many of us are actually sharing our struggles, our victories, and our prayer needs with someone else on a daily basis? It doesn't have to be a 10-minute phone call for accountability to exist, but we've got to care about our spiritual condition enough to tell at least someone what we're facing each day so that they can cover our backs and help us stay on track! Men – if we don't have this accountability, let's start praying that God will provide it – because we can't win a war without fellow Warriors.

Celebrate victories and share struggles with someone.

Accountability will look different for everyone, but a Warrior is aware that someone else has to know our deepest, darkest temptations so that we can receive prayer and encouragement. It might be a text or two in the morning or a message to a buddy saying, "Hey man – I'm home by myself, and I'm feeling some intense temptation to look at pornography...can you say a prayer for me?" It might be a quick call on the way to work to talk about the financial concerns we're having. Or it might be a weekly lunch where we celebrate milestones and spiritual victories but also share the latest on our marriage struggles. Whatever the case – Ecclesiastes 4:9 says it best when it tells us, "Two people are better off than one, for they can help each other succeed." Guys – we *don't* have this on our own. And trying to win the war without other Warriors will land us immobile on the battlefield.

Be completely honest and transparent with someone.

Accountability is inconvenient for our flesh, and it takes effort to initiate. But it is critical that we deliver the unfortunate truth to our accountability. Otherwise, we are cultivating an environment where sin can take root, destroying our lives from the inside out. Transparency isn't fun, but it's a necessity for survival as a Warrior. When we mess up, we fess up. "Hey bro – just lashed out at my wife and said some things I shouldn't have said. Can you just pray that God's Spirit would cover us and help me not to be dumb in those kinds of situations? Thanks, man!" *That's* how we initiate transparency and avoid destruction. Slightly embarrassing? Maybe. But a brief moment of discomfort sure beats a possible lifetime of consequences. When we find the right accountability partners, they'll punch us in the gut and tell it like it is, but they'll also lend a non-judgmental ear and a Biblical perspective that has our best interest in mind.

Transparency is hard, men. It's far from easy to be vulnerable and honest, especially for us guys. And Satan will try to convince us that there are uncomfortable consequences that follow confession, because he knows that exposing sin is the path to eliminating sin! Just like James 5:16 says, confession is what leads us to healing. Warriors – it could be several, overwhelming addictions that we are struggling with, or it could be just one seemingly small habit. Whatever the case may be, it's time to stop settling for less than God's best by concealing those strongholds. Let's tell another Warrior what we're struggling with so that the enemy has no isolated entry point!

Find a spiritual mentor.

We all need that man in our lives who has a résumé filled with an unshakeable faith in Jesus and an unrelenting fight for Jesus. Through the ups and the downs, the celebrations and the tragedies, the prosperities and the hardships they've clung to God's promises and fought for obedience. And they might not have always gotten it right, but they always made it right. I'm tremendously blessed in this area because I've been around this all my life thanks to an earthly father who wouldn't compromise on his principles because he knew his purpose. Whether it's a dad, a brother, a friend, a coach, a teacher, or a pastor – it doesn't matter. We *all* need that role model who has a track record of modeling Jesus' example. It's like any real-world profession; the more we're around experts in a certain field, the more second nature that field becomes to us. Another way of saying it – our chances of succeeding at something increase dramatically when we're around people who have already succeeded at that something. And being a man of God is no exception.

We need to consistently be around men who don't just *say* they love Jesus, but who *live* like they love Jesus. The more we glean from their wisdom, the more we'll realize that they've made calculated decision after calculated decision to live with caution and integrity. *These* are the influences that young Warriors so desperately need – the veteran Warriors who are genuinely passionate about maximizing leadership potential in young men, incessantly grooming replacements so victory on the battlefield extends to the next generation.

It's time to start taking advantage of the wisdom of these battle-tested vets. Proverbs 12:15 tells us, "Fools think their own way is right, but the wise listen to others." We can't underestimate the value of wise counsel through every phase of life, especially when it comes from an experienced spiritual Warrior. Often, his experiences, both successes and failures, can help us discern between choosing God's path and choosing our own. Let's find these men who have consistently stayed close to Jesus and lived in spiritual victory for years and decades. And let's learn from them so that we can become the Warrior example for the next generation!

SUMMARY

+ Time – A Warrior makes time in his daily routine to invest in his relationship with Jesus knowing that time is the vehicle God uses to get our hearts.

+ God's Word – A Warrior reads and reflects on something in God's Word on a daily basis understanding that this is the only way to truly know Jesus.

+ Prayer – A Warrior communicates constantly with Jesus through prayer knowing that continuous connection to His Holy Spirit is the only method of survival in the spiritual fight.

+ Worship – A Warrior uses music to enter into God's presence daily to gain the supernatural perspective, passion, and peace that comes from the Holy Spirit.

+ Accountability – A Warrior initiates accountability for himself by being transparent with someone about every detail of his spiritual struggles and victories.

RESPONSE

Jesus, I know that relationships all start with investing time. And God, I ask that You would give me the daily desire and discipline to invest time in our relationship. I already know that it's going to have incredible return on investment when I do. And although I'm not really sure what this is going to look like in my already crazy daily routine, I ask that You would reveal the practical time for me to spend in Your Word, in prayer, and in worship daily. I don't want to neglect this relationship, because it gives purpose and peace to literally every other aspect of my life!

Give me the courage to have the conversation with my family about beginning fresh and letting this become a staple in my household – to read and reflect on Your Word, to become constant pray-ers, and to spend time worshipping in Your presence! I'm not sure what this is going to look like, but I know that it's simply a lie of the enemy to make me fearful of stepping out and being the Warrior I need to be for my family, friends, and others You put in my path.

Jesus, I just want to know You. And because You are the Word, I pray that You would make me hungry for the Word each and every day. God, give me the discipline to feed my spirit even on days when it's not easy, and to speak Your Word over every situation and every temptation knowing that Your Word is truth and is more powerful than anything I face! Help me to be a Warrior who uses his sword to obliterate every lie and worldly persuasion that comes my way!

Lord, I may not be the ideal pray-er, but it's time I step it up and engage in constant spiritual combat by talking to You all the time – whether audibly from my mouth or silently in my spirit. I know that spending designated, structured time in prayer is critical for me to win the daily battles. But Jesus, I also want to be a Warrior who prays about literally everything, whether it seems spiritually relevant or not. I want to be a leader who confronts every thought of every moment as it comes into my head making sure it aligns with Your Word! Make me into a specimen pray-er who uses the unmatchable name of Jesus to face every fear and temptation, and let Your Holy Spirit give me power and discernment in every thought I think.

God, Your presence is something I want more than anything, because it gives me supernatural peace and perspective on the situations I face every day in this world. Guide me to some life-changing worship music, and help me to insert this powerful weapon into my practical daily routine as a safeguard from the deception, discouragement, and false reality of the world.

Lastly, Lord, let me embrace transparency and accountability as I begin this new journey of investing time in our relationship. I know this spiritual war can't be fought alone, so I pray that You'll provide me with a couple of Jesus-loving friends that I can confide in through thick and thin. Remove all fear, embarrassment, and awkwardness in Jesus' name when it comes to being transparent and sharing my struggles and downfalls. I want to be a Warrior who embraces uncovering darkness so that light will overtake these areas in my life!

Make my daily regimen all about knowing You and obeying You, Jesus!

CHAPTER 4

CONFRONTING THE HEART

Winning the spiritual war requires keeping our hearts and habits pure.

So far, our main focus has been on *thinking* like a Warrior and *preparing* like a Warrior for the daily spiritual battles we face. But now it's time to start looking at the tactics that our opponent will use against us to render us ineffective on the battlefield. It begins with putting our spiritual health under a microscope and examining where we are uniquely vulnerable to attack. For most of us, there is at least one area where the enemy has infiltrated the front lines and has taken control, and the scary thing is we might not even know it!

Men – our opponent needs only *one* blind spot, just *one* entry point, to prevent us from reaching our fullest potential on the battlefield and experiencing the spoils of victory in our day-to-day lives. He just needs *one* area where we are still trying to gratify our flesh and live according to our feelings to keep us from going "all in" and experiencing God's best. And I'm convinced most of us never even come *close* to fulfilling God's purpose or experiencing God's peace, because we won't remain completely pure long enough for God to reveal it to us! It only takes a little sin to steal a lot of purpose! Romans 8:13 (NIV) warns us against providing that single foothold for the enemy saying, "If you live according to the flesh, you will die; but if by the Spirit you put to death the misdeeds of the body, you will live!" Our flesh, if left untamed, will kill us. Or we can "put to death the misdeeds of the body," and experience life as it was intended to be.

Guys – the ultimate goal of this journey is excellence. And excellence boils down to this: we need to start using our energy to *find* something wrong with our hearts rather than using it to defend what's not wrong with our hearts! Whatever that one habit or stronghold is that we've let fester – *that* is what is holding us back from being used to our fullest potential. Once we surrender it to Jesus – *that* is what will ultimately unlock the abundance and peace that we're all looking for. So let's stand on Psalm 5:12 knowing that the Lord "bless[es] the righteous and surround[s] them with [His] favor as with a shield!" Let's pursue *complete* righteousness and receive that shield of favor. It's time to go to war and confront the enemy!

Self-Indulgence – Know who we are and know our standard.

Ephesians 2:3 "All of us used to live that way, following the passionate desires and inclinations of our sinful nature. By our very nature we were subject to God's anger, just like everyone else."

If we want to end up miserable and miss out on God's purpose and peace, we simply need to live by what our feelings tell us. Self-indulgence is the motto of our world today, and everyone is telling us (just like its definition says) to "gratify our own appetites, desires and whims!" And there could be nothing further from God's Truth. In fact, 2 Timothy 4:3 warns us of these times: "For a time is coming when people will no longer listen to sound and wholesome teaching. They will follow their own desires and will look for teachers who will tell them whatever their itching ears want to hear." We need to know who we are, and know that our ultimate standard is the Word of God. If it isn't in the Word, it's just an opinion. And if it's just an opinion, it simply doesn't matter. It seems that all we hear in today's culture is that we should follow every feeling we have, because those natural tendencies are what make us unique. That is laughable though, because this is the *opposite* of what God's Word tells us!

Warriors – this is the perfect point to pause and just acknowledge that our emotions are a fragile, formless, ever-evolving, impressionable, unsubstantiated amoeba that can be changed secondly by even the weakest of external influences! So no – emotions are *never* a wise motivator for our decisions. They'll almost certainly lead to second-guessing and regret at some point down the road! It's much more advisable and beneficial to live by a set of unchangeable truths.

But emotions are enticing, and it's exceptionally easier to live by our feelings indulging in food, sex, money, possessions, thrills, popularity, and power. What makes it even tougher is that we can't control how we feel;

however, we *can* control whether we pray about how we feel! Guys, we can't control what our emotions tell us, but we can pray that God will *change* those emotions and help us manage them according to His Word.

Bitterness / Hatred / Revenge – Choose to forgive immediately, and let God handle the situation.

Luke 23:34 "Jesus said, 'Father, forgive them, for they don't know what they are doing.'"

Undoubtedly every man reading this has experienced a moment of complete disdain for another person at some point. I'm talking about that feeling where we'd love to punch them square in the face and kick them once they're on the ground. Everyone knows what I'm talking about, and it's an almost uncontrollable sensation of adrenaline and restlessness based on how we were wronged or mistreated. Whatever that experience looked like for us, be it a friend who stabbed us in the back, a coworker that gossiped about us to our boss, or a family member who stole something from us, it is the easiest thing in the world to harbor bitter feelings and let a small seed of unforgiveness bloom into an entire forest of hatred. Boy, am I glad Jesus didn't do that after we threw a crown of thorns on His head and started ripping apart His back!

We don't need to go into an essay about why we should forgive immediately. It can be summed up in just two words by the example of *the* greatest Warrior of all time: "The cross." I'm sure Jesus was tempted to hate us as we spat in his face, mocked him, hammered nails into His hands, and stuck a spear in His side. Yet *still* Jesus set the ultimate example when He looked us right in the face and said, "Dad – I forgive them!" Sheesh. If that doesn't serve as a motivation to just let that person (or people) off the hook for what they did, then I don't know what else to say. Hey, guys – let's take 1 John 4:20 seriously: "If someone says, 'I love God,' but hates a fellow believer, that person is a liar; for if we don't love people we can see, how can we love God, whom we cannot see?"

My precious wife sure isn't a liar by 1 John 4:20's standard. She immediately forgave a man who gruesomely slaughtered her brother along with three other victims in a house. Think about that – her own brother was murdered by another man, stabbed a dozen times with a butcher knife. Yet, Brooke Ingram decided that she was going to *pray* for this murderer's salvation instead of harboring hatred. Wow. What a picture of Jesus' love and forgiveness lived out before my eyes. What's our excuse? It's a choice, guys. Let's pray that God would give us supernatural power to let whoever it is off the hook. Right now. Let's instead pray blessings over that person and not let even one more conversation or thought please the enemy with our view of that person. Let's ignore what the world says about being entitled to holding a grudge, and let's demonstrate the same love that Jesus demonstrated for us on the cross. It doesn't matter what they did. Jesus didn't have an excuse, nor should we.

And why not take that a step further? Let's continue to think the best about people even when we've seen them at their worst. Let's give them the benefit of the doubt time and time again. When someone wrongs us, let's fight that urge to "get even" by living out Proverbs 20:22, and let's just "wait for the Lord to handle the matter." Talk about a challenge for us as men! We always want to go and fix everything, but God tells us that a Warrior doesn't look for revenge. We let *God* fix situations because one thing is certain: He can handle it better than we can! That's why it's *always* best to hold our tongues and say a prayer even when the world tells us our anger is justified.

Warriors – it's uncomfortable for our flesh to choose forgiveness. *Super* uncomfortable. But as Pastor Chris Hodges says, Warriors "travel light" and shed the baggage that we're carrying – the grudges, the frustrations, the records of wrong. And when we get rid of the weight, we experience freedom. We find out instantaneously that we've been punishing *ourselves* by keeping a tight grip on that animosity. Because it is the offended that benefits most from forgiving the offender!

Pride / Vanity / Narcissism – Get over ourselves and be humble.

Philippians 2:3 "Do nothing out of selfish ambition or vain conceit. Rather, in humility value others above yourselves." (NIV)

To say that our culture has become consumed with self is a comical understatement. Look no further than social media outlets to see self-created virtual shrines that oftentimes do nothing but feed our egos and offer an altar for others to admire us. Let's take a step back and examine how bad this has gotten: we consider it *normal* to capture 24/7 videography and photography of ourselves so others can provide instantaneous feedback on our every move! It's bizarre. And no matter how normal this becomes in our culture, it's narcissism at its worst. No, there's nothing wrong with social media, but it is a perfect snapshot of the self-centric epidemic in our society – we're obsessed with ourselves, and we're fixated on our world and our world only.

It's worth asking – are we more concerned with gaining followers for ourselves or gaining followers for Jesus? Let's drop the façade and admit that we *all* occasionally struggle to keep humility intact. Whether it's pride in our accomplishments, appearance, wealth, position, popularity, or intelligence, we *all* have moments where we are just plain impressed with ourselves. Meanwhile, God's shooting us straight in Romans 12:3 (NIV) when He says, "Do not think of yourself more highly than you ought." Guys – it's time that we hop off that high horse. It's a deliberate choice to be humble or to be proud. It's a choice to exalt others above ourselves even when the world's standards deem us superior. It's a choice to intentionally stop feeding those thoughts that glorify our talents, attributes, and accomplishments. When we choose to keep those narcissistic thoughts alive instead of putting them to death, it shows.

Many of us eat it up when people look over at us because of our notoriety, popularity, or our physical attraction. We love the attention of commanding a room…and that's *vanity*. It's finding satisfaction through worshipping self. Philippians 2:3 (NIV) talks about this form of pride saying, "Do nothing out of selfish ambition or vain conceit." Hey, men – it might seem petty, but God doesn't like it when our excitement is rooted in attention for ourselves – even for a brief moment.

We need to get over ourselves. I know there are some guys who have it going for them occupationally, monetarily, aesthetically. But what a sign of shallow, immature thinking to believe that we are superior to someone based on an item on our résumé, a number in our bank account, or the structure of our physical bodies! This type of prideful perspective is the root of mistreating others too. How many of us have ever *not* interacted with others in a situation based on their inferior position? Or awkward appearance? Or differing personality? Or lower intelligence? Or lack of success? Let's get real – we've *all* had thoughts that said we're better than the employee at the bottom of the totem pole, the strange-looking, weird guy that we avoid at church, and the uneducated motor mouth that annoys us at the gym.

Let's call it what it is – it's *pride*, and God doesn't like it! A Warrior doesn't base the credibility of others on externals and worldly status symbols. A Warrior sees every person as valuable and more important than himself regardless of what worldly measuring sticks are telling his intellect! Speaking of intellect, what about the pride of those of us who know more than everyone else? We won't listen to *anything* from *anyone* because we've heard it all. This "know-it-all" mentality is rampant among men. And when we're easily offended, it's indisputable evidence of pride in our hearts. Warriors know that we can learn something from every person we encounter, and like James 1:19 says, we are "quick to listen" and "slow to get angry" when we receive advice or correction. Guys – let's not get offended by criticism. Instead, let's celebrate it as a chance to grow! *That* is humility.

It's one thing dealing with *our* pride, but how about the doozy of dealing with someone *else's* pride? Come on, men – we *all* like to be the alpha, don't we? And we sure don't like being challenged, stepped on, or walked over. We're wired to crave respect from others, and when someone fails to deliver, we don't take well to it. Our flesh absolutely hates being disrespected. Yet, this is exactly what Jesus wrestled with during the last week of His life: prideful people who deep down He knew were far inferior to Him, spitting on Him and beating His body to a pulp. It makes you wonder how in the world He didn't snap. Jesus faced unthinkable pride and still demonstrated a perfect humility. This is the kind of backwards thinking Warriors possess. We embrace the moments when someone considers themselves better than us or disrespects us. Those moments aren't excuses to get fired up and show another person who's superior. No – those moments are opportunities to exhibit the uncommon, uncompromising humility that the Man Himself demonstrated on this Earth.

Judgmental Spirit – Love people.

Matthew 7:3 "And why worry about a speck in your friend's eye when you have a log in your own?"

I don't know about anyone else, but I used to have a PhD in pinpointing the shortcomings of others. I remember the days of high school and college when my favorite course of study was the sin of my peers. I was the master of scoping out others' weaknesses from a mile away but was as blind as a bat when it came to identifying my own. And one day I realized that I was the subject of Matthew 7:3, constantly worrying about the specks in the eyes of others. Meanwhile, I had a tree trunk in my own. I had forgotten the inconvenient reminder of Romans 3:23 – that I was a part of that "all" that had sinned and fallen short of God's standard. I was that guy – the religious, holier-than-thou, hypocritical, judgmental "Christian" that spent his time educating others on their imperfections. Ouch. I needed to hear the hilariously profound quote, "Don't judge others because they sin differently than you." Boy, if we were all as concerned about our *own* spiritual condition as we are about everyone else's.

It is a strange phenomenon that has developed in church culture. We look at the sins of others and become obsessed with how they are not obeying God. It's almost as if we are miserable obeying Jesus' Word, and we want others to be miserable with us! A right relationship with Jesus will give us nothing but love and grace for others – not animosity toward them. Mark 12:30-31 tells us simply: Love God. Love others. Period! It doesn't say "Love God. Accuse others." Billy Graham knocked it out of the park when he said, "It's the Holy Spirit's job to convict, God's job to judge, and my job to love." Grand slam.

A great litmus test for our hearts as Christians: Does someone else's sin spawn a desire in us for them to experience the *love* of God or the *wrath* of God? Unfortunately, a lot of us might not want to answer that question honestly because it would contradict everything about the Man we say we live for. We need to check our perspective, guys. Some of us seriously want to see others pay for what they are doing, and that is an anti-Biblical attitude.

I totally used to be that guy who made it my top priority to tell others what was wrong with them and how they needed to fix it. I was missing the boat on my God-given assignment: to give people love before giving them a lesson! Yes, we need to hold friends accountable for the sin in their lives, but relationship comes before retribution. And kindness precedes criticism.

Warriors love. We don't judge. We've got as much room for improvement as anyone! Let's do our job and let God do His!

Worry / Fear / Doubt – Trust that God is in control.

Philippians 4:6 "Don't worry about anything; instead, pray about everything. Tell God what you need, and thank Him for all He has done."

One area where I've struggled immensely in my past? Not truly trusting that God's got every situation in His hands. I was good at *saying* I trusted, but my emotions and thoughts were *gripped* with fear. Am I going to get into a head-on collision driving there? Is she going to break up with me? Am I going to find someone new if I obey God and end this relationship? Is this sickness something serious that could take my life? Am I going to have enough money to make it through next month? How in the world is God going to turn this possible lawsuit into something good? Fearful thoughts can consume us and convince us that God isn't bigger than our situation. They can even throw us into deep depression. And guess what. It doesn't change the reality that God is sitting on His throne able to do *anything* and *everything* He wants *whenever* He wants. Our worrying doesn't change the reality of God's omnipotence over the universe. It just pointlessly ruins our days on Earth.

Guys – we can't worry and pray at the same time. So instead of investing a thought into what might happen, let's invest a prayer into declaring faith in who can make anything happen! Let's be pray-ers who confront every worry or fearful thought with a simple declaration of trust in God's power! This isn't easy, especially in the valleys of financial struggles, health issues, family tragedies, career uncertainties, or relational challenges. It's downright painful to deal with these situations. But Warriors live by faith, not by feelings, and we *know* that according to Psalm 23:4, God is "close beside [us]" and will protect and comfort us in every situation! It's time to abandon the lie that worrying is a habit that we inherited through our family tree or some trait that is out of our control. When we replace worrisome thoughts with prayer and Scripture, God *will* intervene.

Discouragement / Depression – Have faith that God is with us.

Deuteronomy 31:8 "Do not be afraid or discouraged, for the Lord will personally go ahead of you. He will be with you; He will neither fail you nor abandon you."

It was June of 2008 when I decided to take the big step of starting my own marketing and web technologies business. There I was a couple of years out of college with an intense passion for sports and an eagerness to get my foot in the door in the college sports industry. I took the plunge, and within two weeks, I had received an opportunity to create an online showcase for the UAB Blazers football team, a project that would help sell their program to recruits. I was elated! I had my shot, and I *wasn't* going to disappoint!

Fast-forward three months to October of 2008, a month after completing a beautifully elaborate project for the Blazers. I was fresh off of probably my greatest professional accomplishment to date, and then the phone rang. And it wasn't good. It was one of the UAB coaches, and all he said was, "Hey Lance – we need to take the website down immediately." What in the world was going on? I was freaking out inside, and my heart sank through two stories of our apartment complex. Then things got worse. Naïve me didn't know that copying design elements of the Florida Gators' website was a big no-no. Apparently, ignorance doesn't pardon stupidity, and I was now in the midst of a potential lawsuit. It might not seem like a big deal to anyone else, but just picture this: I've voluntarily left the corporate world to give it a go on my own, and I'm literally on my first big job with over 200 hours of work invested – all of it now down the drain. To add insult to injury, I quickly received a "cease and desist" letter from the sports design company that I dreamed of becoming – all because I had imitated their work.

My world was crashing down, and I was completely and utterly devastated. My thoughts raced for two straight weeks waiting fearfully to get the verdict from UAB on whether they would even allow me to redo the project. I hardly slept. I worried. I cried. I played out every possible negative scenario. I was in a deep state of depression because in my mind, my business was history. And even if it survived, there was no way I would ever get a sports team to trust me again. After all, the most prominent Southeastern Conference school at the time had pegged me as a plagiarist. Not to mention, I had embarrassed an entire athletics program!

It was an awful time. But what's the response when we're hopelessly discouraged? We absolutely smother our feelings with worship to regain proper perspective! And that's what I did. I can still remember every detail of the exact moment when I turned on some worship music, hit my knees, and completely unloaded the situation on God. I kid you not – within *seconds*, I felt physical weight lifted off my body! The moment I surrendered the depression and the discouragement to Dad, He handled it. And not only did my business survive that situation – it thrived after that situation. I was able to redesign the UAB football showcase, and God just showed off by allowing me to receive a prestigious advertising honor for my new, *original* design!

That depression was real, and for those who have experienced the isolation and uncertainty that accompanies the darkness of depression, it's overwhelming. We've probably all faced these moments and seasons that brought about unspeakable hopelessness. For some of us, we didn't even know *why* we were in that depressed state. In fact, those situations seem to be the worst of all, because we can't pinpoint the source of that discouragement.

But whatever the case – even when we feel like the walls are caving in on us – God is *there* with us. And even when we don't see light, we declare truth. Warriors stand on Deuteronomy 31:8 knowing that God will "neither fail [us] or abandon [us]." Our heavenly Dad is just waiting for us to hand Him our most devastating circumstances so He can show off with His power and shower us with His peace. Warriors – Psalm 34:17 tells us that God hears us when we call to Him for help, and He rescues us from all our troubles. Let's be men who call on God *first* and invite Him immediately into our bad days. Let's just tell Him that we need Him to intervene – even before we reach out to spouses, friends, and pastors – and *especially* before we try to deal with situations on our own. Then just wait – because when God gets involved and sends His army into the combat zone, He annihilates the darkness, and John 1:5 tells us that His light can never be extinguished!

Regret / Unworthiness / Guilt – Declare that God has redeemed us.

Psalm 103:12 "He has removed our sins as far from us as the east is from the west."

We've *all* got skeletons in our closet. We've *all* made plenty of unspeakably stupid decisions that still bring us embarrassment and shame. But those ignorant moments and idiotic choices in our past do not define who we are now. And when we let our past tell us who we are or let guilt convince us that our mistakes are unforgivable – we're minimizing the power of Jesus' death and resurrection. Warriors – we don't slight the cross. We know the magnitude of the cross of Jesus and the significance of His resurrection. It has covered every sin we've ever committed and every sin we will commit – no matter how atrocious or sick those sins seem to us. Regardless of how filthy our yesterday might be, nothing can withstand the cleansing power of the blood of Jesus!

Ephesians 1:7 assures us of this, and that God "purchased our freedom with the blood of His Son and forgave our sins." It's very simple – when we repent, God removes our sin *completely*. And Matthew 3:8 tells us that God just wants our obedience from that point forward saying, "Prove by the way you live that you have repented of your sins and turned to God." God doesn't care about yesterday. He just wants our hearts today!

Warriors – we need to remember the profound truth in Romans 8:28 that God uses *everything*, even our missteps, for His purpose when we follow His calling. And if we really want to ruffle the feathers of the enemy, we'll use our past stupidity to help prevent someone *else's* future stupidity! Be encouraged because God doesn't know the word "irreparable!" And we're not going to buy into the enemy's lies to condemn us for how we messed up. God is not only going to restore us to completeness, but He is going to turn what the devil intended for evil and use those past struggles to help others struggling in the same way! Warriors – yesterday's mistakes are nothing but a platform for today's ministry!

Negativity – Choose joy.

1 Thessalonians 5:16 "Always be joyful."

Is there anything more draining than being around a person who always dampens the mood with a glass-half-empty perspective? We all know that person, and no matter how ideal a situation may seem, they'll be sure to burst that bubble and remind everyone that they're not impressed...with *anything*. Negativity is exhausting, not to mention contagious. And it can siphon joy from even the most optimistic people. The question is – are we the ones that are siphoning the joy from our wives, our families, coworkers, and friends? Negativity can kill a household. It can destroy an office. It can ruin any relationship. Men – we can exhaust, discourage, and frustrate others with our attitudes, or we can energize, encourage, and inspire others with our attitudes. Either way, it's a *choice*. We as men hold the ability to completely transform every environment with our attitudes, so let's not waste it!

The Bible spells it out simply for us in 1 Thessalonians 5:16 telling us to "always be joyful." That is a weighty responsibility that can only be accomplished by incessantly focusing on the positive no matter how grim a situation looks. See – Warriors know that no matter how hopeless a circumstance may seem in the natural, the supernatural power of God is infinitely bigger, and He can change any situation in an instant! Guys – it takes no effort to succumb to pessimism. In fact, it's downright lazy. And any of us who ridicule steadfastly joyful people and call them "fake" is likely just annoyed at the fact that we're too immature to do the same! What the world calls fake, Warriors call leadership! Because unwavering joy requires remarkable effort and maturity.

Insecurity – Be confident in God's unique design and flee comparison.

Ephesians 2:10 "For we are God's masterpiece..."

Insecurity might be a topic that our culture typically associates with women, but they aren't the only ones who struggle with feeling like they're not good enough, talented enough, smart enough, or special enough. That gut-wrenching feeling of uncertainty about who we are is just as poignant for men as it is for women. The enemy knows it, too! Remember – Satan's greatest tactic is deception, and he'll whisper lies to us to get us down in the dumps, temporarily paralyzing us and preventing us from operating in the role God placed us. The enemy knows that if we will buy into his lie that we're insignificant, we will automatically compensate by seeking significance and security from some worldly calling card or comfort. I feel irrelevant, so now I'll go find something that makes me feel relevant! Misplaced identity.

We are the worst at this. We will go find some title or profession or attention-getter to hang our hats on. Or we'll go and sedate our self-doubt with thrills – alcohol, drugs, sexual pleasure, food, money – *anything* to ignore the pain of feeling unimportant or insignificant. Attention and affirmation through social media have become a go-to medication for our culture. And isn't it a comedic irony that we build a picture-perfect virtual façade to mask and medicate a miserable reality? We put every detail of our seemingly splendid, problem-free lives on display, gauging interest and receiving feedback that alleviates our insecurities – until the next day when we retreat to the same remedy again!

But cyber assertion – just like any other worldly solution – will eventually leave us miserable. That's because our design makes us incapable of finding security in how we look, what we wear, what we drive, how much money we have, how much we accomplish, or how much attention we receive from others. True significance comes from knowing that we were uniquely woven together by the Master Tailor, and that His perfect plan involves us doing a job that no one else can do, in a way that no one else can do it. God made me like me for a job no one else can do like me. Grasp this and it'll transform our view of self! Psalm 139:13 tells us that God "made all the delicate, inner parts of my body and knit me together in my mother's womb." We might be far from what the world considers "perfect," but that's the problem – the world isn't our standard! God is the Master Craftsman and intentionally put each one of us together.

It bolsters both a substantial confidence and a steady humility knowing that I, Lance Ingram, all of 5'6" and 140 pounds wearing shoes and soaking wet, was dynamically engineered for a purpose that no one else on Earth could do as well as me. And the areas where I'm not in line with the world's prototype were calculated choices by the Creator to keep me from doing something *other* than my job! How liberating that even what the world calls a weakness was a premeditated decision by God to keep us from doing something He didn't intend for us to do!

Theodore Roosevelt said it best: "Comparison is the thief of joy." And when we compare ourselves to others, we not only lose our joy, but we insult our Creator. We might not be as talented as our friend on the football field. We might not have as much skill on our instrument as the person beside us. We might not have as much money or as nice of a house as our neighbor. We might not be as successful in our career as our brothers or sisters. But God didn't *want* us to be them. God wanted us to be us. He wanted us to be who we are because we are equipped to do completely different things than that person who, in our minds, has superseded us.

Someone will *always* be better than us by the world's standards, but Warriors combat feelings of insecurity with confidence in how we've been wired for a task that only *we* can do. When we feel inadequate in our appearance, our talents, our accomplishments, our popularity, or find ourselves on the slippery slope of comparing *our* lives with someone *else's*, let's quickly recognize that this is an attack from the enemy to distract us from God's tailored assignment for us. The truth is when we don't feel good enough, our perspective isn't Biblical enough!

Warriors – comparison is the path to defeat or conceit. Neither is where God intended us to be. So let's stand on Ephesians 2:10 remembering "We are God's *masterpiece*." And the One who holds all power in His hands took the time to architect every detail of our bodies – all to accomplish a uniquely dynamic assignment here on Earth! Let's stop second-guessing the expertise of our Artist!

Dishonesty – Honor commitments and live with integrity.

Proverbs 12:22 "The Lord detests lying lips, but He delights in those who tell the truth."

Has anyone noticed how the world's standard is relative? It will tell us we're doing a lot better than the next person, so we're good to go. Too bad that's not how the Lord's standard works. Sin is sin to Him, and it's all equal. And while most of us probably aren't in the habit of blatantly lying to those around us, there are plenty of us who will conveniently omit details to save embarrassment, embellish a story to avoid an argument, miss a deadline because of laziness or procrastination, or lock the bedroom door to hide something shameful that we shouldn't be doing. These habits are no big deal to culture, but they're detestable in God's eyes (see Proverbs 12:22).

Proverbs 6:16-17 warns us that the Lord "*hates* a lying tongue," and it doesn't give exceptions to the rule, nor does it categorize lies based on their severity. A lie is a lie, and Warriors don't mislead with our words or our follow-through. God is looking for those He can trust even in the most seemingly irrelevant situations and conversations. If we say we are going to be at a meeting at 8:00 a.m., let's be there at 8:00 a.m. If we tell our child that we are going to go play with them after work, let's go play with them after work. If we mention we are going to cut the yard and take out the trash, let's cut the yard and take out the trash. And if we commit to being a faithful husband, let's be a faithful husband who hides *nothing* from his wife even when she's not around!

Let's be men who take our words seriously. Far too many of us have become flippant with our words and just plain lazy with our commitments. 2 Corinthians 8:21 describes the conscientious communication of Warriors saying, "We are careful to be honorable before the Lord, but we also want everyone else to see that we are honorable."

Guys – every letter we utter is an extension of our testimony. The question for us is: are we being *"careful"* to honor God with our words and commitments? Honesty is the concrete footing on which relationships are built. And even a hairline crack in that foundation could *destroy* the entire structural integrity of those relationships! Let's be men whose promises are predictably reliable and whose integrity is boringly certain. Let's be more concerned about God seeing our dishonesty than a camera, a teacher, a boss, or a wife! Honesty isn't about getting caught externally, but about being clean internally.

Jealousy / Coveting / Greed – Choose contentment and be generous.

1 Thessalonians 5:18 "Be thankful in all circumstances, for this is God's will for you who belong to Christ Jesus."

It seems like we're never content with what we have. Whether it is eyeing something that someone *else* has or salivating over something that we *don't* have, our flesh is a bottomless pit of desire that can never be filled. We all *know* that, yet at this very moment every one of us probably has our eye on attaining something we don't have. And it's because the thrill from the *last* thing that we finally got only lasted for a brief moment. We may as well get used to this, because no matter what we get, whom we marry, or how much money we make, our flesh has only one response: "more."

Our desire for more is a lot like a toddler's dissatisfaction with a toy after just a moment of play. Our flesh is always saying, "Where's the next toy?" and, "Take me to do something else." Just like it's not in a toddler's DNA at 12 months to be content with anything for more than a brief second, it's not in our DNA to be content with a person, a house, a position, a number in a bank account, career success, or anything else we're striving to attain. The enemy knows that if he can entice us with the house our neighbor has, the vehicle our friend just purchased, or the success our coworker has achieved, then we will waste our lives chasing worthless bait.

Guys, we can't depend on what we have to fill us up. The answer to battling this never-ending journey to gain more than what we currently have is to choose contentment and pray specifically that God's supernatural presence provides true inner peace! Sound familiar? It's a choice – a choice to "be thankful in all circumstances" like 1 Thessalonians 5:18 tells us, and put our wish list in the back seat where it belongs. Warriors don't fixate on objects. We fixate on obedience. And crazy enough, God enjoys rewarding us with those objects we want as they become secondary in our hearts (see Matthew 6:33). But the key is keeping our motives pure!

Let's aggressively battle against greed by following Proverbs 11:24, and "give freely" to God and to others. The Lord promises us that when we are generous with our time, talents, money, and resources, we will "gain even more!" If we truly appreciate the abilities and resources that God has given us, we won't be tight-fisted with them. Instead, we will be focused on blessing others with them. Then just *watch*. When we get into the habit of being generous with our resources – giving to God instead of gratifying self – God is going to prove His promise in Proverbs by pouring out *even more* to fund His mission!

Anger – Pause, pray, and practice self-control.

Proverbs 16:32 "Whoever controls his temper is better than a warrior, and anyone who has control of his spirit is better than someone who captures a city." (ISV)

It takes one second to ruin a testimony that has taken years, or even decades to build, guys. And anger does just that every day in the lives many men. I've seen firsthand in my marriage how destructive anger can be and the ridiculously powerful grip that it can have on our bodies during a moment. I remember one specific instance a few months into marriage when I was so livid with my wife that I threw my glasses on the ground, got about six inches from her face, and screamed *the* harshest things I could say to expose her insecurities – an inexcusable verbal knockout intended to administer the deepest emotional pain possible. I'm completely embarrassed by that night, and it saddens me to even recall that moment when I saw her in tears because of the violence of my demeanor and the sharpness of my words. I share this instance to demonstrate the rapid and volatile nature of anger. It can strike fast. And it can strike unexpectedly. We've *got* to be prepared.

Men – the constricting grasp that anger has on us during moments of rage is a scary phenomenon. It will convince us that the only way to eradicate it is to act on it. But God doesn't want us to release it on someone; He wants us to relinquish it to Him! It's a discipline to have the presence of mind to pray immediately in those moments when our emotions are fuming and our nostrils are flaring. But that's what Warriors do. We pause to tell the Holy Spirit to calm us down, and we pray while we grit our teeth and clench our fists. That adrenaline might be rushing through our gut, but we nip fits of anger right in the bud with a white flag raised to Jesus. This is what Psalm 16:32 (ISV) is all about when it says, "Whoever controls his temper is better than a warrior!" We defeat anger by letting Jesus take command in the moment.

Some of us are in situations right now where if we don't give Jesus the reins on our anger sooner rather than later, we're going to make the devastating mistake of *physically* abusing someone. Warriors don't claim the loving name of Jesus while dominating and demeaning other people. And we don't follow the unbiblical gender stereotype our culture has sold us – the arrogant, testosterone-driven, domineering man who takes offense to any challenge of his authority. God designed us to rule over the earth, but He never intended for us to abuse others in the process – neither verbally nor physically. Just look at Jesus – a man who had *all* authority over this world, but we never see Him misuse that authority by mistreating people!

Whether our own earthly fathers or father figures set the right example or not – we can still look at our Heavenly Father as our prototype. And Psalm 145:8 says that He "is slow to get angry and filled with unfailing love!" I sure am glad that's true about our Dad. We can be in the process of screwing up royally, and He is *already* welcoming us back with open arms. Why shouldn't we be that same way to our children, our coworkers, our bosses, and our wives? Do people fear coming to us when they've wronged us? Do they dread being honest with us because of our aggressive retribution? And do they get scared when they fail to meet our expectations? They shouldn't, but they likely do if we aren't staying connected to the Holy Spirit in the frustrating moments. Let's be men who reflect before we react. And let's literally vocalize the name of Jesus when we find ourselves tensing up, because He will extend our fuse when it seems to be burning uncontrollably to an inevitable explosion!

Anger towards others is not the only anger we need to keep in check. Some of us are angry with *God* right now because life's not going the way we wish it would. But here's the brutal truth: God already gave up His child for us, and no matter how much hardship we face here on this fallen planet, He owes us nothing! God's love has already been proven by the perfect sacrifice, and it is outlandish for us to have an attitude towards God that is contingent on our earthly enjoyment.

Warriors – we all need to hear this: Tragedy and trials are not a sign of apathy from God! The enemy will deceive us into thinking God doesn't care when we face suffering. But we know better! And as Warriors, we combat these potential seeds of anger and doubt with God's Truth and declare trust in God's plans for us. We shove those feelings aside knowing that John 16:33 already warned us about this when Jesus said, "You *will* have trouble," in the world! Too much of the time we expect a perfect situation on Earth, but God never promised us that. In fact, He promised us the exact opposite! So next time we begin to get frustrated with God because we're having a rough day or season, let's stop focusing on what we're going through and start reflecting on what He went through watching His Son be beat to a pulp on our behalf.

Impatience – Trust God, endure the test, and keep obeying.

Romans 5:3-4 "We can rejoice, too, when we run into problems and trials, for we know that they help us develop endurance. And endurance develops strength of character, and character strengthens our confident hope of salvation."

We are wired as men to crave control, efficiency, progress, and quick fixes. But let's get real – life usually doesn't go according to our plans and expectations. And there are times when we have zero control over our circumstances. So we have to *wait*. And what man doesn't hate that word? We don't like it when we can't take control and fix the situation quickly. And when we're dealing with a discouraging diagnosis of a family member's health, facing financial instability, or searching relentlessly for a new job, time often feels like it is standing still. But just as we see in the story of Job in the Bible, these are the times when God simply wants us to stand firm in obedience and develop patience and endurance.

There's no one that battles impatience more than I do. My flesh is not a fan of Romans 5:3 when it challenges us to *celebrate* the hard times saying, "Rejoice...when we run into problems and trials, for we know that they help us develop endurance." Pardon me if I don't want to throw a party when we're caught in traffic for two hours. Or when our child won't stop crying at 3:00 a.m. Or when we are struggling to pay the bills for the sixth straight month because business isn't coming in. Or when we're still waiting after five years for God to provide a baby. These aren't the moments where I want to pull out the kazoo and drop the confetti. And God isn't expecting us to do that. But He does desire for us to trust that He's allowed it for our growth. It's not so much about reveling in the feeling of frustration for our flesh, but more about recognizing the potential for growth in our spirit! And sometimes that means enduring. Comforting advice, right? Sometimes Warriors just need to endure it and trust that God's in control. Warriors trust His timing. We know that both the brief moments and the prolonged seasons are just tests for us to grow unwavering trust and unshakeable obedience.

We are infamous for getting in God's way and delaying His timeline for our growth. Inconvenience usually leads to impatience, and impatience leads to independence. We face a problem. We want a quick resolution. We get tired of waiting. We try to fix it with our own solution. And we fail to see God's intent behind allowing the problem in the first place! It's a dangerous domino effect when we interfere with God's timing, because where we think we've expedited the elimination of a problem, we've just delayed the revelation of its purpose. Let's be composed and controlled in the unbearable moments, and confident and courageous in the upsetting seasons. And as Psalm 27:14 says – let's just "wait patiently for the Lord" to move on our behalf.

Addictions – Starve the temptation, endure the pain, pray, and run away.

1 Corinthians 10:13 "The temptations in your life are no different from what others experience. And God is faithful. He will not allow the temptation to be more than you can stand. When you are tempted, He will show you a way out so that you can endure."

Every human being in this world medicates discontentment with something. It just so happens that men gravitate toward a lot of the same medications – drugs, alcohol, pornography, sports, gambling, eating, materialism, spending, music, media, social media – but we're all looking for the *exact* same thing: a proximal thrill to motivate us to get through the day. We just need *something* in our near future to look forward to that will give us a satisfying high. Who cares if the feeling of contentment is short-lived, the dopamine high quickly subsides, or the adrenaline rush goes away after a minute or two? At least we had a moment on the mountaintop and got a break from the stress of reality! Thank goodness for that brief second when I experienced some relief from my boring routine!

This is us, men. It's sad – and frustrating – all at the same time. We can call them hobbies. We can call them thrills. We can call them highs. We can call them enjoyment. But in a lot of cases, we should be calling them *addictions*. It's time we get real and acknowledge this sobering fact: we've become dependent on that next thrill to motivate us. Tomorrow's indulgence has become our reason for existence. And we will come back to them over, and over, and over again. Deny it all we want. We're addicted. But it's okay. The first step to recovery is admitting we have a problem, right? Medical experts and doctors tell us that addictions are medical conditions that run in families. But in reality, an addiction is nothing more than letting our feelings call the shots and then growing accustomed to the resulting habit. Yes – we might have a predisposition toward a certain struggle because of our genetic makeup or family history. But addictions are simply a dependence on some *thing* that we've been habitually feeding our flesh, and these habits are super painful to break.

While our predispositions and struggles might not be the same, the sensation that accompanies each temptation is the same. 1 Corinthians 10:13 says we all face something in our lives that tempts us almost to a place where we feel powerless, and it is "no different from what others experience." What we all feel – it's all the same, guys. The only difference is some of us are not confronting that feeling with the power that supersedes every temptation! We've succumbed. We've surrendered to the feelings, so it's no wonder we have been overwhelmingly defeated up to this point! But when we introduce the name of Jesus, watch out! Because the power of Jesus' resurrection can obliterate whatever it is! And in the unanimously powerful name of Jesus, He is greater than any addiction or temptation that we face. No prescription from a doctor or treatment from a medical expert can even come close to what Jehovah Nissi, our Victory, can do to our greatest temptations.

Warriors – we've all got predispositions to certain struggles, and some of them we've gotten way too comfortable with. They're so deeply embedded in our habits that we don't even realize they're there. It's time to start considering those dependencies that motivate our existence. Let's look for them, and even if there's nothing, let's find the closest thing to it. It's time to arrange a meet-and-greet for our "addictions" to shake hands with the Man who defeated the grave. And it's time to run away from the lusts that are stimulating our senses. Starving a habit is painful, but Warriors are willing to endure the discomfort to unlock true peace!

Lust / Sexual immorality – Confront every thought with Jesus' name and run!

1 Corinthians 6:18 "Run from sexual sin! No other sin so clearly affects the body as this one does. For sexual immorality is a sin against your own body."

It's a rare occasion to find a man who is *completely* sexually pure – both in action *and* thought. Sexual impurity is absolutely crippling our generation of men all because it just feels so good to indulge in sexual pleasure. I know firsthand how sexual immorality will destroy us from the inside out. I'll admit it – this used to be my "struggle." I had pretty much everything else in my life in line with God's Word, but thinking about women sexually was a habit that I had settled into believing was okay. Hey – we all have that one "struggle," right? And besides – I wasn't having sex, so it wasn't that big of a deal!

I was the master at just looking at something on my computer or phone a couple of times a week, or just using a mental image that I had stored in my mind. I wasn't hurting anyone or performing sexual actions with anyone to satisfy my sexual desires, so it was harmless. Or at least – it wasn't as bad as what *other* men were doing.

My sin doesn't compare to his sin. And it's *just* my thoughts! What dangerously erroneous theories administered by Satan himself. It's exactly why the enemy is dismembering us in this battle. We are losing the war for our *thoughts*. And when we lose the war for our thoughts, we will eventually lose the war for our actions!

Chasing sexual temptation has become the norm, even for men who claim to be Christians. We've discarded Matthew 5:28 which tells us that even *looking* at a woman in a sexual way is committing adultery. Instead, we let our minds quietly entertain sexual temptation when we're watching commercials, walking in public, hanging with our girlfriend on a Friday night, or browsing the Internet with no one around. The list goes on and on. Those split-second thoughts that we entertain – quiet as they may be – are reeking deafening havoc on us. And those visuals that we store in our intellect for the next moment we are behind closed doors – they're putting us on a destructive path that demands completion!

Guys – a thought eventually demands an action. And whether we like it or not, we lose the battle with sexual sin when we flirt with just one thought. Once the thought process commences, the urge to satisfy our pleasure becomes almost uncontrollable. We are going to talk more details later in the Warrior study, but it's time we train our eyes to look away immediately, fight by using Jesus' name to skewer sexual temptation the moment it arrives, and start running from the situations that lead to sexual indulgence. For some of us – we need to put a filter on our computer and phone so that someone receives all of our online activity. For others – we need to cut off a relationship that is leading us to sexual impurity before marriage. For some married men, it's time to starve that nasty habit of fantasizing about being with someone other than our wives. Or maybe we need to end an adulterous emotional or physical relationship or social media conversation that has gone too far already.

It takes some major fight and discipline to tame our sexual desires. But none of us will defeat this without having the supernatural power of Jesus leading the way. I tried *so* many times to conquer this struggle on my own, but it took God's Holy Spirit power and conviction to give me the fuel to get my tail out of that desk chair, "x" off my browser, and flee the cancer that was stealing my peace and identity. I still remember confronting those temptations with the Word, a prayer, Jesus' name, and even physical movement away from the situations. There were moments when time seemed to stop while my body felt almost paralyzed as I stared at the screen on my laptop quoting 1 Corinthians 10:13 standing firm on the fact that God would show me a way out, and give me the strength to endure! The battle is hard. It's dirty. It's uncomfortable. It's downright miserable during certain moments – for our *flesh*. But if we can stand on God's Promises and stay obedient in the moment where our flesh is starving for satisfaction, God is going to bless us with an abundance that we've never experienced before in our spirit.

Filthy Speech / Language – Pray before we speak, and keep our words pure.

Ephesians 4:29 "Don't use foul or abusive language."

Plain and simple – some of us need to clean up our mouths. From using curse words, to insulting others, to joking inappropriately, all of us probably have an area where our tongues are not glorifying Jesus. Our words absolutely matter, and when we scream profanities in a heated moment, hurl an insult at someone in the middle of an argument, or tell a joke that involves crude language or sexual humor just to get a laugh – we are misrepresenting our Savior and misusing a weapon that God designed to bring life. And it is entirely too easy for us to do.

We are all going to face the angry moments when we are itching to use a couple of choice words to tear someone down – but we can burn bridges in one second with our tongue that might take decades to rebuild. Proverbs

18:21 reminds us of the power that our words possess saying that "the tongue can bring life or death." The question is – are our words bringing life, encouragement, and love to those around us in the middle of a disagreement with a child, or parent, or spouse? Or, are we flippantly saying whatever comes to our minds and translating our feelings with our mouths in moments of frustration? Warriors pause and pray before we speak the words that come to our minds – especially in heated conversations. *That* is deep Christianity.

And how about the casual hangouts with the guys? Most of us *love* to either tell or hear an inappropriate joke or story for humor or entertainment's sake. I'll be the first to admit I struggle from time to time with stepping over that line, and the struggle is only magnified when you add the components of live radio and a massive, national audience. It's an issue I pray about a lot because I recognize just *how much* satisfaction I receive from getting a good laugh in my college football, comedy routine!

But guys – that brief adrenaline rush is *never* worth relinquishing our eternal testimony. Let's not cheapen the importance of our relationship with Jesus by smearing it with vulgarity. Let's not stoop to that place where flattery from our friends or entertainment for our coworkers becomes more valuable to us than pleasing our Savior. Let's always remind ourselves of Ephesians 5:4 – that "Obscene stories, foolish talk, and coarse jokes – these are not for [us]."

Gossip – Shut our mouths, encourage, and pray for others.

Proverbs 10:19 "Too much talk leads to sin. Be sensible and keep your mouth shut."

Society stereotypically associates gossip with women, but plenty of us shatter that stereotype daily. Proverbs 18:8 (NIV) says, "The words of gossip are like choice morsels," feeding our desire for entertainment and for self-security. Men – when we talk about someone else's family problems, mistakes, or struggles, it serves *zero* purpose unless it results in encouragement and prayer for those involved. To discuss others' drama or misfortune for the sake of being entertained is wrong, and it's simply a mask for our own discontentment and insecurity. News flash – when someone enjoys talking negatively about others, all they're wanting is to gain some false sense of superiority over those that they're insulting. It's human nature to compensate for our insecurities by tearing others down. Instead of addressing my own weakness, I'll just convince myself that someone else is even weaker than I am!

Warriors – let's not be men who enjoy the sensation of excitement of talking about the problems and drama of others. It's our job to set the example and just "keep [our] mouth[s] shut" like Proverbs 10:19 tells us to do, because we don't use people as punching bags to make us feel better about ourselves. When we find ourselves in a conversation where someone else is being insulted, let's just *not* participate. Let's speak life over the insulted with our tongues. And like Proverbs 18:21 says, let's pray blessings over every person who is being torn down. When all the guys are talking about how they just can't believe Andy cheated on his wife and arrogantly laughing about how he is an idiot for doing what he did and how he got caught – that's when a Warrior steps up humbly and says, "Man, I've gotta say that we are all just a split second away from being in Andy's shoes, and I am hurting for him and his family right now. I'm gonna be praying for him!" Warriors hijack gossip with words of humility, vulnerability, encouragement, and prayer. We don't participate in or contribute to conversation that tears someone down for our entertainment or security.

Materialism – Don't obsess over things, but use things to influence people.

Matthew 6:19-20 "Don't store up treasures here on earth, where moths eat them and rust destroys them, and where thieves break in and steal. Store your treasures in heaven, where moths and rust cannot destroy, and thieves do not break in and steal."

The promise and excitement that comes from finally getting that new boat, that custom-built house, that big-screen TV, or that stylish suit is sensational, is it not? There's something about the notion of having that next *thing* that gives us a romanticized perspective of life. We always convince ourselves that life will be incredible upon its attainment, but it never is. However, that doesn't stop us from dedicating our passion and energy toward obtaining that next materialistic item! The sad reality of reaching our goal to get the "thing" that we've been working for is that 100% of the time it can offer only a transient thrill. And once that fleeting moment is over, it never fails that we are left wanting the next thing.

Later in this study, we are going to talk more about the specifics of materialism and not obsessing over the accumulation of *stuff*, but right now we need to come to grips with the fact that it doesn't matter *what* it is that we're wanting, or *how* great that thing may seem. It *will* leave us discontent. That's because we weren't made to be fulfilled by things. 1 Timothy 6:9 warns us that our desire for materialistic riches will "plunge [us] into ruin and destruction." Just look at the Hollywood culture for the proof in that pudding. So many celebrities with every materialistic possession under the sun, but they're miserable, just searching for some kind of substantial, lasting peace.

Peace and contentment don't come in the form of a fancy house, a hunting rifle, or designer clothes. There's nothing wrong with enjoying these things, but there's a *major* difference between enjoying things and being motivated by our desire to get them. If my excitement and hope when I wake up each morning comes from my desire to get closer to attaining some *thing*, then I'm now being driven by materialism. That's called an *idol*. We all have some desires and dreams that probably involve materialistic things. And that's fine. But we don't abandon our principles to get them, nor do we allow those things to be our incentive to get out of bed every day. A Warrior's wish list doesn't dictate our attitudes, our choices, or our relationships. We operate on Matthew 6:19-20 knowing that true treasure is rooted in living according to God's Word and receiving the rewards of our permanent home.

Let's stop settling, guys. It's time to confront materialism as our source of passion for life. Let's face the truth – that thing we've got our eye on right now probably won't even excite us *next month!* Warriors know that possessions are nothing but resources to influence people to know Jesus!

Laziness / Selfishness – Stop idolizing convenience and start sacrificing for others.

2 Corinthians 5:15 "[Jesus] died for everyone so that those who receive His new life will no longer live for themselves. Instead, they will live for Christ, who died and was raised for them."

Living for ourselves is insultingly easy to pull off. In fact – it takes no effort whatsoever. That's why it's the norm in our fast-paced culture to live in our own little world and hardly acknowledge others. Our activities revolve around satisfying our pleasures, our comforts, and our interests. And we participate only in the activities that are convenient and make us comfortable. From sitting idly on the couch every night to skipping out on church on Sunday because of the weather – our routines are controlled by what's easiest. And while it's one thing to relax and refresh occasionally, it's a whole different deal when we become slaves to comfort and *exist* to relax and refresh.

We've lost the discipline of getting out of our bubble and sacrificing for others. Sacrifice isn't convenient – hence its name – but it's the key to influencing people! It might be visiting a new friend in the hospital on a Friday night when we already had plans. Or maybe it's shutting down the TV or the hunting trip on a Fall Saturday to spend time doing something that our wives want to do. Or maybe it's giving one night of our week to serving our church or investing our talents in the next generation. Or perhaps it's altering that family holiday tradition in order to accommodate the in-laws. Whatever the case – it's time for us to stop worshipping convenience.

For a lot of us – the sacrifice and effort needs to begin at *home*. It is outlandish how lazy some of us have become in our marriages. We will complain all the time about our marriages struggling or going through countless rough seasons. But when was the last time we went out of our way to encourage and love on our wives? We will talk about specific ways that we can do this later in the Warrior study, but right now we need to be praying that God opens our eyes to selfish habits in our marriages, and that He gives us fresh ideas about how we can make our wives feel special.

We might also need to consider how we can *help* our wives around the house instead of always sitting on our tails. I'll be the first to admit that at the end of a workday, it's much easier to lie down on the couch and relax than help my wife make dinner or unload the dishwasher. But I might relieve a ton of her stress just by considering her comfort instead of my own. If we can master this perspective of constant sacrifice, we will be amazed at how simply considering someone else's feelings over ours will transform a relationship. Warriors always keep our eyes and ears peeled to pinpoint opportunities where we can lend a hand and make someone else's life easier!

And fathers – how about our children? Making time to spend with our children is sometimes inconvenient. Turning off the sports news channel, putting down the fishing pole, rescheduling that important early-evening meeting – they take effort – as does intentionally engaging in meaningful, spiritually-directed conversations with our children. These investments are downright uncomfortable at times! But time and spiritual direction are the greatest investments we can make into our kids. That's why a home environment just feels healthier – both emotionally and spiritually – when our time is focused more on our families' spiritual condition than our own physical convenience!

One perfect example of how convenience can disconnect us from God is our Sabbath Day. Men – we aren't doing our families any favors by being lazy on Sundays and treating church as optional or seasonal. Letting comfort and convenience become our god will lull our families into isolation and ultimately leave them miserable. That's because our spirit is not satisfied by a couple extra hours of sleep or a day on the lake! As much as the kids might celebrate staying home from church, they have absolutely no clue what's best for their overall spiritual, emotional, and even physical health! Every human being needs to be consistently connected to other believers and be in God's presence regularly to experience true fulfillment.

Warriors are focused on being spiritually useful, not physically and emotionally comfortable. And we've got to be on guard because Satan's greatest tool to rendering us spiritually ineffective is oftentimes our own comfort! Warriors – inconvenience is a *safeguard* from our selfishness and laziness. Let's embrace it and recall 2 Corinthians 5:15 in times of untimely interruptions remembering "those who receive [Jesus'] new life will no longer live for themselves." What a simple and versatile piece of Scripture. When we know Jesus, we aren't selfish. Not very tough to interpret!

Religion / Works – Get close to God instead of getting busy for God.

Ephesians 2:8-9 "God saved you by His grace when you believed. And you can't take credit for this; it is a gift from God. Salvation is not a reward for the good things we have done, so none of us can boast about it."

It isn't our place to judge whether someone knows Jesus or not, but God makes it clear that one day many will not be with Him in Heaven simply because God never had a relationship with them. My heart feels like it's carrying a 10,000-pound weight when I think about the moment when people will come face-to-face with God and will be turned away from eternity with Him because they spent their *entire lives* going through the motions of church and religion. And sadly, some of us might *be* in that category of religious rejects – because we haven't really connected with Jesus relationally. We know *about* Him. We tell people *of* Him. We do things *for* Him. But we just don't *know* Him. God, Jesus, Church – they are merely ritualistic inclusions, not relational intimacies.

Church attendance, weekly Bible Studies, prayer, and worship – they are all powerful entities of a relationship with Jesus. But they are no good if they're merely check boxes for us. Yes – God *wants* our *effort*, and He *definitely* wants us to serve Him. But our salvation inherently has nothing to do with our church attendance or our ministry résumé. It sounds crazy, but we can spend decades relentlessly doing things for God and never actually know God. We can be a pastor, a minister, or a worship leader right there in the middle of the church hustle and bustle, even *leading* people to God – yet still have had *no* encounter with the power that comes only through a relationship with Jesus!

Guys – it's time to drop the act. God doesn't want us to produce fruit *for* Him. God just wants our hearts so He can produce the fruit *in us!* What a relief it is to know that all we need to do for God is humbly position ourselves before God – as pliable, moldable, usable vessels – every day! We can relax on the résumé-building, guys. We don't have to create impressive results. We just have to remain impressionable receptacles. That means placing ourselves in front of the bloody cross of Jesus on a daily basis and coming face-to-face with the incomparable power of our God in Heaven. The result? Our agenda automatically defaults to *pleasing Him*, not building a portfolio *for* Him. Because when we are close to Jesus, the fruit produces itself. All we have to do is keep the garden open for watering so that it's *His* fruit, not ours, that is being produced.

And for what it's worth – we'll find that God's fruit is much more appealing than the crop we try to cultivate on our own! Many more people will be attracted and impacted by God's organic produce than our artificial junk! Warriors – religion says obedience is an action to impress God, but relationship proves obedience is a fruit of knowing God. Let's get close to God and let our obedience become a result of the overflow of our relationship with Him. It's time to stop following rules and just follow God!

Physical Apathy – Balance our pace, exercise, and diet.

1 Corinthians 6:19 "Don't you realize that your body is the temple of the Holy Spirit, who lives in you and was given to you by God? You do not belong to yourself."

So many men don't want to hear this, but it needs to be said: Our physical health is spiritually relevant. Period. We can deny it all we want, but the truth is our physical neglect can negate our spiritual impact. Let's all take a second and come to grips with this reality. It's uncomfortable and inconvenient, but it's true. And while it's difficult to precisely pinpoint the magnitude that proper physical care has on us, its effects on our spirit, our attitudes, and, in turn, every person we are around, are undeniable. Our physical health affects the quality of our energy, our thoughts, our emotions, our confidence, and ultimately our ability to influence.

Later in the Warrior study, we'll talk details about the repercussions of poor physical health as it relates to maximizing our spiritual potential. But for now, it's worth asking ourselves whether we are treating our bodies as highly valuable, one-of-a-kind vehicles to transport God's Spirit. Humbling to think about it – my body is the only one made with its configuration, and it's the only one that I get. And its purpose is one-fold – to chauffeur *the* most powerful, prestigious, prominent, pristine Person where He wants to go! You think we'd have that vehicle in tip-top shape at all times. After all – it can be embarrassing to drive someone around in a dilapidated clunker. If someone gave me a luxury sports car without asking for anything in return, I would be obsessed with making sure that the oil is changed routinely, the inside and out are always spotless, and the gas tank is topped off and ready for use. And God did exactly that. Yet – we act like our bodies are dumpsters that sit idly, consuming and accumulating whatever trash is thrown their way.

Most of us don't do enough. But for a rare few, we're *overdoing* it physically. We have a pace that is so rapid that we aren't eating and sleeping enough. And as well-intended as we might be in our busyness, apathy can come in the form of under-eating and overexertion as well. But whether our pace is too swift or too sluggish, it's urgent that we do whatever is necessary to stay nourished and balanced in our physical routine. It's time to make some changes, men. If we truly believe that our bodies are valuable and were "bought with a price" by Jesus' sacrifice on the cross, then let's start paying a little more attention to our pace, our diet, and our exercise.

SUMMARY

+ A Warrior aligns his heart and every habit with God's Word, knowing that purity and obedience in every area is the key to experiencing complete spiritual fulfillment and victory in the spiritual war.

RESPONSE

God, I'm nowhere close to perfect right now, but I want to do better. And I sincerely want my habits to align with Your Word as I pursue perfect obedience of Your commands.

Yes – it's incredibly easy to allow my comfort and my convenience to dictate my choices, but I want to live by Your Word, not my feelings. Jesus, I need Your Holy Spirit to convict, strengthen, and direct me to think like You, act like You, and depend on You in every area and every season of life.

No temptation that I face, addiction that I have, or habit that I've developed can compare to the power of Your resurrection, which means I can overcome literally anything with Your supernatural power within me. God, I believe that at the name of Jesus, every addiction and unhealthy habit will bow down. I claim that name over every struggle, worry, frustration, and discouragement that comes my way.

Lord, let me look like a Warrior in everything I do. Let me set the example in every circumstance, every environment, every habit, and every thought, remembering that this life is all about knowing You, trusting You, and obeying You.

CHAPTER 5

FRIENDS AND ACCOUNTABILITY

Survival in the spiritual war requires surrounding ourselves with the right people and initiating accountability.

We've probably all heard it before: "Show me your friends, and I'll show you your future." And if observation alone isn't proof, we can look at statistics that show indisputable evidence that John Kuebler knew what he was talking about: We become who we are around. The influence that our circle of relationships has on us is incalculable. Our friends determine the complexion of our home environment, our topics of conversation, our approach on marriage, our response in trials and tragedies, our perspective of money, and our decisions on parenting. The list could go on. Friends have immeasurable impact on who we are and who we become.

Friends – Choose friends who make us more like Jesus, not friends who make us feel comfortable.

1 Corinthians 15:33 "Don't be fooled by those who say such things, for 'bad company corrupts good character.'"

Whether it is our buddy from work, a family across the street, or one of our children's classmates – every person will either push us to God or pull us away from God. There is no in between. And far too often we settle for the comfort of having common interests rather than face the challenge of finding common character. It's time to reevaluate the people we're doing life with and make some tough changes to our circle of friends. Because as important as it is to have common interests with our closest friends, a common spiritual foundation is far more important than the common bond of pledging the same fraternity or loving fishing, hunting, or video games!

Yes – it's inconvenient, uncomfortable, and even difficult at times to find friends that sharpen us spiritually, but I'm living proof that when we consider worldly commonality as secondary and place spiritual commonality as the priority, God will bless the *secondary* as well! This is yet another example of how God fulfills the promise of Matthew 6:33. Seek first God's character as we're finding friends, and the common interests will be added. Guaranteed. So then how do we set ourselves up for success in finding spiritually like-minded friends?

Disconnect from the wrong places.

It's obvious that we need to connect to the right places to find the right friends. But what often prevents that from happening is our unwillingness to disconnect from the wrong places. Now it's not my job nor someone else's job to decide what situations are spiritually helpful or harmful to each of us. That's the Holy Spirit's job to provide the discernment on what's glorifying to Him. However, there are plenty of situations that are obvious breeding grounds for sin that we need to stay away from. Going to the bar, the club, or the house party on Friday night probably isn't connecting us with friends who are going to positively impact our spiritual purity. And no offense, but having the mentality that we're going to be the Christian influence that saves people at the bar at 1:00 a.m. is usually just a cop out to be where the party is. Yes – God can save people anywhere, anytime in any way He wants, but let's use common sense – revival is probably not going to break out at the bars where worldly indulgence is the agenda.

If we have a longing to be included in what the popular crowd is doing and we have trouble letting go of the social settings that involve the "who's who" of our network, we might just have an addiction to socializing. I've been there. I've experienced the paranoia that comes from even the *mention* of missing out on the latest social developments. That's because socializing had become a vicious idol, and one that needed to be confronted with the name of Jesus! Men – let's remember that our identity and relevance are not dependent on being socially included or socially informed.

Then there are the less-obvious social situations that can lead to sin. Hey, men – if taking a road trip to the game with our buddies causes us to tell nasty jokes or succumb to the social pressure to indulge in alcohol, then maybe we don't need to go there. Or, if going over to a friend's house after school leads to searching for pornography on his computer while his parents are at work – then we need to get away from there. The location and activities of our friends will tell us where their priorities are. And if any location or activity cultivates addictions, debauchery, fornication, crudeness, gossip, immaturity, or irresponsibility – we need to *avoid* them at all costs! 1 Corinthians 15:33 warns us that "bad company corrupts good morals," so no matter how well-intended we are in these sinful situations – we *will* eventually be influenced by the worldly pressures they bring.

We've been flirting with these worldly settings long enough, and it's time to nip them in the bud and pray for new friends that don't need to participate in the cultural norms to have a good time. We need to take 2 Corinthians 6:14 seriously when it says, "Don't team up with those who are unbelievers. How can righteousness partner with wickedness? How can light live with darkness?" Warriors can't coexist with worldliness. We've gotta get serious and get away from the people and places that are encouraging us through word and deed to indulge in what feels good. This isn't about being legalistic, basing our group of friends on whether they sin or not. We all sin, so that's not what this is about. This is about making sure that we are constantly in tune with where God wants us and with whom God wants us around. There's a huge difference between occasionally committing a sin and deliberately living in sin. We're all going to mess up at times, but Warriors avoid situations where we are being persuaded to participate in habits that are out of line with God's Word.

Connect to the right places, pray, and obey.

So we've disconnected from the wrong places, but now what? Or better yet – who? We've got no friends, and the world is coming to an end! Where are we going to meet anyone? And who are we going to hang out with now? Our enemy knows *exactly* what to whisper in our ears in times of uncertainty and isolation. He even *welcomes* the challenge that follows our obedience of disconnecting from the wrong places. Because now he has a *new* objective – to convince us that it will be impossible to find people our age that have our beliefs. And one of his go-to tactics is to make us believe that the only way we will meet people is by going right back to the places from which we just disconnected! He'll tell us that the only outlets for social connectivity involve revisiting the same secular gathering places and popular hangout spots.

A signature Satan move – persuade us to revert to old habits so we stay on his never-ending merry-go-round of misery. But we don't fall for that. We know that our God is laughably larger than our fears of isolation. He is God. And we seriously think that He is going to have trouble finding us some like-minded friends? Come on, guys. God tells us in Ephesians 3:20 (ESV) that He has "abundantly" more than "all that we ask or think." Men – God has more than we could imagine waiting for us relationally. He has friends that exceed every expectation in our minds. But He's waiting for us to proactively give up the wrong relationships and ask Him for the right ones. Then while we're waiting on God to provide those friends, He is watching for us to remain obedient to His Word, plugged into a healthy church, and full of faith that He *will* fulfill His promise. Obedient *choices* always precede God's abundance, and it's no exception as we search for the right people to do life with!

Cut off the relationships that are leading to sin.

If we want to experience God's best, we've got to be systematic about eliminating sin from our lives. A lot of the time that involves distancing ourselves from *people* who are influencing us to sin. It's painful to cut off relationships, especially with those we love so much. But if our mission is holiness, sometimes relationships become casualties of spiritual warfare.

Sin is exceptional at camouflage, and it has a sneaky way of seeping its way into any relationship and making itself at home. If it isn't addressed upon arrival, sin will quietly sprout into a stronghold, and we will adjust to its presence. We all know about this. The first time sin enters a relationship, we always feel guilty. The second time, the guilt isn't quite as overwhelming. And the more frequent that sinful habit becomes, the less sensitive we become to its companionship. We sin until conviction has been stifled. Then one day we look up and realize that we're in a deep, intimate relationship being suffocated by sin. Sin is either put to death on arrival, or it will numb us into a tangled mess.

For many of us, we're smack dab in the middle of relationships defined by that tangled mess. And it's time for us to put our emotions aside and pray for supernatural empowerment to remove ourselves from those relationships that are causing us to sin. This especially goes for any type of sexual sin. If we want to be miserable, just let sexual impurity fester in a relationship.

And no – we don't have to be unkind or judgmental as we sever certain ties with people. That's a ridiculous misconception and lie from the enemy. There is nothing "unkind" or "judgmental" about passing on the campsite invite if we know that the people present will pressure us into sinful choices. A decline doesn't mean we don't care about people. It just means we're avoiding opportunities to sin.

Create alternative social environments conducive to purity and relational depth.

So if the campsite is a breeding ground for irresponsibility and indulgence, then why not create our own get-togethers? Why not create alternative locations and activities with these same people, but make the environment more conducive to innocence and purity?

For instance – Stuart might want me to head out to dinner with him and his unsaved buddies and then hit up the bar on Saturday night. But what if instead, I created an environment at my apartment where we cooked out with several of my solid Christian brothers, and we invited Stuart and a couple of his friends to join us? This is a perfect example of creating an alternate social environment conducive to purity and relational depth. Not only am I now in a pure situation that I can control, but I'm also in the majority and have created a setting where meaningful, spiritual conversation can take place if the Lord opens that door.

This is what the ideal social environment looks like to a Warrior – a holy location, pure activities, controllable content and conversation, and a solid Christian majority! This recipe is rooted in giving the Holy Spirit full reign to move in relationships if He desires to. Otherwise, the environment caters more toward our desires rather than God's. Conversation that involves spiritual focus, transparency, and honesty is the ultimate goal of a Warrior's relationships and gatherings. And the content from our conversations will usually pinpoint whether our relationships are focused on God's purpose or our pleasure.

There's nothing wrong with having conversations about sports, music, entertainment, news, hobbies, and interests. To be honest – these are some of my favorite things to discuss. But conversation about worldly topics cannot create deep relationships. Eventually, depth requires revealing our spiritual journeys – both our struggles and victories. And there's nothing like the freedom and the bond that God creates when we are united spiritually with other friends and families. That's because God designed us as spiritual beings with a spiritual purpose and a spiritual void that can only be filled by living lives that acknowledge our spiritual journey. Real relationships require us to be real. And realness is activated more by authentic words than alcoholic beverages. Don't tell that to the world though!

Here's the question to ask about our best friends: "Do we ever have raw, transparent, authentic spiritual conversation with each other?" And if the answer to that question is "no," then it's probably time to find some different friends – for ourselves, our wives, and our families – that will sharpen us spiritually and challenge us to live obediently. Let's not allow convenience, ease, and comfort to be the determining factors of our closest friends. Let's do whatever is necessary to connect to the places and people that are focused on living for God's purpose, not their pleasure. When we do this, we're going to discover that contrary to popular belief, we don't have to sin to have fun! We can be content without compromise!

Find friends that base their advice on God's Word, not their own opinion.

No matter how much we know or what we've experienced, we all occasionally need direction and advice from others. When we're struggling with our marriage, facing a difficult situation with our employer, making a life-changing decision for our future, or wondering how to deal with a person who has hurt us – we're going to need direction at times. And that direction typically comes from our closest friends, which begs the question: Do our friends point us to God's Word or just pose their own opinions?

There are a lot of smart people in the world, and there are even more clever quotes, feel-good theories, new theologies, and ever-evolving opinions on how we should approach morality, marriage, family, sex, career, money, and health. But all of them have one thing in common: they aren't the Word of God. And no matter how smart or well-intended our friends may be, if they are giving us advice based on anything but the Word of God, it is irrelevant and toxic to God's will for our lives. That's why Warriors surround ourselves with friends who are constantly pointing us back to God's Word and using *it* as the Standard. Otherwise, we are listening to lies that will quickly carry us off track from God's plan. We all tend to gravitate toward friends who tell us what we *want* to hear rather than finding friends who will tell us what we *need* to hear. But Warriors pursue spiritual brothers who direct us straight to God's Word no matter how it makes us feel. If our lifelong friends or closest buddies are not pushing us back to God's Word, then it's time to find another source for spiritual guidance.

Avoid cliques and exclusion.

Just as soon as we are blessed enough to develop that tight-knit group of friends who love Jesus, we quickly build walls that prevent others from joining us! It's a speedy, seismic shift from desperation to delineation. There we are – desperate to find the right friends – but once that is accomplished, we immediately become territorial and exclusive with our friend circle.

Guys – let's not forget how it felt to be met with resistance as we feverishly and fervently sought out Godly people to do life with. There are countless other men, couples, and families looking to find what we are blessed to already have. And it's up to us. We can allow cliques to form where we exclude others from our "circle," or we can be on the lookout to include other impressionable candidates seeking Godly relationships.

A discerning insulation is definitely a necessity in any circle of friends – because we surely don't want to allow toxic relationships to infiltrate and corrupt a purified network. But most of the time, our exclusivity has zero to do with their toxicity and everything to do with our comfortability! We don't want those people in our group because we don't want that new family to complicate the chemistry we've already established! How ridiculously selfish. This happens all the time in the Church and among groups of close Christian friends. Yet – it is the antithesis of who Jesus is. When you look at Jesus throughout the Bible, He was approachable, humble, and, like Acts 10:34 (ESV) says, "showed no partiality."

Philippians 2:4 outlines the system to look like Jesus and show God's love to others. It says, "Don't look out only for your own interests, but take an interest in others, too." It doesn't matter how perfectly compatible we are with our current group of friends, how long we've known them, or even how strong the bond is with them. Let's not be so immature that we turn our noses up at those who are "outside" of our established circle of friends, or exclude them because they are "new" or "different." Rather, let's set the Warrior example and always be looking for opportunities to meet, love, include, and "take interest" in others.

It's time to do away with the impermeable holy huddles in the church – the Christian cliques with self-centered, feel-good relationships – and be aware of the multitude of outsiders who are in dire need of the right support system. Instead of getting obsessed with our segregated circle of tight-knit traditions, let's lead the Church toward looking less like a country club and more like a hospital. No requirements or exemptions – *everyone* is welcome to come in and get healthy!

Be an example, be a gatekeeper, be a disciplinarian, and pray for our children's friends.

If children are great at one thing, it is observing what mom and dad do. And for those of us with kids, the greatest thing that dad can do is to be sure our children are observing obedience! Luke 6:43 conveys the importance of our *example* and the impact it can have on our offspring: "A good tree can't produce bad fruit, and a bad tree can't produce good fruit." And while discipline and instruction will help set boundaries for our kids, there's nothing more effective than *modeling* what we teach. Whether we like it or not – if we aren't hanging out with the right people, we can't expect them to do so either! Our example is far more powerful than our words, and that's why the most effective parenting tool is simply to be who we ask them to be. Being a "good tree" will produce "good fruit." That means surrounding ourselves with the type of people – both adults and kids – that we want them to be around. Our relational associations should match our spiritual aspirations. And we absolutely cannot substitute character for comfort when it comes to our friends or our families' friends, because what our kids see – they are going to replicate. Let's be men who typify what we teach.

While setting the example is critical, there *will* be times when we set the right example and teach the right lessons, but still watch our children go down a path of disobedience. That's why we can't overlook our responsibility as a gatekeeper. We can't control everything, but as fathers, it is *our* responsibility to monitor our children's friends, and to cut off relationships that involve dangerous, sinful habits. Being ignorant, naïve, or apathetic about whom our children are hanging out with is neglecting our role as gatekeeper. As shepherd and protector of our children, there are going to be times when we need to put a stop to certain relationships. It might be an unhealthy boyfriend/girlfriend relationship, a group of friends from our son's football team who use filthy language, or the kid down the street who has an anger problem. There are so many situations that should have us on high alert in order to protect our kids from the wrong habits.

As a side note: fathers – let's be *very* wary of sleepovers, slumber parties, and spend-the-nights that are not under our roof. Extremely wary. Our pastor introduced us to this "no sleepover" parenting policy, and I had a profound revelation about the amount of complete filth that I was exposed to during my childhood and teenage years when I spent the night at friends' houses! I began recounting all of the nastiest, most sinful moments of my upbringing, and sure enough, every one – literally all of them – were the nights when I was removed from the Godly shelter of my parents' authority. The porn, the promiscuity...it was never under Burr and Jan Ingram's roof.

A "no sleepover" policy might not win many brownie points with our kids. And the sobering reality is we will probably become unpopular with our kids for enforcing rules, imposing consequences, and making tough choices. But honestly – our favorability rating shouldn't matter to us. God didn't position us as fathers to be popular with our children, and occasionally, our love will result in their dislike. But we aren't here to be liked by our kids; we are here to be their spiritual guide. And it's well worth bearing their temporary criticism if it prevents their permanent corruption.

Let's be diligent in praying for our children's friends regularly – that God surrounds our kids with young men and women who genuinely love Jesus and understand the magnitude of what He did for us. Ultimately, that Holy Spirit power is the game changer in providing both the discernment for us parents, and the discretion for our children.

Accountability – Initiate transparency and accountability with other Warriors.

James 5:16 "Confess your sins to each other and pray for each other so that you may be healed. The earnest prayer of a righteous person has great power and produces wonderful results."

It's not difficult to pinpoint why most men cringe when we hear the word "accountability." We take on enough responsibility as it is at work and home. The last thing we want is to be crowded with even higher expectations and inconvenienced with more limitations. So we sit back, relax, and get comfortable with apathy altogether avoiding the transparency and boundaries that accompany spiritual maturity.

Warriors *crave* accountability, because it is the necessary push that develops us into prototypical Warriors who fight to stay close to Jesus every day. We need the push, guys. We need even the most marginal advantage to fend off the tenacious attacks from the enemy's arsenal. And our teammates will make or break us in the battle. If we want excellent results, we must surround ourselves with men who are excellent. That means they are more passionate about living according to God's Word than they are about the beer they are drinking during the game, or the boat ride they are enjoying on the lake, or the hunting trip they are taking to the ranch.

If we haven't done this already – it's time to find at least *one* Christian brother who cares more about Biblical obedience than feeding his flesh. Just one man who stays connected, shoots us straight, prays with us and for us, and encourages us through the struggles and the victories alike. Do we have this type of accountability in order? We touched on these principles of accountability in chapter three, but now it's time to discuss the details of making them happen!

It is my responsibility to keep myself accountable.

If we really want to avoid accountability, we can accomplish this without any effort at all. We can withdraw. Clam up. Isolate ourselves. But it takes a *true* spiritual Warrior to initiate the accountability himself. It shows that we *want* it. It shows that God's purpose is worth the inconvenience and it's worth the blood, sweat, and tears that come with the fight. And it shows ownership – that we've taken responsibility for making sure someone knows where we're winning and losing. We are men! And we don't depend on someone else to come and ask us how things are going.

Self-accountability. It is the mark of a Warrior because it is the only *true* accountability. Think about it – no one else knows the exact moments when we're being tempted, nor do they know the exact moments when we've fallen. And these are the two situations when we need accountability the most! If I'm struggling, it's up to *me* to let someone know! And that would be ludicrous on my part to think that it's someone else's responsibility to do *my* spiritual inventory. I am the only person that can initiate communication during my moments of temptation or after my moments of indiscretion. The realities of transparent accountability are repulsive to our flesh. That's a surefire sign that something is tremendously beneficial to our spirit! And James 5:16 confirms it – bolstering the power of accountability in our moments of both temptation and condemnation. It's during the moment of temptation that we need another man of God praying for us, because "the earnest prayer of a righteous person has great power and produces wonderful results!"

But what if we've fallen? What if temptation has given way to condemnation, and we're now ashamed and chagrinned? James 5:16 yet again points to accountability as the pathway to renewal saying, "Confess your sins to each other and pray for each other so that you may be healed!" It is confession that leads to healing. But confession requires connection!

Whether we're on the brink of stupidity or we've already stepped into it – reaching out to another Warrior for support is the smartest move we can make. Yes – exposing the filth of our flesh is extremely difficult to do – both *when* we're being tempted and *after* we've given into temptation. But the discipline in these tough moments is what differentiates a Warrior from other men. It is where the rubber meets the road.

Warriors – let's not be so lazy to allow sin to overtake us without at least getting a brother to fight the temptation with us! Let's care enough about glorifying Jesus to actually put up a fight! And if we do fall, let's not dare buy into that preposterous lie of condemnation letting guilt erode our identity because we're embarrassed to tell someone. It's time to embrace vulnerability and implement the trusted twofold system of James 5:16 remembering that "wonderful results" and "healing" come from prayer and confession.

Celebrate victories and share struggles with someone.

It cannot be emphasized enough, men. We. Need. Each. Other. And isolation will always eventually lead to destruction. Even the greatest Warriors can make shockingly regretful decisions when we are separated from the pack. It only takes a moment. Even 364 days a year of being connected to other Warriors is woefully dangerous – because it only takes that *one* day of reclusive behavior to reap disastrous consequences. Besides, if we only want convenient accountability, we'll become victims of seasonal connectivity. That's where many of us are. We try to front-load accountability from New Year's to Easter and then live off of the surplus in our reserve tank during the spring and summer months when we "disconnect" from everything! Sounds silly, but this typifies casual Christianity. That said, effective accountability doesn't work that way. True accountability doesn't get breaks.

Proverbs 18:1 (ESV) warns us that "whoever isolates himself seeks his own desire." And we are notorious for isolating ourselves when the accountability becomes inconvenient. Hey, it's summer, and I sought God and stayed connected to my Christian brothers from January to May. I think I'll take a couple months to detach and relax. This kind of inconsistency in accountability leads to susceptibility. And just like physical war – if we wander off from fellow soldiers even for a second – we can be blown to smithereens. Don't miss this – a momentary lack of protection can lead to lasting devastation. And relaxation is always the first domino.

It's prom night, and my girl is looking gorgeous. I think I want to go find a private hang out spot after the dance ends and enjoy some one-on-one time. No, I'm not going to bother getting prayer tonight because I really just want to satisfy my desires tonight. Fill in the blank with a scenario. They all fit. When we cut off accountability, when we isolate from the group, when we relax for a season, when we indulge for a night, it's a sign that as Proverbs 18:1 says, we're seeking our own desire! Let's be on high alert when our flesh is despising the thought of accountability – that moment when we're sighing, rolling our eyes, and shaking our head because the last thing we want is for some "spiritual truth" to rain on our indulgence parade – because *that* is the moment when our spirit needs accountability the most. *That* is the moment when we find out who the *Warriors* are.

Are we fighting to remain connected even when we don't want to fight to remain connected? We all need at least one spiritual brother who is there for us every day, because even the most content and confident man in the world still needs a buddy to give him a fist bump after an accomplishment, say a prayer for him in the tough moments and seasons, and punch him directly in the gut with brutal honesty on occasion. And to the skeptics who want to keep their struggles private – Galatians 6:2 disagrees by encouraging us to "share each other's burdens." God didn't design us to face life's challenges alone. He put us around each other specifically for mutual support.

Be completely honest and transparent with someone.

The effectiveness of accountability can only be as great as our level of transparency. And if we aren't willing to share *our* most shameful secrets, we can't expect *God* to share His most abundant blessings. God is looking for men who hide *nothing*. And I'm convinced that God is awaiting a transparent troop of men willing to be real – a collection of guys who might have a disgustingly dark area but are confronting it instead of concealing it! There is no point in even having accountability if we're not committed to complete transparency. The whole objective of accountability is to expose sin and eradicate it – so if we're leaving certain sins unaddressed, and we're unwilling to come face-to-face with the filthiest of filthy, we might as well not have the accountability to begin with!

If we're not all in, we might as well not be in at all. Casual accountability serves no purpose whatsoever other than checking off a box to make us feel like we're being obedient when, in reality, we're just wasting our time playing Christian charades. It's time to abandon the draining misery of covering up sin – even if it's just one struggle – because Proverbs 28:13 assures us that "people who conceal their sins will *not* prosper, but if they confess and turn from them, they will receive mercy." God's Word makes it so simple: don't hide sin, but expose it and get away! Men – concealing sin is cancerous! And *any* omission in confession leads to corrosion. Transparency is indeed *the* only path to peace. But the question is – does someone know about the darkest of our dark intentions, tendencies, and struggles? No, that doesn't mean airing our dirty laundry to the world. But it does mean sharing our darkest secrets with someone!

So how do we handle becoming the Biblical accountability for someone *else?* Luke 17:3 tells us that "if another believer sins, *rebuke* that person." No, that doesn't mean jumping all over a brother while looking down on him for his mistakes or being harsh with him because of his poor choices. But it does mean voicing the truth even when the truth hurts. Painful truth can still be delivered with a kind heart. And we can still call out sin while loving the sinner! Galatians 6:1 outlines this for us, urging us to "gently and humbly" help other believers "back onto the right path."

Men – we've gotta do better at calling other men out and upholding the Word of God as our non-negotiable standard of living. But as we confront, let's remember that our divine assignment is to support a brother before trying to change his behavior. As Pastor Chris Hodges says, it is absolutely essential to "*connect* before we *correct.*" Warriors – it's time to start fighting this battle of accountability together. The enemy fears Biblical confrontation and exposure – because he knows that once our sin is uncovered, it can then be eradicated. The question is – are we bringing our darkness into light by telling another Warrior about our most shameful secrets? We can't expect to enjoy God's best until we're willing to expose our worst.

Find a spiritual mentor.

I thank God every day for the blessing of growing up around an earthly father who always looked like Jesus – not just in *word* but in *action.* I'm beyond thankful for the wisdom, guidance, and example that Burr Ingram set for my two brothers and me – because there's nothing like having a living, breathing model of the content that we have been taught to live. Being an eyewitness takes away a whole lot of guesswork. And this firsthand example of God's Word being lived out in front of us – it is something that every man needs. It might indeed be our earthly father that fills this role in our lives, but it could also be a small group leader, a coach, an uncle, a grandfather, a youth minister. It really doesn't matter what their "title" is – it just matters that they live a life of closeness to Jesus, love for others, and true obedience of God's Word.

Regardless of our age or spiritual maturity – we *all* need the wisdom and example of accomplished men of the faith. In fact, the Bible tells us this is essential for spiritual victory. Proverbs 24:6 says, "Don't go to war without wise guidance; victory depends on having many advisers." If we want to win in spiritual battle, we need to involve proven men of Biblical obedience in every choice we make and circumstance we face! Whether it is a rough patch in our marriage, an important financial decision, or confusion about a career path – the last thing the enemy wants is for us to seek the wisdom of men who have been there before and possess the experience to know how to handle those situations maturely and Biblically. Consulting the wise is the safeguard for successful plans according to Proverbs 15:22. So let's consistently consume the counsel of Warriors who have fought the war victoriously for years and decades. Their spiritual savvy propels our spiritual success!

SUMMARY

+ A Warrior disconnects from the wrong places in order to find friends with common character instead of settling for the comfort of common interests.

+ A Warrior is extremely careful about choosing and monitoring friendships, understanding the incredible influence that they can have on his family.

+ A Warrior initiates accountability and transparency, sharing his victories and struggles with other Warriors knowing that exposure of sin and connection to wise counsel leads to healing and peace.

RESPONSE

Jesus, the people I am around have more impact on me than I realize – and I just want to glorify You when it comes to the friends that I choose and the relationships that I cultivate.

While it might be difficult to disconnect from the wrong places at times, God, I need You to provide the conviction and the power to stay away from places that cater more to satisfying my flesh than growing my character. Give me the strength to cut off any and all relationships that are leading to sin, and provide me with the supernatural strength to walk away from them immediately!

Lord, let every environment that I am in be pure, and allow opportunities for me to develop transparent, Jesus-centric, Bible-focused relationships. Surround my family and me with friends that care more about Your Word than their pleasure or opinion.

God, surround me with Warriors who won't look down on me for my sin, but who will still keep me accountable to obeying Your Word. Give me the power to be transparent and honest about my victories and struggles, and help me master the discipline of self-initiated accountability. Break any fear of embarrassment, and bring peace as I share my shameful choices and filthiest habits with other Warriors. And Jesus, I declare right now that healing comes from exposing my sin and covering it with the blood of Your cross. I ask that You would provide the right brothers to support me in my spiritual journey.

Jehovah Jireh, my Provider, I pray that You would provide me with at least one spiritual adviser who models what Your Son looks like. I pray that You would open the right doors for me to connect with a true spiritual giant who has followed You steadily and uncompromisingly for decades. And allow me to soak up his wisdom and experience so that one day, I can also leave a legacy as a spiritual mentor for a young Warrior.

CHAPTER 6

MARRIAGE AND FAMILY

A Warrior's greatest responsibility is fighting for spiritual victory in his marriage and in his family.

It cannot be communicated enough that our most pressing assignment as Warriors is fighting to stay close to Jesus. That proximity to Jesus has incalculably far-reaching effects – the most obvious of which are seen in our family environment. And no matter where we are in the spectrum of life – whether husbands, fathers, sons, or a combination of the three – we all have the responsibility to be leaders in our homes and set the example of excellence in our families. Whether that means reflecting the selflessness of Jesus in our marriage as a husband, or mirroring the leadership of Jesus as a father, or having the humility of Jesus as a son – Warriors exist to lead our families! I'm blessed to say I was raised by a father who did just that!

Burr Ingram is a true Warrior prototype. Not only was he an honoring son to Edith and Bob Ingram, but he has led my precious mom as a dynamically selfless husband for their 40-plus years of genuinely happy marriage. Not to mention, he has fathered three sons to *obsess* over Jesus, prayer, and the Word of God, all while *living* what he taught us. Oh, yeah – and he's done all of this while working his tail off as a vice president of one of the nation's top hospitals for nearly three decades. My dad is a rarity – a fighter who has lived for Jesus as a son, a husband, a father, and a leader out in the real world for more than half a century! I'm just thankful to have been a spectator to see how it's done.

Guys – even if these roles aren't relevant to our current phase of life – one day they will be. And we've got to be ready to dominate our assignments on the home front when that time comes!

Husbands – Love our wives like Jesus loves us.

Ephesians 5:25 "For husbands, this means love your wives, just as Christ loved the church. He gave up his life for her..."

Outside of our relationship with Jesus, there is no relationship more paramount than the one we have or will have with our wives. And honestly – there isn't even a close second. Kids, parents, siblings, lifelong friends – they all pale in significance to the uniquely-designed woman that God entrusted to each of us to love here on Earth. This is evidenced by the job description we are given as husbands in Ephesians 5:25 – to "love [our] wives, just as Christ loved the church," by giving up our lives for them! Is there any way we can understand the weight of what Ephesians 5:25 is asking us to do? Just think about what Jesus' love for His Church looked like: He allowed his body to be butchered for the very people who were butchering Him! To think that we stood there and spat in His face, shoved nails in His hands, and laughed at Him as we pressed thorns onto his innocent head. Yet He took it – while looking us right in the eyes!

Unfathomable love. Jesus truly did the unthinkable. He sacrificed everything – even His physical body – just to show us that we were His priority. He did what was best for us when it was the last thing we deserved, and He honored us when we were far from honorable to Him. Now does *that* sound like us as husbands? Is *that* kind of love present in our marriage? It's definitely an inconvenient commitment because it demands giving up our rights, our power, and our agenda. But Warriors – when we start prioritizing our wives' needs above ours, and start exhibiting a love that will not budge in the face of mistake or mistreatment – our marriages are going to be absolutely transformed. Guaranteed.

Value our wives.

So, we're called to love our wives following *the* most selfless example in the history of the universe. But where do we even begin to show this type of sacrifice to our wives? A good place to start is making her the undisputed #1 in our rankings. If there's one universal attribute about every female in the history of the world, it's that they all desire to be #1 in the eyes of the leader they've chosen to follow. Guys – women aren't complex. They're actually insultingly simple. And they're *all* just looking for one thing – for someone to consider them more important than anything else. To be *the* priority. This is the definition of value, and it's what every wife is longing for from her husband – to be first. That's it! When we make our wives feel like they're the princesses worth giving up everything for, and that nothing – not other women, not money, not sexual pleasure, not cars, not sports, not hunting, not work – can knock them out of the #1 spot, we'll peel back all of the layers of complexity that have built up in our marriages. Or better yet – prevent them from accumulating altogether!

Like it or not, observation alone is proof. A marriage that is complicated usually involves a wife that is neglected. And the reason there are so many difficult wives out there is because there are so many neglectful husbands out there. Guys – if we want a marriage marked by simplicity, it starts with a wife who is confident that she is *the* priority. Husbands – it's worth asking – is my relationship with my wife getting more passion, more attention, more time, and more effort than competing influences? And when I think about my wife, do I honor her as my most valuable prize?

It's hard for some of us to value our wives because of how we perceive them. We entertain thoughts on a regular basis that paint our wives as inconveniences, as naggers, as annoyances, and dare I say – as baggage! Our thoughts are so focused on the nuisances we forget that a wife is a sign of favor from God! Proverbs 18:22 reminds us that "the man who finds a wife finds a treasure, and he receives favor from the Lord."

This should be a sobering wake-up call for us because God considers your wife and my wife as "treasures!" And if *He* thinks they're treasures, why in the world would we be so arrogant to believe otherwise? That's *exactly* what we're doing when we dwell on even one thought that paints our wives in a negative light. Sure – the enemy wants to throw an emotional breakdown, an insulting comment, a frustrating conversation, or a hormonal moment our way to shift our minds from treasure to torment. But Warriors don't fall for that bait. And in the same way that Jesus graciously considered us treasures when we didn't deserve it, we do the same thing for our wives when *they* might not deserve it. She may have snapped on me, but she's still my most valuable treasure. She might have disrespected me in front of the children, but she's still my most valuable treasure. And she may have insulted me in front of all my friends, but she's still my most valuable treasure. *Nothing* my wife can do can change my perspective of her. That's Ephesians 5:25 right there.

Husbands – it's time to re-program *our* thoughts to match up with *God's* thoughts about our wives and frequently remind ourselves of the favor that we've found in receiving our spouses: "My wife is God's treasure, and she is my best friend, my teammate, and my first priority. I will always be honorable in how I think and speak about her – and if anyone does dishonor her, I will kindly, but firmly, defend and protect her – as she is a unique, delicate gift that the Lord entrusted to me to love and lead."

Lead our wives.

We love our wives by valuing our wives. But we also love our wives by *leading* our wives. And guess what? They're waiting to be led. God wired them that way – to follow us. And Ephesians 5:22 (NIRV) instructs them to do just that, telling them to "follow the lead of your husbands as you follow the Lord."

Now guys, I don't know about you – but if I'm driving across the country, and my wife is trailing behind me in a separate car depending on me to safely and smoothly navigate her to our destination, I am going to be sure that I know where I am going! And if she is following close behind me, mimicking every start, stop, and turn, trusting me to protect her along the journey – you better believe I am going to do some research in advance to check weather conditions and potential hazards that could put her in danger! Leaders prepare accordingly to protect their followers. And this is a perfect snapshot of Warrior husbands. We take our responsibility as spiritual navigators and protectors extremely seriously, because our wives have placed a delicate dependence in our hands, counting on us to lead them carefully. Even if they don't know it, every wife is looking to follow a man who's carefully following *the* Man!

Pastor Jimmy Evans, founder of the internationally known *MarriageToday* ministry, illustrates this picture of marriage beautifully saying husbands are like the sun and wives are like the moon – the moon just reflects what the sun is showing. And guys, I hate to tell you – but if our wives are always selfish, frustrated, irritated, or angry – it's probably because *we* are selfish, frustrated, irritated, or angry. It's time to stop getting mad at the dark moon and instead increase the brightness of the sun because they're just reflecting us! As leaders, we are going to be held accountable for the influence we have on our wives' behavior. That's a poignant reminder not to abuse our leadership role in a marriage.

One inexcusable habit that we've developed in our marriages is extorting our God-given honor to lead by dominating our wives as if they are the inferior beings. We suppress their desires and manipulate them into thinking that since *we* are the leaders – what *we* say is what goes! And this kind of domineering dictatorship could not be further from God's intent! 1 Peter 3:7 clearly defies this type of abuse saying, "She may be *weaker* than [we] are, but she is [our] *equal* partner!"

Warriors – we weren't given a leadership role to flaunt it and to "show" our wives who's the head of the household! Our wives' submissiveness isn't an invitation to oppress, control, overpower, overshadow, and over-masculinize our role as the stronger figure in a marriage! It is an opportunity to demonstrate how to put someone else's interests before our own! God gave us authority so that we would make our wives the priority! And *that* is what leadership in a marriage looks like! Is our leadership reflecting that our wives are the priority? Are we exemplifying the attitude, the forgiveness, the grace, and all the attributes that we want from them? It's time to work on the sun in the mirror if we want to see an improvement in the moon's reflection!

Listen to our wives.

The title of this section is cringe-worthy for us as men because most of us are awful listeners. But as much as we sometimes cannot stand to focus and listen to the details of our wives' conversations – it is critical to a healthy marriage to conscientiously *absorb* our spouses' thoughts and feelings! We are wired to be fixers, but that is *not* what our wives are looking for when they are telling us about the dramatic developments of the day, the relational challenges among friends and colleagues, or the emotional toll that someone's comments have taken on them. Our wives need our ear and our attention – not our solution to their situation. It's elementary in theory, but quite the accomplishment to execute, because this requires biting our tongues to squash our problem-solving tendencies. Most of the time, women just want to be heard. And simply sharing with us makes them feel better. It makes no sense to us, but it makes perfect peace for them! So, next time we go into "fixer" mode, it might be worth reminding ourselves that our wives usually just need us to be a *sponge*, not a *handyman*.

However, when our wives *do* look to us for counsel or feedback, we have one responsibility – to incessantly lead them to be the example of Jesus. That means whether our wives' feelings have been hurt by a friend's words, or she has been discouraged by a sibling's selfishness – we gently lead her away from bitter thoughts or any line of thinking that supports a grudge against someone. We always encourage immediate forgiveness, softly nudging our wives towards being the mature example in *every* situation. Guys – this is a biggie. We hold the power in our households to divert gossip and distract from tearing down others. And it is our responsibility to help our wives look at others with compassion and maturity. We *all* have our moments of weakness when we get fed up with others, and during those exasperating days, it sure does help to have a counterpart who is pointing us back to our spiritual purpose before the "venting" becomes "bashing." Part of pointing our wives (and children) back to the path of spiritual perspective is helping them see past their pain to sympathize with someone else's pain!

The enemy desperately wants to entangle us in the surficial bickering of how we've been offended so that we never get around to praying supernatural blessing over the offenders! Satan is clever, and he loves for us to get caught up in the petty, trivial, nonsensical, back-and-forth jabbering about others because it distracts us from the substantial spiritual war waging underneath! Let's have our ears peeled for those subtly sneaky moments when the enemy tries to worm his way into our conversations and convince us that trashing others is justified. Instead of getting hung up on someone else's malicious mistreatment, let's remember the old adage that "hurt people hurt people." And above all else, as Luke 6:28 says, let's "*pray* for those who hurt [us]!"

Pray with and for our wives.

I used to consider it an overused cliché in the church to say "just pray about it." But once we have experienced the real, tangible, life-changing, situation-altering power of prayer in our lives, we realize just how mighty and relevant our God is! And once we experience firsthand the presence of Jesus and the reality of His control over literally everything, we will stop trying to fix things for our wives. Instead, we will rest in the fact that God's totally got it.

Look, guys – we naturally gravitate toward putting out fires, solving problems, and implementing solutions. And that's why it is incredibly difficult for us to pause in the midst of those teeth-clenching moments and just say, "God – this issue is driving me *crazy* – and it's the last thing I want to do, but I am going to be still and let You handle it." 2 Chronicles 7:14 offers us the best advice for those tense, heated instances saying, "If my people...will humble themselves and pray and seek My face...then I will hear them from Heaven." A Warrior is humble enough to pray and seek God's face when every part of his body is restless with a desire to fix situations and resolve frustrations. Hear this, men – most vulnerable situations just need a Holy Spirit intervention, not our hasty interruption!

I will be the first to admit that when there's an unsettled situation that involves my wife, it will be accompanied by an almost uncontrollable desire inside of me to do something about it! It's like I go stir-crazy if I'm not taking a step to alleviate the existing dissonance. It is almost an obsession to at least be progressing toward a solution. But while this mentality might be a strength in our business profession, it is a weakness in our marital position. Prayer expedites resolution. And when God sees us acknowledge that He is in control – right smack dab in the middle of that tense juncture – He is going to honor us. Instead of taking control (and often making a mess of things), sometimes we just need to say, "Lord – I hate this situation. I don't get it. I don't like it. But I *trust* You with it. And God – help us to look like You through it!"

Warriors – it's time to become pray-ers, not fixers. Praying *with* our wives, *over* our wives, and *for* our wives on a daily basis is the sign of a *true* Warrior husband. We can't underestimate the power of audibly covering our spouses with God's Word. Because when my wife hears me building those supernatural barriers around her day, her influence, her safety, her health, her job – this has indisputable impact on her sense of protection and security. That's because she knows she is in *much* better hands when I put her in *God's* hands.

Cherish our wives.

When was the last time we actually *did* something to appreciate our wives? We're talking something out of the ordinary and outside of the box. Something that involved deviating from the everyday routine and required that extra effort to pull off. Our wives desire to be cherished the same way we desire to be respected. And when we get off our tails to make even the slightest sacrifice to demonstrate worth to our wives – that little bit will go a long way. Because when our wives feel like they're being honored, they will reciprocate the effort by honoring us. Our investment becomes our benefit!

But what if we give and they give nothing back? I mean, it's exhausting to produce but never consume in any kind of relationship – especially in marriage where we are around our counterpart all the time. At times, it can feel like our spouses have become a parasite, not a partner! But even in these rare occasions where our wives don't seem to be shadowing our sacrifice – we keep on keepin' on. We continue cherishing them until God breaks down any walls of frustration, selfishness, and laziness in our marriage! This is a much more advantageous approach than the alternative.

Marriage can turn into a mutual waiting game if we're not careful. We both just sit there and spectate, waiting on the other to show some interest in the relationship – and this is a guaranteed recipe for deterioration of a marriage. A relationship that God intended to be a continuous cycle of giving becomes a continuous cycle of waiting! It's time to break that cycle because that's not how we operate. We don't sit around waiting for things to happen. Yes – we let God do His part, but we do all we can do in the meantime! I sure am glad God's love for His church wasn't dependent on reciprocation!

But what if we just don't *feel* like doing special things for our wives? Well – we do it anyways – because investment breeds interest! And sometimes we need to just obey regardless of how we feel because that's what God asked us to do. We set aside feelings and align our choices with the Word knowing that eventually we will receive that breakthrough in our emotions. But never – *never* – do we wait for the emotions to come first. Once again – choices lead, feelings follow!

So the question is: what are some practical ways to *cherish* our wives? Well – a great place to start is by using our words! Men – we are most affected by what we see with our eyes, but women are most affected by what they hear with their ears. Every woman might have different interests, but they all have one thing in common – they are moved by words! So why not begin by writing our wives a random note or two about how much we value their friendship, their sacrifice, their hard work, their parenting, their beauty, their patience, or their trust? Simply recognizing the details and appreciating the effort behind the investment that a wife makes will do wonders for a marriage – whether written or spoken! Don't believe it? Just try it! But fair warning – be prepared for the benefits that follow!

Words are just the tip of the iceberg though. Action on our part would be nice on occasion too. How about surprising her with a bouquet of $10 flowers from the grocery store with a card telling her how beautiful she is or how spectacular her eyes are? Or giving her a top-25 list of reasons she's loved? Or dropping off her favorite coffee or snack at work? Guys – it doesn't matter *what* we do – it just matters *that* we do! It is time to start putting the same thought and creativity into cherishing our wives that we put into playing our music, customizing our 4-wheeler, and planning our road trip with the fellas. Our wives aren't secondary, so let's stop giving them secondary effort!

And another thing – let's be sure to pinpoint the dynamic expressions that speak most powerfully to our wives. For me, I knew on day one that my wife responded most favorably to me when I gave her my time! When I spent time with her, she translated it as the highest articulation of love. And when I invested time, it propelled our relationship more efficiently than any other deposit I could make. But – when her tank was running low on quality, one-on-one time, our relationship suffered severely. That would always indicate to me that scheduling some time with *just* her and me – without any interference or distraction – was eminent. It didn't matter what that time involved; it just mattered that we got it on the calendar immediately! Whatever it is that makes our wives weak-kneed – let's exploit the fire out of it! A Warrior husband discovers the unique desires of his wife and strategically targets those areas to add equity to his marriage. It's a simple, but effective, strategy. And every one of us can make it happen. It just takes a little effort.

Romance our wives.

The more effort we invest into appreciating our wives, the more eye-opening the difference will be in our marriages. And this goes for the *romantic* side of the relationship as well! Most of us have probably heard the comparison of a marriage to a wood-burning fire and how both require constant, often inconvenient, efforts to keep the flames strong. But this analogy is dead on. Marriage is a wood-burning fire, not a gas-lit fire. We can't expect the romance in our marriage to survive off the spark that started it years or decades ago! It needs new kindling *every day* to maintain that healthy fire! Sure – removing the ash, hauling in fresh firewood, supplying air to the flame, stoking the embers – they're messy, and they're a hassle. But man – that cozy, toasty, crackling, sizzling, soothing reward – it tends to nullify every troublesome step we took to get there! Marriage is no different, men. The payoff justifies the pain of the payment plan!

But how do we maintain the fire in our romance? And what if that fire has been extinguished for *years?* Well, the first answer is prayer! God is going to honor us for realizing that He is the Answer to supernaturally igniting our marriages with romantic desire. This whole mentality of "we've got this" translates to so many areas where honestly "we don't got this!" Pardon the grammar, but the point is God's intervention is *always* more effective than our investment! Let's not miss the boat on what a Warrior looks like – a man who is close to God, understands God's limitless power, obeys God, and relies on God as the Supreme Catalyst for change in *everything* he faces.

Men – we pray first when we want to see sexual revival in our marriage! We pray that God instills in us an unbridled passion for our wives and vice versa. We pray that Jesus breaks down every emotional void and every physical insecurity to create purity and tranquility in the marriage bed. And while God does what only He can do, we get busy doing what He wants us to do – pursue our wives! We already discussed the idea of thinking of ways to appreciate our wives – whether it be cleaning the house for her, surprising her at work, or leaving a sweet note on her bathroom mirror – but *romancing* our wives goes deeper than kind gestures. It demands that we remain in the "dating" mindset – when we would do anything and everything just to have one more moment with our sweethearts – for the *entirety* of marriage.

I still remember all of the ridiculously silly things I did for my wife before we got married, and how annoyingly giddy we were to everyone around us. But the excitement of that season didn't happen because of youth, newness, or emotional chemistry. No – it happened because there was an inexhaustible fight to capture my prized possession, a strategic plan to schedule everything around the girl of my dreams, and an obsessive pursuit of time with the beautiful Brooke Gilleo. The problem is – this radically romantic mentality can dissipate once the conquest of marrying our sweetheart has commenced!

It's time for men to start acting more like boys in this part of our marriage – to be cheesy, spontaneous, and thoughtful as we pursue our wives the way we did before we said "I do!" So what if it wears out our hands and forearms to give our wives that 20-minute massage to relax them. So what if it takes a little time to go put on a stylish suit, fix our hair, and spray on her favorite cologne to show her that she's still worth impressing. So what if it requires an extra trip to the store to go buy a dozen roses and spread rose petals around the bedroom. Let's show our wives that they're worth being romanced! It really doesn't matter what we do as long as we are trying! Guys – can we just try? Can we stop talking about the right things, and just *do* them? Let's catch our wives off guard, and let's stoke the fire by returning to the dating scene!

But let's not stop at praying and pursuing, because God-ordained romance demands protecting our minds as well! And if there's one thing we all need to hear, it's this: investing thoughts in other women will not only destroy marital romance, but it will destroy a marriage in its entirety! Way too many of us are in the habit of contriving admirable thoughts about women that aren't our wives – and sadly, it has become a second nature habit! And to every one of us I say, "*Grow up* and stop being so selfish." It's time for us to stop flirting in our minds with fantasies that involve any woman except our wives. This is not just referring to sexually immoral thoughts. When we let our minds curiously entertain scenarios of spending time with other women, communicating with other women, living with other women, and even having sexual encounters with other women, it is like attaching a stick of dynamite to our marriage. And romance? It is an inevitable casualty of the devastation that will ensue when we don't guard our minds from intruding daydreams.

Men – we have cheated our wives of the mental, emotional, and sexual thoughts that belong to them. We have chased seemingly innocent, complimentary thoughts of other women that are doing nothing but deteriorating our marriages. And even with the most silent, minuscule, endearing thought that we give to another woman – whether on her appearance or personality – we steal that value from our wives and add it to something that pulls us away from purity! When we see that attractive young lady walking in the store, and we think, "Wow, she is gorgeous," or let our hearts indulge in the whim of, "I wonder what she's like" – we have now considered an alternative, entertained a scenario, and invested emotionally in a relationship outside of our wives. That can all happen in a second, and this is anything but innocent. This is sin. This is robbery. And this is a big deal!

Guys – Satan wants us to compliment other women, deposit thoughts into "what if" scenarios, and chase those curious, emotional sensations, because he knows that it subtracts from our marriage. So what do we do when He tries to steal from our marriage? We *confront* him and declare contentment elevating our wives to a place of incomparability!

Laugh with our wives.

It is hard to have a healthy marriage if there is no humor in a marriage! And as we return to the dating scene with our wives, let's also return to laughing with our wives! We need to learn how to laugh again with our spouses, even in the moments when we don't feel like laughing! Laughing relieves stress, refreshes perspective, renews positivity, and even reduces defensiveness. Scientific studies even show that laughter can deter burnout and depression in a marriage! And I believe it. In fact, I've seen this firsthand for decades in my parents' marriage, which seems to consist of 90% laughter and 10% talking! Maybe we need to stop taking ourselves so seriously and start adding a little bit of childishness back to our pursuit!

Communicate clearly with our wives.

Another crucial component to leading and loving our wives is communicating effectively with them, because all relationships function more efficiently when expectations are clearly defined and potential points of conflict are thoroughly discussed. Yes – it might seem impossible at times to get on the same page as our wives, but it's a Warrior's responsibility to initiate the conversations and create a healthy communication culture to ensure we remain tight-knit units with our significant other.

One fundamental dynamic of effective communication involves *clarifying expectations*. When expectations are clearly defined, we will save our marriages from a whole lot of headache! Some of our marriages are like quiet volcanoes with hot lava boiling under the surface, and if the toxic issues aren't resolved sooner rather than later, there will be an explosion with catastrophic consequences. It's time we bring up the issues that are causing dissension in our marriage and resolve them with prayer, patience, conversation, and compromise.

The most destructive moments in my marriage have all been products of differing expectations. My wife is expecting to do things one way, while I'm expecting to do things another way. And this is a recipe for some serious tension. This is the way the enemy works. He just wants conflicting expectations, so that someone's expectations will be unmet. Because where there are unmet expectations, there will be disappointment. And Satan knows that disappointment leads to division, and division leads to arguments, anger, and ultimately – resentment. So what is the safeguard from conflicting expectations? Clear communication. Every marriage has its own unique set of dynamics, and every marriage has *that* issue – the radioactive one – the one that has created arguments *time* after *time* in our marriages. But it's time to prayerfully initiate the conversation to get on the same page with our spouses when it comes to *that* topic. Whatever *that* point of conflict is, it probably falls under one of several categories. But even if it doesn't, these subjects are worth a sit-down discussion with the wife to establish uniformity and consistency.

Common Sources of Conflict:

- Responsibilities at home (cleaning + yard work + dinner + dishes + laundry + car maintenance)

- Parenting responsibilities and disciplinary techniques

- Church commitment and involvement

- Money (tithing + saving + spending + eliminating debt + giving + planning for the future)

- Sex (frequency + responsibility / obligation to our spouses)

- Social schedule and interaction (introverts / extroverts)

- Extended family (siblings + parents + in-laws)

- Holidays (time + location + extended family involvement)

For what it's worth, unmarried men can benefit from discussing these aforementioned subjects (minus the "Sex" – save that one for marriage) as interview material for potential wife candidates. It never hurts to know the philosophical differences in marital dynamics before they slap you right in the face after the honeymoon!

Guys – these points of conflict can hijack our marriages and create dangerous division, none of them more so than our extended family. Look – this is a sensitive topic in most marriages, but we need to be reminded that our immediate family (brothers, sisters, fathers, mothers) becomes extended family when we get married. And our extended family is always secondary to our wives. Always. It doesn't matter that we have spent decades with our parents and siblings by our sides. Genesis 2:24 tells us that we leave our fathers and mothers and become one with our *wives!* We all have different family situations and face vastly unique circumstances, but God gave us the responsibility of being our wives' teammate at *all* times. So even if we disagree with our wives on certain matters, or feel a pull to "side" with our family in a discrepancy, we need to rebuke that in Jesus' name, and "hold fast" to our wives like Genesis tells us to do. Warriors do *whatever* it takes to stand with our wives, even at the expense of hurting our family's feelings. And here's a useful tidbit: let's just avoid drama altogether by *never* involving extended family in the disagreements that we have within our marriages. It does nothing but create chaos and discord. Let's just settle the disparity internally, and leave the peanut gallery out of it. Warriors don't entangle extended family in our marital disputes. Period.

When it comes to extended family, we can still invest in those relationships without involving them in our hardships. And as Warriors, we do just that. We put that effort in to cultivate healthy relationships with extended family – and that goes for our spouses' families too! Guys – it takes a true Warrior to invest in his wife's family the way he invests in his own. No, we might not have decades of memories and nostalgia with our in-laws, but new relationships can only be as strong as the time and effort we invest in them. Warriors understand the importance of balanced investments with both sides of the extended family and are even willing to sacrifice tradition to meet the needs of our wives. No, we might not always "feel" like leaving our parents' house to go over to her parents' house on our favorite holiday, but we do it with a great attitude because that's what an adaptable Warrior does.

Communicate gently with our wives.

Even with clear communication and defined expectations, there will inevitably be disagreements within our marriage. And there's an epidemic among men in how we handle disagreements. We're aggressive, controlling, and dominant toward our wives, attacking her weaknesses to compensate for the respect that we are looking to gain. We are notorious for going into attack mode if our expectations are not met or our wives have disrespected us. Men – it takes zero effort to launch an offensive against our weaker counterpart. It takes zero effort to let our adrenaline and testosterone call the shots. It takes zero effort to point our fingers at our wives and verbally chokeslam them so they know "who's in control." But Warriors don't get combative with our *wives*...we get combative with the *enemy!*

Guys – when we're close to Jesus on a daily basis, His Holy Spirit is going to give us patience and discretion during moments of rage and frustration. But we have to listen to His Spirit and actually obey His leadership in those moments. This is where practical meets principle! In the heat of the moment, a Warrior seeks to understand more than to be understood. A Warrior masters the discipline of shutting his mouth instead of causing irreparable damage to his marriage with one flippant, emotionally driven comment. A Warrior is on guard, especially when he is tired, knowing that the enemy loves preying on the exhausted. A Warrior has the maturity to know when to walk away, pray, and cool down. A Warrior knows how to admit fault and take responsibility for his mess-ups. A Warrior *protects*, not *exposes*, his wife's insecurities in a dispute. A Warrior is marked by gentleness in conflict with his wife.

Ephesians 4:26 cautions us to be heedful of the power of anger saying, "'Don't sin by letting anger control you.'" Guys – this describes *exactly* what anger is doing if we in *any* way try to maim our wives (or anyone for that matter) physically or emotionally! It is "controlling" us. And this isn't us, guys! Warriors allow the Holy Spirit to control our anger, and we demonstrate self-control during conflict. But Ephesians 4:26 doesn't stop there. It jabs us again in the gut saying, "Don't let the sun go down while you are still angry." Warriors resolve conflict before going to bed. What an arduous task to tackle! The *last* thing we want to do when we are not seeing eye-to-eye with our wives is communicate with them. But this is what separates the Warriors from the rest of the pack. It doesn't necessarily mean that everyone is happy when our heads hit the pillows, but it does mean that we value our wives, our families, and our obedience of God's Word enough to listen, pray, and at least seek to understand the situation.

It is a big deal not to resolve the underlying issues, guys. A major danger of unresolved conflict in our marriage is the division that is slowly created over time. It happens one small step at a time, and before we know it, Satan has introduced us to the word "divorce." Real talk, guys – the "d" word shouldn't even exist in a Warrior's vocabulary. Divorce has unfathomably crippling, multi-generational ramifications on our families, and that's why all throughout His Word, God discourages us from ever going this route. There may be men reading this right now who are considering divorce, and in Jesus' *powerful* name, I'm praying for healing, forgiveness, and the love of the cross to shelter that marriage. I'm also praying that you have the strength as Warriors to work through the pain, infidelity, and wrongdoing so that unity is restored! Just know that God *wants* to restore your marriage!

If divorce seems to be the final decision, just remember – the more *time* and *prayer* we give every choice, the more *clarity* and *wisdom* we will experience. Before we make any big decisions, it is best to just stop! And when we stop, we pray. And we pray some more. And then we find a spiritual advisor who Biblically pushes us toward forgiveness, patience, reconciliation, unity, and the Word of God.

For those who have walked through the painful process of a divorce, there is no reason whatsoever to be discouraged. God doesn't care about our past mistakes – He just wants our future decisions! And He promises us in Revelation 21:5 (ESV) that He makes "all things new!" So if we've been a part of an adulterous relationship or walked through a divorce – He tells us in John 8:11 to "go and sin no more!" Wow! Just think about that. Regardless of how horribly we've messed up in our marriages, God isn't focused on our wrongdoing. This is the most liberating and peaceful promise for all of us – that our Dad just wants us to start new today.

Stay committed to our wives no matter what.

Divorce isn't a part of a Warrior husband's vocabulary simply because we are committed to our wives. And there is *nothing* they can do to change that. Commitment means that we are willing to be absolutely miserable for moments or seasons while we work things out with our wives. There are going to be challenging, trying, unhappy, frustrating, pull-our-hair-out, utterly wretched times in marriage. And Warriors are okay with that! In fact, it's a part of what we sign up for when we say "I do" at the altar and make a promise that we are there "for better, for worse!" We don't budge in the "worse" moments because those are the very ones when our spouses need us the most. Not to mention, those are the moments that define the legitimacy of our commitment! And, boy, is "worse" no fun. Sometimes "worse" might even involve forgiving a wife who has been unfaithful to us. And in these terribly painful cases, it is only the supernatural grace of Jesus Christ *in* us that can lead us to live out what we say we believe.

And when we are experiencing these indescribably infuriating, downright depressing moments in our marriage, the *last* thing that we do is seek solace by entertaining scenarios and conversations with other women or run through fantasies in our minds that involve us leaving our wives. We immediately hit our knees, open our Bibles, and reach out to our Warrior brothers to combat these destructive temptations in prayer! There *will* be miserable moments, but we have got to be armed for spiritual war and committed to fighting in the very first moment of their arrival! These dangerous moments in marriage are when prayer, worship, the Word, and accountability are literally our lifelines for survival! God is going to honor unwavering Biblical commitment to our wives in marriage as it is following His Son's example on the cross, which is summed up in the miracle of Romans 5:8 (NIV): "While we were still sinners, Christ died for us!" Warriors – let's become the Ephesians 5 example of a husband and remind our wives often that there is nothing they can do to ever change our commitment to them.

Fathers – Live the example we teach.

Proverbs 20:7 "The godly walk with integrity; blessed are their children who follow them."

It won't be long before we are gone from this Earth. And when we *do* make our exit, we can only leave our families one thing that matters – and that is a legacy of living for Jesus. It sounds cliché, but anything else – no matter how well-intended or admirable it may be – is useless. We can raise children with textbook manners, impressive accomplishments, dynamic talents, outstanding work ethic, and even a laundry list of selfless deeds. But – all that is *worthless* if we haven't taught them where true identity, substance, and satisfaction are found – in knowing and obeying Jesus! *That* is the measuring stick of success in our fatherhood!

Psalm 127:4 says, "Children born to a young man are like arrows in a warrior's hands." Fathers – we have these shapeable arrows in our hands just waiting to be sharpened into versatile weapons in God's army, and it's time we start treating fatherhood as a training ground to craft the arsenal of future generations! It's time to wake up and realize that our purpose as fathers is to simply set the example of integrity, excellence, and closeness to Jesus so that the next generations are exposed to the same peace, power, purpose, and promise that a relationship with God brings!

Men – we are here to provide direction, and it is up to us to navigate our families to the right destination. We need to take this task very seriously, guys, because without *our* example, we could cost our children, our grandchildren, our great grandchildren, and beyond a chance at knowing Jesus and spending eternity in paradise. Think about that! What a responsibility – to know that *our* example (or lack thereof) could determine whether our families' families' families receive the only thing in life that matters – a relationship with Jesus! This just isn't a responsibility to take lightly.

Be the example for our children.

A lineage that lives for Jesus starts with us living for Jesus. And there is nothing that will influence our children more than simply *living* what we tell them to live! Because whatever we are *doing* is going to trump what we are *saying*. Behavior will always outweigh teaching. Fortunately, I was blessed with an earthly father whose actions nearly always matched up with the words that he taught my brothers and me. He taught us to treat Mama like a queen, but more importantly – he *treated* Mama like a queen! Proverbs 20:7 doesn't tell us to "talk about" integrity. It tells us to "walk with" integrity and that our children will be "blessed" by that example. It doesn't matter how many mind-blowing proverbs and truths we tell our children; it matters that we *live* them. We can't expect our kids to live something that we are not living. Let's be the example and model what we want our children to look like, because there is much more power in our *actions* than there is in our *words*.

Be there for our children.

The influence we have on our children can only be as great as our time invested in them. If we aren't spending time around our children, we can't expect to have influence in their lives. Love is demonstrated to a child through time, so our presence is essentially the gateway to influencing our children. Quality time alone isn't enough. Our children need *quantity* more than anything. I'm blessed to have had parents who were always there, and their presence is what gave, and still gives, them credibility. I never had to question the sincerity of their words or suspect some ulterior motive in their parenting, because they showed they cared by being there! I never had to wonder if Dad would be at my practice, because he was usually the coach wanting to invest in me!

This is the example Warriors set for our children. Warriors are there. And there is *never* a doubt in our children's minds, because they know that they are more valuable than our career, our money, our hobbies, and our agenda. Hey, men – it is inconvenient at times to be there for our children's special moments, and we might not be able to make it to every event, but it's a Warrior's priority to make choices that put our *children's confidence* ahead of *our convenience*. Sometimes that might even mean getting interested in our kids' interests even if they might not be our cup of tea!

If we want to step up our commitment to be there for our children, then we better step up our commitment to be there for our *spouses*, because there is an unavoidable correlation between our faithfulness to our spouses and our ability to even be involved in our children's lives! Hey, men – maintaining a pure and faithful marriage protects our freedom to be around our kids. And we can't forget that. The seemingly innocent flirting with a coworker could eventually lead to our children being miles away from us. The friendly conversations with the cute friend at the gym could begin the journey that results in seeing our children once every two weeks. And while God can restore and bless the broken situations in our lives, it is a lot easier to just protect them from breaking in the first place! So next time we start flirting with marital infidelities, let's remind ourselves of the domino effect that those seemingly unrelated casual conversations and computer clicks can have on accessibility to our children!

Sacrifice for our children.

Setting the example for our children means making decisions that put their desires ahead of ours. Philippians 2:4 (NIV), which we discussed in chapter five, can be applied on the fatherly front as well. It urges us not to get caught up in our interests but to look to "the interests of others." And there is no better example of someone who gave up his interests for his children's interests than my father. Burr Ingram was the epitome of sacrifice, spending very little time and money on himself. He never chased his own pleasures and agendas at the expense of compromising the principle of selflessness that he taught us. He was a true man – because like 1 Corinthians 13:11, he had the discipline to "put away childish things" to be the Warrior father God made him to be. He was *always* about his wife and his children and what was best for us. That is a true manifestation of Jesus' example!

Guys – a Warrior understands that life as a parent isn't convenient, and he embraces the inconvenience of sacrificing for his children in every stage of life. No, it's not convenient to get up four times throughout the night to change a diaper on a two-month-old baby or to spend that $200 on the prom dress our teenage daughter has been wanting instead of the newest gadget that we've been wanting. It isn't convenient to be at our baby girl's ballet recital and miss the big game on TV or the trip with our buddies. And it isn't convenient to get the family around the table every morning for a 5-minute devotion and prayer to start every day. It just *isn't* convenient to be a Warrior father and sacrifice time, effort, and money for our children. But inconvenience is what we *do!* It is what Warriors thrive on – the challenge to shatter the norm! We sacrifice our fleshly desires and our comfort, day after day, knowing that we are setting the example of Jesus' sacrifice and investing in the influencers of the *next* generation!

Set boundaries for our children.

Speaking of inconvenience, it sure isn't convenient to constantly monitor what our kids are doing. But setting boundaries is non-negotiable if we care about our children, and it does not matter what kind of attitude or pushback we receive by doing so! It is a Warrior father's responsibility at all times to know what is going on in his children's lives, to set Biblical boundaries, and to make unpopular decisions if necessary.

Just like it is our job as parents to keep our naïve 18-month-old away from electrical outlets so he doesn't get electrocuted, it is also our job to monitor our 17-year-old's phone and social media outlets to prevent him from promiscuity. The same way we guard our toddlers from random strangers, we should guard our adolescents and teenagers from having the wrong friends. And the same way we shield our five-year-old from the vulgarity of certain TV shows or pop music, we should do the same for our 20-year-old junior in college. We don't parent based on age – we parent based on *purity!* And at no point in our children's lives does our responsibility as a monitor and gatekeeper expire, because purity is age-irrelevant.

While there *is* a point in life when our children no longer "have" to abide by our rules, there *isn't* a point at which they stop needing our discernment and discretion. Even when a son or daughter becomes independent and wants nothing to do with a parent's guidance, it is still our responsibility as fathers to lovingly push our children towards Biblical living. We cannot let our fear of annoying, frustrating, or embarrassing our children prevent us from boldly and gently fathering them toward the purity of Jesus. A Warrior isn't concerned about being a popular father; he is concerned about being a *protective* father. Guys – Satan just needs one outlet, one friend, one relationship, one iPhone app, or one social media post. He just needs *one* opportunity to infiltrate our children's minds to get them off track. Let's be awake and aware of potential impostors and pray relentlessly for discernment from the Holy Spirit to protect our kids from disguised sin.

But here's the challenge: boundaries and lazy parenting cannot coincide. Too often our convenience and inconvenience become the gods that keep us from parenting responsibly and adhering to the parameters we have set for our children. For example, if we let our six-year-old son play video games upstairs for five straight hours to keep him from "bothering us" while we are hanging out with friends, we are parenting irresponsibly to cater to *our convenience.* Or if we snap at our two-year-old daughter and scold her because she interrupted our football game on TV with her crying, we are parenting not based on her disobedience but on *our inconvenience.* It's time for fathers to grow up and act like fathers. Let's not lazily abandon Biblical parenting to preserve our leisure.

Discipline our children in love.

Setting boundaries is one thing, but enforcing them is a whole other ball game. Disciplining a child has to be the most undesirable part of parenthood because it is no fun for either party. That said, it is an absolute necessity as a Warrior father to administer consequences when our children choose to live outside of God's parameters. God's Word takes this a step further in Proverbs 13:24 telling us, "Those who spare the rod of discipline *hate* their children!" "Hate" is a word that should get the attention of every apathetic, lazy, immature father who is more concerned with his children's approval than his Heavenly Father's approval! The Bible makes it clear: what we see as "staying on our children's good side," God sees as *hating* our children!

Proverbs 13:24 goes on to say that, "Those who love their children care enough to discipline them." Society might tell us that "kids will be kids" and that we should "let them be who they are" allowing poor decisions to slide without any consequences. But the Bible tells us that "letting it slide" is a sign that we don't care about them at all! Hear this, men! Hebrews 12:6 says that even God "disciplines those He loves and punishes each one He accepts as His child!" Now if *God* translates discipline as love, that is enough reason for us to do the same!

Discipline is essential, but its *delivery* is everything. We have a nasty tendency to misuse discipline as a stage to show off our authority instead of using it as a tool to protect our children's purity. Our longing for respect and control often leads to an over-masculine, aggressive, angry approach in our correction. But disciplining our children's wrong choices in anger is fighting sin with sin! Ephesians 6:4 warns us against this kind of parenting saying, "Fathers, do not provoke your children to anger by the way you treat them. Rather, bring them up with the discipline and instruction that comes from the Lord." Discipline isn't about us changing our children's behaviors by oppressively leading them to fear. It is about God changing our children's hearts by gently leading them to the cross! Love and gentleness should characterize us as earthly fathers and disciplinarians, because that's what characterizes our Heavenly Father.

But what does Biblically based discipline look like? Well – it may come as a surprise to some, but Proverbs 23:13 (ESV) says, "Do not withhold discipline from a child; if you strike him with a rod, he will not die." Now as comical as this verse may sound, it touches on a serious point in our parenting – spanking our children. And believe it or not, the Bible advocates it. No – the objective of spanking isn't to hurt our children, nor is it to serve as an outlet for our anger or some retaliatory avenue to unleash our displeasure. But the Bible clearly supports physical disciplinary action as long as it is a calm, controlled decision, not an aggressive, knee-jerk reaction. It is simply a tool to demonstrate that unruly behavior leads to undesirable consequences.

Ultimately, it is the attitude and explanation behind the physical discipline that should speak louder than the punishment itself. Yes, there is value behind firm, restrained, responsible physical discipline. Proverbs 29:15 (ESV) reminds us that "the rod and reproof give wisdom." But – our primary goal in discipline isn't to punish. It is to *look* like Jesus' example while we *lead* to Jesus' example.

Let's not be hypocrites in our own houses by dictating behaviors with intimidation. Instead, let's always conclude disciplinary action by tying our lessons to Jesus' living. By targeting the heart and the "why" behind every correction, our children will one day hopefully abandon the "I *have* to do this" mentality and embrace the "I do this because *Jesus* did this" mentality!

Be transparent with our children.

It's all about the heart, guys. As we discipline, we are targeting the internal motives, not the external actions. This is also our goal as we cultivate relationships with our children. If we want to get to our children's hearts, we must establish a foundation built on unfiltered openness and steadfast kindness. The healthiest relationships are marked by an honesty that allows one another to expose the filthiest things knowing that transparency will be met with love and approachability. 1 Peter 4:8 is a sobering reminder for us as parents, especially when our children have made a choice that has driven us to rock-bottom discouragement: "Most important of all, continue to show deep love for each other, for love covers a multitude of sins."

If we want to reach our children's hearts and see them exhibit transparency, vulnerability, honesty, and desire-driven obedience, then we need to show them that *they* are more valuable to us than their behavior. Yes – it's our responsibility to keep our children on the right path, but it's even more critical for us to be there for them and love them through every peak and valley. This means supporting and loving our children even when they are choosing to live in sin, because there's a massive difference between *loving a child* and *loving a child's sin*. The best way to say it is: our children aren't their sin. Our children are our children, and sin is sin. And while we hate the sin that's in them, we can still love them despite it. When we live out this extremely challenging principle, God will honor it because that's the exact same kind of love Jesus exhibited for us on the cross!

Extending love and grace to our children will help us establish a healthy, honest, open communication culture. And when we tell our children that we only expect *honesty*, not *perfection*, they will be liberated to a new level of honor and respect for our authority. We will be amazed at the depth of our relationships as love becomes the first reaction from dad instead of anger. Suddenly, our children will be drawn to us instead of being terrified of us, because they know we have their best interest in mind! That's a phenomenal principle right there from Pastor Chris Hodges.

But what about *our* transparency? A Warrior father owns up to his parenting mistakes and is humble enough to admit fault if fault exists. News flash – we will inevitably mess up in our parenting efforts on occasion and mishandle a situation or two along the way. But there's nothing more impressionable and impactful on our children than looking them in the eyes and genuinely saying, "I'm sorry how I handled that. I was wrong. Will you forgive me?" God will bless this kind of raw authenticity and candid humility when we've blown it with our kids. Let's be approachable, humble fathers who are there to listen to our children, love them through the difficulties and mistakes, and admit wrongdoing when it's needed. Let's have open ears, open arms, and open hearts for our children so that they see us as a reflection of Jesus!

Speak life over our children.

Our children are watching to see how daddy responds to their successes and failures, but they are also *listening* to *hear* what daddy says about their successes and failures. Men – we have no idea how consequential our words are when it comes to our children's self-worth. The words that we voice define what our children believe about themselves, because what daddy says about them is absorbed as truth! When our words speak insults, inadequacy, negativity, discouragement, doubt, frustration, anger, oppression, and disappointment over our kids – we program them to believe they are failures! It is inexcusable to abuse our role as protectors and become the *perpetrators* of our children's deficient self-worth, but it's a reality in way too many households.

Our words foreshadow our children's future. And as Warrior fathers, we may use our words to condemn what a child *did*, but we should never use our words to condescend who a child *is!* It is our responsibility to regularly remind our children that the mistakes they make are *not* who they are constantly reinforcing the separation between indiscretion and identity! A Warrior father knows that what a child does doesn't define who a child is. And just because a child *has* a failure doesn't mean that child *is* a failure! So instead of bashing our children when they mess up, let's tell them that they are better than that! Let's use our tongues to bring "life" like Proverbs 18:21 tells us to do. And let's be careful with our words to distinguish that division between *behavior* and *being*.

Be consistent with our children.

There is comfort in consistency, and Hebrews 13:8 provides a comforting truth about the consistency of our Savior – that "Jesus Christ is the same yesterday, today, and forever." There is such a peace in knowing that Jesus is *always* there for us, and that we *always* know what to expect! I'm so thankful that I don't have to guess what mood my Heavenly Father is in today or whether He is going to love me after what I did yesterday. There is relaxation in the predictability of our Father's attributes and behaviors, and our children need this same predictability from us! Whether they realize it or not, our children need to watch us be the rock of the family during trials time after time. They need to see us working hard to provide for the family month after month. They need to see us treat our wives like queens year after year, decade after decade. They need to be annoyed when we wake them up 15 minutes early to pray and read the Word with the family day after day!

Our children *need* to see constants amid an erratic culture. The way we provide this is by consuming the Word, living the Word, and teaching our children the Word. Children find comfort in our consistency and the consistency of pointing to God's Word, because it provides structure and dependability. So as we navigate the challenges and trials of being a father, let's *always* point back to that trustworthy, absolute standard, the Word of God, as our constant compass. And let's stand in confidence on the promise of Proverbs 22:6 that if we "direct [our] children onto the right path, when they are older, they will not leave it."

Pray with and for our children.

We have talked ad nauseam throughout the Warrior study about the power of prayer, but it's worth mentioning again that prayer outdoes anything we can do on our own. Without God's power and presence going before us, we will exhaust ourselves as parents, seeing marginal results. But if God's hand is involved – just watch out! We may fail miserably as fathers on our own accord, but we will inevitably succeed if we follow 2 Chronicles 7:14, and "pray and seek [God's] face" about every little detail of our children's lives! *This* is where we see undebatable results.

Warriors pray with our children. And we pray God's protection over *every* aspect of their existence. We pray Deuteronomy 28:13 over them – that God would make our children "the head and not the tail." We pray that our children would have unexplainable impact for Jesus, that they would never enjoy sinning, and that the Holy Spirit would guide them in situations where peers are pressuring them to follow the cultural norm. We pray that our children would be surrounded with like-minded friends who hate sin and love Jesus. And we pray that our children are one day led to spouses that love God and live for God. Men – we pray because it is infinitely more effective than even our perfect parenting!

Sons – Appreciate the parents God chose for us.

Exodus 20:12 "Honor your father and mother. Then you will live a long, full life in the land the Lord your God is giving you."

It is no accident that we have the parents we have. And if we *believe* that our God knows what He is doing, then we should thank God every day for the parents He provided for us. Because whether our parents have or haven't been model mothers and fathers, whether they were present or absent during the milestone moments, or whether they remained committed or walked out on us during our childhood – God *knows* what He is doing. Unsympathetic as it may sound, the specific undertone of our upbringing is irrelevant, because whether positive or negative, it is a preordained part of God's plan for us as sons! And whether our upbringing has been pleasant or painful – there is purpose behind what we've experienced as sons.

Psalm 139:16 is a comforting reminder that God has intentionality behind our story line: "[God] saw me before I was born. Every day of my life was recorded in [His] book. Every moment was laid out before a single day had passed." God knows what He is doing! And whether our parents have been helpful or harmful to our journey, God knew what He was doing when He handpicked them. We know that God's plan is preordained with a perfect purpose, so it's not our job to ask *why* we should honor our parents. It's our job to just *do* it!

Obey our parents when we are young.

Being honorable sons in our youth means respecting our parents' positions as uniquely chosen, God-anointed authorities. This respect translates as obedience. It's simple. And for young men living under the roof or provision of a parent or parents, it is our Biblical assignment to heed parental instruction and abide by their rules. Colossians 3:20 makes it clear: "Children, always obey your parents, for this pleases the Lord." It's probably not what a lot of the young men are wanting to hear, but when we're ticked off because our parents are asking us to do something that we vehemently do not want to do – we *bite* our tongues, *thank* Jesus for His chosen authority in our lives, and *abide* by the rules that our parents have set for us. Period.

Warrior sons flee rebellion and we do what our mothers and fathers ask of us. Of course there are going to be moments when we just plain don't like what our parents are telling us or the boundaries they are setting for us. But we need to *get over it* and realize that obedience isn't always going to be the most pleasant experience for our feelings! Maybe we really want to see our girlfriend later tonight, or we really want to listen to that pop music album, or we really want to hang out with the guys on Friday night at that house party. Whatever the case – we default to our parents' judgment because that's what God asked us to do. That's what honoring sons do!

As annoying as it is to concede to this fact – when our parents "inconvenience" us, they are usually just *watching out* for us. They are trying to protect us from potential strongholds that we aren't perceptive enough or experienced enough to foresee! Those boundaries they set are walls of wisdom built from their mistakes and experiences to simply save us from our ignorance – not to impose their will or make us miserable! Guys – there is a lot more knowledge behind our parents than we realize. And even if we don't agree with them or understand them, we can still obey them. Warriors see past our feelings and realize that our parents are our chosen, ordained authorities. And they're typically our biggest fans, greatest protectors, and most dependable supporters.

But obedience is as much about exuberance as it is abidance. In other words, our *countenance* is as important as our *compliance.* Yes – honor involves a purposeful action, but it requires a positive attitude. It's not honoring to our parents when we sit at home and pout all night because we couldn't go on that date or to that party, because while we're technically complying with their rules, we're not truly considering the love behind their boundaries. Honor means obeying while having a joyful attitude and an appreciation for how much our parents care. Warriors make the right choice with the right attitude.

But what about those of us who have been raised or are being raised by selfish, immature, irresponsible parents who have contributed to serious pain and countless, horrific memories? The reality is some of us come from situations where parents are the source of depression, hate, and hurt. But no matter how much pain we are holding because of how we were mistreated, neglected, or even abused – God *wants* that pain. And He *wants* us to *forgive* our parents as a step of obedience to reflect His Son Jesus. Because even in broken parental situations, young Warriors can set the example of Jesus and *choose* to let them off the hook for their mistakes. Even in our youth, we can *choose* to honor the dishonorable! 1 Timothy 4:12 reminds us, "Don't let anyone think less of [us] because [we] are young, but be an example to all believers...in the way [we] live!" Young Warriors – we can set the example even for the superiors in our households!

Being the example of Jesus in our youth is often a difficult thing to do, but Warriors relish the opportunity to be one of the rare examples for our friends. We are the exception to mediocrity. We are the guys on the baseball team who don't bash our parents because of their boundaries. We are the guys who don't insult our mom because she embarrassed us by showing up at the school dance. We are the guys who actually listen to our dad's advice on dating the right girls even though we feel like we know everything at age 20. We are the guys who get home at 10:25 p.m. because our curfew is 10:30 p.m. We are examples of honor because our peers need to see a living example of Exodus 20:12. Plus – our parents *deserve* that honor for all that they've given just to raise us. What a slap in the face it is to our parents to act like we don't care about all of the sacrifice they've made to invest in us. Every last one of us should go out of our way to tell mom and dad "thank you" *today* for all they've done for us. It honors them, and it honors God.

Listen to our parents when we are older.

Being an honoring child doesn't expire with age or independence. As sons, we are called to honor our parents no matter how old we are or how self-sufficient we become. Guys – our independence doesn't merit arrogance toward mom and dad. And just because we live under another roof doesn't mean we're suddenly exempt from respecting their role as our navigators. All throughout Proverbs, God urges us to listen to our father's teaching. Proverbs 23:22 actually specifies the importance of doing so later in life saying, "Listen to your father, who gave you life, and don't despise your mother when she is old." God's Word is clear – honor doesn't have an expiration date! And even in those frustrating moments when we might not agree with our parents' two cents, or we just flat out don't want to hear it, *these* are the "make or break" tests for the Exodus 20:12 honor of a Warrior!

Guys – we are *never* too old to receive wisdom from our parents. Job 12:12 tells us that "wisdom belongs to the aged, and understanding to the old." We are foolish if we don't heed the advice rooted in decades of experience from our parents – even as we become autonomous, self-supported men. Warrior sons *never* stop learning from our elders because we can *always* become wiser. Just look at Proverbs 9:9: "Instruct the wise, and they will be even wiser. Teach the righteous, and they will learn even more." Regardless of our age, it shows wisdom to seek wisdom. Sure – we might occasionally receive advice from our parents that we disagree with, but we can still honor the heart behind their message – because their guidance is almost certainly rooted in love. Our parents don't enjoy disagreeing with us, nor do they find pleasure in making decisions difficult for us. They just don't want us to learn from experience by getting burned like they did! We need to stop getting offended, skeptical, or critical of the guidance given by our parents, and instead thank Jesus that they care enough to advise us!

Warriors – let's appreciate when our parents protect us with their discernment and discretion, even *later* in life. And the next time we're annoyed at our parents' message or its delivery, let's at least honor the heart behind it. Because contrary to what our feelings might be telling us, the vast majority of the time parents just want what's best for *us*, not for *them!*

Leaders – Reflect Jesus' example with excellence.

Joshua 24:15 "But as for me and my family, we will serve the Lord."

It is a gargantuan responsibility to lead a family and to be the catalyst that establishes a Jesus-centered environment for our households. And while this responsibility is largely rooted in being the Warrior husbands, fathers, and sons that God desires, we can't overlook our all-encompassing role as leaders of the household. Reality check: A Warrior can't lead a generation if he can't lead his own family. In fact, 1 Timothy 3 tells us that in order to be a leader in the church, a man "must manage his own family well" living "above reproach!"

It's an inconvenient truth, but when Paul calls us out to live "above reproach," he's telling us to live blameless, flawless lives as they relate to God's Word. He's calling us to be the exception and to be living, breathing shadows of Jesus' example. Talk about a serious assignment. This isn't for the fair-weather, lukewarm, semi-committed, one-foot-in-one-foot-out man. That's why there are so few of us actually *living* above reproach! Guys – it is our responsibility to lead our families by following Jesus' example in everything. John 3:30 is our mission every day as leaders of our households – to let Jesus "become greater and greater" while we "become less and less."

Talk passionately and constantly about the power of Jesus in our homes.

What does our conversation consist of at the beginning of every day around our homes? How about at the end of the day? One telltale sign that Jesus is the most important focus in our homes is when our conversations focus less on the literal and more on the spiritual. Instead of just talking about the latest happenings at school and work, we are more focused on what God is teaching us in His Word and how we can use it to bless people. The conversation culture of a Warrior's household is focused more on others' eternity than our entertainment. And like Deuteronomy 11:19 says, we talk passionately and constantly about God's Word – "when [we] are at home and when [we] are on the road, when [we] are going to bed and when [we] are getting up."

The conversations that take place inside a home are a reflection of its leader's focus. And it's up to us to consistently celebrate and discuss the name of Jesus – the healing, the forgiveness, the love, the mercy, the provision, and the realness of His power! I want to be a husband and father whose conversation is obsessively fixated on hearts that matter for eternity, not things that won't matter tomorrow.

It's fine to talk about the latest news, events, gadgets, and fashions, but let's make sure that Jesus' name continuously gets the conversation, the credit, the excitement, the smiles, the cheers, the celebrations, the faith, and the trust that it deserves around our homes. Let's interject Jesus' example and eternal perspective into literally *everything* we talk about, because He is relevant to *every* topic and *every* area of life! And let's always remind our families that the name of Jesus holds more weight than *any* obstacle we encounter! What a blessing we will be to our families when they hear us habitually voicing our confidence in Jesus when even devastating challenges arise!

Spend daily time with Jesus in prayer, worship, and the Word.

Our leadership is an extension of our time with Jesus. And if we aren't praying, worshipping, and reading the Word, we can expect our homes to have more complaining, more arguing, more worrying, more anger, more discouragement...more of everything we *don't* want. Mark it down. Every day, week, or season that we experience depression or frustration in our families – it is almost always a reflection of *our* empty spiritual tank. When the Warrior of the house is running on "E," the tone of the household will usually magnify that deficiency. So, if nothing else, let's make sure that the head of the household is spending time being fed so that the family is being fed through him!

Men – we are the *protectors* of our families. And the greatest way we protect our wives and kids isn't through having guns and alarm systems in the house. It is through battling the enemy with prayer, worship, and the Word *every* day, even when they might not see us fighting for them behind closed doors. It is our responsibility as home leaders to have that time with God *for* our families by putting on the armor daily and asking God's supernatural presence to protect them. They may not realize it, but our families are desperate for all the benefits that come from our connecting to Jesus because He equips us to lead gently and consistently!

As leaders of the house, let's create a family dynamic where it's completely normal to say little prayers all throughout the day, even if the subject matter isn't all that serious! If we're running out the door and saying bye to the wife, we can stop for two seconds and say "Jesus – be with my wife... cover her throughout the day and keep her safe!" If our child is discouraged about striking out twice at his baseball game, we can spend 10 seconds saying "God, encourage my little man right now, and help him realize that he is a winner and that he is going to have the game of his life next time he steps on that field! But help us remember that life is about so much more than baseball! Amen!"

Make church a priority.

When you look at it on paper, it seems so elementary to make church a priority. But when Sunday rolls around, suddenly that vacation, lake house, sports event, family time, cold weather, or rainy forecast...*they* become deciding factors. Guys – we all know that attending church doesn't make us Christians, but Hebrews 10:25 says, "Let us not neglect our meeting together, as some people do, but encourage one another, especially now that the day of His return is drawing near." Jesus is coming back soon, and I want to be living the life He has called me to live surrounded by people who keep me focused on the *eternal!* Hey, guys – there's a reason why the football games on television, the trips to the mountains, and the days at the pool all look so appetizing on the *weekends*. Because Satan does *not* want us to be around other believers in God's house! The enemy will do *whatever* he can to coax us to other places so that we don't encounter God or unite with other believers.

And has anyone else noticed how when we *do* miss one week of church, we suddenly don't want to go the following week because it was "nice" to relax? Then after two or three weeks of missing it, the enemy has captured us in the isolating web of comfort and we dread going back. Meanwhile, our family seems more on edge. There's more bickering. We all feel more isolated and disconnected. And for some reason, we aren't experiencing as much peace and excitement in every area of life. Why is this? It's because God created us to connect with Him, connect with others, and connect with His purpose of serving others. And without church and its accountability, we will be lured toward uselessness by our comfort and convenience.

Look – there's nothing wrong with missing church on occasion to rest, reflect, or just enjoy unplugging from everything. But missing church should be the *exception*, not the norm! Our kids should be caught off guard when we miss church, not expect it half of the time. On Sunday mornings, they shouldn't have to ask whether the family is going to church...it should be a given. Warriors don't let conveniences or inconveniences determine our weekend schedules!

So, let's just get over our desire to sleep in on Sundays and treat it like a vacation day. Let's get up and get moving early enough to have our families there to learn and grow each week. Let's set the example of commitment to a church body and serve that collection of people *especially* when it's not convenient. It's time to get involved in church activities and small groups that regularly realign our families' focus on why we exist!

Be the gatekeeper and moderator of influences in our home.

We set the tone of our homes, guys. And a huge part of setting the tone is filtering and monitoring what *enters* our homes. We hold the responsibility of keeping watch over every influence that comes through our doors, because it only takes one impostor to create toxic situations within the walls of our homes. But *people* aren't the only influences. It's time we start paying attention to the *media* influences around our homes. Music, Internet, television, movies, social media – there are so many opportunities for trash to enter our homes, and we have to be on guard, snuffing out *any* dangerous spark that could ignite a flame.

Music, for one, can change the entire atmosphere of a household in a matter of moments. And when we shut off the secular music and crank up the worship music in our houses, its impact is inarguable. The same can be said about the television. It's our responsibility to block that channel, turn off that show, or just shut off the TV altogether if it's delivering filth. We've become so desensitized to the gross behavior and moral standard of our world that we're starting to compromise if it's not *extreme* filth. As long as it isn't *way* over the line, we'll leave it on. As long as they've got their clothes on, it's okay. As long as they're bleeping out the cuss words, we're good. And as long as it's not *too* bloody, *too* gory, or *too* evil, we'll keep it on.

James 1:21 says, "So get rid of *all* the filth and evil in [our] lives." I mean, how much clearer does God's Word need to be? Let's stop flirting with the world's way and protect our families from consuming even *small* doses of filth. We don't eat just a little bit of the waste out of our garbage cans as a dinner appetizer, nor do we allow our children to put just one piece of trash in their mouths when they've found their way into the compactor – because that's absolutely disgusting! Not to mention, it's hazardous to our physical health! So then why are we okay with doing the equivalent with our eyes or ears if it's hazardous to our spiritual health? We cannot underestimate the demonic forces that try to hitch a ride into our homes through television, movies, and music. And it's just not worth giving the enemy a foothold by flirting with even the most finite amounts of filth. Warriors are intentional about protecting the presence of God in our homes by finding the innocent alternative to that song, channel, show, or movie.

And let's not even get started on the worldwide web. Goodness gracious – the Internet has become the greatest funnel for filth of *any* of the media influences. Web and social media have stockpiled a landfill of readily accessible content – from pornography, to movies, to music, to games, to even virtual friend networks. With so much opportunity for infiltration, it's more crucial than ever to monitor the devices that connect us to this content. Hey – if it requires doing a little research and spending a few extra dollars to put firewalls and filters on our web browsers, then that's what we've got to do. If it prevents a potential addiction to pornography in our families, then you better believe it's worth every second of our effort and every penny of our investment! And if getting our children's phone passcode plummets our approval rating and likability factor – then so be it. Warrior leaders do what we have to do to ensure that the Internet isn't piping filth into our homes!

Equally as important as keeping the wrong media out is moderating the right media coming in. And for some of our families, we just need *less* media. Even the most wholesome shows on TV need to be consumed in moderation. Too much time consuming media equals too little time spent with our families!

The unfortunate reality is, it might be *us* spending too much time checking social media, the stock market, the latest on our football team, or the breaking news headlines! Or maybe it's *not* us. Maybe it's our wives or children who won't get off of their phones. Either way, studies show it is impossible to be simultaneously present in a physical environment and a cyber environment. Our focus is either on the virtual world, or it is on the real world, but it can't be both! Let's be sure our families aren't in this nasty habit of being "alone together!" We can lovingly encourage everyone to participate in meaningful media-less time together as a family by shutting off our TV's and phones! Just put them down, and slowly back away. Then let's invest in relationships that actually matter, and create memories that we'll remember for decades – not social media interactions that we won't remember in seven minutes!

Be predictable and trustworthy.

Our families need a *rock* that they can depend on to be a flesh-and-blood example of what Jesus looks like. Our kids shouldn't have to wonder if their dad is being faithful to their mom. Our wives shouldn't have to worry when they're out of town about whether we are watching pornography on the TV or computer. Our families shouldn't be uncertain about how we are going to handle unexpected financial hardship. Families of Warriors know that the leader of their household is staying close to Jesus daily, so his choices are predictably pure and mundanely trustworthy! And while our physical bodies might change over time, our choices remain constant and reliable giving a much-needed sense of security and stability to our family sentiment.

Be responsible.

Being responsible isn't fun a lot of the time. Responsibility takes tremendous discipline, planning and attention to detail. But Warriors do whatever it takes to manage our time, work, home activities, money, and health with excellence. Colossians 3:17 reminds us that "whatever [we] do or say, [we] do it as a representative of the Lord Jesus Christ..." We need to remember that we represent the holy, set apart, perfect nature of Jesus in carrying out the responsibilities in our homes, and it absolutely matters how we do things!

Time

How we manage our time has more of an impact on our families than anything. Our families need to *know* that they are more valuable to us than any other entity that demands our time. And the way that we achieve this is by shutting everything else down, quieting the noise, and intentionally creating quality time for our families to communicate and have fun. Our phones, work, cars, hunting, video games, sports, and friends – these are great in moderation. But let's be sure that meaningful relationships aren't getting the time left over from our investment into meaningless things. It might mean staying up fifteen minutes later after a tiring day to listen to our wives tell us about *their* days. Or it might mean planning something enjoyable for the family to do together one night a week. Whatever the case – let's take some initiative and be present where our families need us. And let's also go out of our way to have fun with our families! Creating memories makes families immeasurably stronger, so let's think outside the box, suggest exciting outings, and say "no" to potential conflicts to show our families that *they* are the top priority of our time! Our families are our greatest assets, so let's be sure to give them our greatest investment!

Work

We as Warriors invest time into our families, but we also invest hard work. As leaders of the home, we work as hard as we can to provide however we can! And this doesn't necessarily mean bringing the most money into our households, but it does mean putting forth the most effort for our households. Guys – even in situations where we might not technically be the most lucrative breadwinner of our household, it's the effort that counts. Being a hard worker means we don't take shortcuts to do as little as possible to get by. We don't arrive late and leave early. We don't sit on the sidelines while others are growing and excelling. And we definitely don't sit on our rear ends without work because we refuse to lower ourselves to do a certain type of work! Warriors are humble enough to work whatever, whenever. When we work, we strive for best, not bare minimum! So whether we have an eye-opening deposit statement on payday or not, it's our *effort* that matters! Ecclesiastes 9:10 (NIV) says very simply, "Whatever your hand finds to do, do it with all your might!" As

Warriors, we work with *all* our might. We go above and beyond to set the standard instead of following the standard.

Home Activities

Working hard extends beyond getting a paycheck though. Warriors set the example of hard work at home as well. Once again, 1 Timothy 3:5 reminds us just how important managing our home environment is saying, "If a man cannot manage his own household, how can he take care of God's church?" Hey, guys – if we are gonna wear the Jesus jersey, we need to make sure that we're busting our tails to manage things around the house with excellence. God tells us that how we manage *our* house is directly related to our competence to take care of *His* house! Here are some areas where we need to pay attention to excellence around the home. And be forewarned – being a Warrior isn't very glamorous!

> *Caring for Babies and Children*
>
> There are countless opportunities to help with babies and children in practical ways. Babies need to be fed, changed, bathed, dressed, and rocked, and you never know what time these needs will arise! While most moms want to handle a lot of these duties on their own, Warriors don't just abandon ship and let them fend for themselves! We are willing to help out with *all* of it, no matter the hour! And it doesn't stop with babies, because toddlers and children need outfits prepped, lunches made, rides provided to and from destinations...the list goes on! As Warriors, we capitalize on these opportunities to serve our wives and lend a hand where we can.
>
> *Doing Yard Work*
>
> How we manage our property says a lot about our emphasis on excellence and our attention to detail. Our yards are not only an extension of our work ethic, but they are also a reflection of our abilities as managers of our household. Are we putting in the

sweat equity to tackle the landscaping duties around our property? Mowing the grass, trimming the bushes, weeding the flowerbeds, weed eating and edging around the yard – these are *our* responsibilities, guys. And whether we like it or not, they are another manifestation of our testimony of excellence for Jesus. So whether we do it ourselves or pay someone else to handle it, let's care enough to keep our premises at least moderately manicured.

Paying Bills

Warriors honor our commitments with punctual follow-through. We pay our bills on time because we represent God's Word by keeping our word! Romans 13:7 says, "Give to everyone what you owe them: pay your taxes and government fees to those who collect them, and give respect and honor to those who are in authority." Men – every action is a reflection of who Jesus is, and overdue invoices, outstanding balances, and delinquent accounts are misrepresenting a Savior marked by integrity and responsibility. Let's be trustworthy in how we handle our debts to companies and individuals.

Taking Out the Trash

There isn't much to say about taking out the garbage other than – *do it!* Let's not wait for our wives to tell us that certain chores like this need to be handled. Instead, let's be ahead of the game in keeping things clean around our homes.

Fixing Dinner

Most of us probably aren't the world's greatest chefs, but we don't have to be culinary experts to fix dinner occasionally. Some family situations or work schedules might prevent this from happening, but spending the time to cook dinner when it's necessary is a massive help to our wives. It's small efforts like this that create a more team-oriented, unified, peaceful home environment – because they show our wives that we value them enough to make a sacrifice!

Washing Dishes

The sacrifice in the kitchen doesn't stop with dinner though, because *after* dinner brings its own set of responsibilities! Wake-up call – washing, loading, drying, and unloading dishes is time-consuming! And we shouldn't just expect our wives or kids to always handle that task. Let's be on the lookout when dinner is done so that we can chip in and help where it's possible. And let's keep our heads on a swivel for when the dishes in the dishwasher are clean so we can unload them and put them in their respective cabinets and drawers. This saves time and effort from someone else having to do it and relieves our wives of the burden.

Doing Laundry

After exiting the kitchen, we can make a stop by the laundry room, guys! Because that's where we'll find yet another way to take some of the load off of our wives – both literally *and* figuratively! Seriously though – every man needs to learn how the washing machine and dryer work and actually wash a load of laundry! Laundry takes more time than we realize not to mention it is a frequently recurring task that we're *well* capable of handling. So why not make a dent in the family to-do list each week by lending a hand? And if we're horrible at folding laundry (I am), who cares! We will just do our best and remember that it's our effort and consideration that matter! Let's keep our eyes and ears peeled for needs like these before our wives even ask, guys!

Cleaning the House

Keeping a house clean can be a daunting task, and that's why a team effort makes a world of difference. Even if our wives don't have out-of-the-home jobs, there is nothing keeping us from grabbing a broom and sweeping the floors or finding a rag and dusting the house. And there's also nothing keeping us from pushing a vacuum or scrubbing a toilet! Let's not be too proud to get our hands dirty cleaning the house if it will de-stress our wives. And let's be sure that when people walk into our homes that they are greeted with cleanliness and organization. 1 Corinthians 14:40 says, "But be sure that everything is done properly and in order" – a principle of worship that can be directly applied to the home front! Let's initiate some serious cleaning and de-cluttering if that's what it takes to get our households "in order."

Cleaning the Cars

This same principle in 1 Corinthians 14:40 can be applied to our vehicles as well. Guys, we don't have to have *nice* vehicles to have *clean* vehicles. I've got a beat-up 14-year-old Honda Accord at the moment, and while it might not be much to look at, it's clean... and it's as well maintained as it can be in its inherited form! Warriors don't allow our cars to become closets or dumpsters. If our floorboard is filled with junk and our back seat looks like a trash bin, it's a contradiction to the excellence and attention to detail that we preach in every other area! Let's keep our cars from becoming landfills or storage rooms and instead represent our Savior with cleanliness and order.

Just because we are the men of the house doesn't mean we can't help with these tasks, even those that have stereotypically (and inaccurately) been associated with women's duties. Culture's gender roles are a bunch of hogwash. Warriors are humble enough to do *anything* and *everything* necessary to help our families. We debunk social theory, dismiss our exhaustion, swallow our pride, and pitch in to help the team no matter what that entails!

Money

Warriors hold great responsibility with our time investment and with our work ethic, but we also hold great responsibility with our money management. We will be talking about this more in depth in chapter eight, but it is our job to steward God's provision well. Proverbs 3:9 tells us to "honor the Lord with [our] wealth," and we do this through prioritized tithing, disciplined saving, wise spending, generous giving, and selfless planning. Money is a powerful force. And it can be a powerfully *positive* force when our perspective of it is Biblical. But money can become dangerously alluring bait when we see it as a superior solution to the One who provided it! As leaders of the home, it's our responsibility to view money correctly and manage it carefully to set up our families for both spiritual *and* financial success. Warriors demonstrate principles like giving God our first 10%, saving for the future, spending smartly, giving to the less fortunate, and planning for future generations.

Health

Then there's the responsibility that many men neglect as leaders of the house – taking care of our physical bodies. We've talked briefly about how our physical health is directly correlated to our spiritual health and we will actually dive into even more of those details later in the Warrior study. But from a family standpoint, we need to understand that *how* we care for our physical bodies has a pronounced impact on our home environment. Because how we manage our physical health will ultimately influence both the *attitudes* and *behaviors* of our wives and children. Here's a perfect example:

From an attitudinal standpoint – if I eat unhealthy meal after unhealthy meal and don't exercise, it negatively affects the way I feel. And when I don't feel well, my attitude usually stinks. When my attitude stinks, my wife and my sons are not going to want to be around me. And if my attitude stinks for long enough, it will eventually influence them to have the same attitude. Once that happens, our home becomes a pretty unpleasant place to be around!

From a behavioral standpoint – if I eat unhealthy meal after unhealthy meal and don't exercise, my wife and sons from observation alone are going to assume "that's just the way we do things!" And the majority of the time, my behavior is going to breed the same behavior from the members in my family – because families typically shadow the fathers!

The bottom line is – our families not only reflect the attitude that results from managing our physical health, but they also reciprocate the behavior that gets us there! That's why it is a Warrior's role to balance our pace, exercise routinely, eat healthy, interact with other Christians regularly, and serve God's house consistently. These practices lead us to physical health, and when we are physically healthier, we are also spiritually, emotionally, and mentally healthier. All of these benefits transfer over to our families when we are disciplined enough to actually live them out!

SUMMARY

+ A Warrior's greatest priority is leading his family to spiritual victory.

+ A Warrior husband loves his wife like Jesus loves the Church, unconditionally giving up his life for her.

+ A Warrior father not only teaches Jesus' example, but he lives Jesus' example knowing that actions influence more than words.

+ A Warrior son appreciates and honors the parents that God chose for him when he is both young and old.

+ A Warrior leader reflects Jesus' example in all aspects of his home environment striving for excellence, predictability, and responsibility in everything he does.

RESPONSE

God, I want to lead my home well. I want my family to know that they're my top priority and that leading them to spiritual victory is more important to me than anything.

Lord, let me be the example for my family, and let it start with being a Warrior husband who loves his wife like You love us – relentlessly forgiving her, valuing her, leading her, listening to her, praying with and for her, cherishing her, romancing her, laughing with her, communicating clearly and gently with her, and committing unconditionally to her. Holy Spirit, I need Your power, patience, and guidance to pursue my wife and to love her the way You love me! Please, God – make me a Warrior husband in every aspect of my marriage.

Jesus – being a Warrior father is definitely a challenge. That's why I need You to go before me, giving me the power to not just teach the example but to be the example! I want to be there for my children. I want to sacrifice for my children. I want to discipline my children in love and have relationships with them built on transparency and honesty. God, make me a consistent father for my kids, and help me to get into a habit of praying with them and for them constantly!

God, also let me be a Warrior son and honor my parents at all costs. You chose my parents specifically for me, so help me to appreciate them and respect them with my words and my attitude. God, I forgive them for any area where they've fallen short of my expectations and declare that they are a gift from You! I pray that You would clothe me with humility, thankfulness, and boldness in any situation where I am tempted to say something disrespectful about my mom or dad. No matter what, they deserve all of my honor. And I'm not going to trade that for popularity or gossip's sake.

Lastly, Lord, let me be a Warrior leader in my household. I want to reflect Jesus in my home, so let that begin with time in prayer, worship, and the Word each and every day! Through my relationship with You, I pray that You'd give me the wisdom and discipline to make church a priority for my family! Give my family Your supernatural desire to commit to meeting with other believers, and give me the discernment to filter every person and every thing that enters our home. Holy Spirit, keep every filthy influence far from our doors and speak to me about influences that need to be eliminated. Make me trustworthy, consistent, and responsible as I lead our home and go out of my way to serve my fami-

ly in the everyday, mundane tasks around the house. And give me the ability to manage my time, work, home activities, money, and health in a manner that aligns with Your Word.

Jesus – thank You for my family. Let me look like You for them!

CHAPTER 7

SEXUAL PURITY

Winning the spiritual war requires fighting for our sexual purity.

Let's just get this over with and call it like it is: Men – we are getting dominated in the battle for our sexual purity. Utterly dominated. We're being preyed on by an enemy who is effortlessly exposing our most glaring weakness – our desire for sexual pleasure. And it's a critical issue. Satan has cast his most beautiful bait for us, and we've fallen for it – hook, line, and sinker. And now we've got this hook in our mouths that we just can't seem to break free from. So we've given up and settled into a lifestyle of eternal impotence. Meanwhile, the erosion of our sexual purity is leaving the carnage of devastated marriages, divided families, and dysfunctional relationships across the board!

Hear this, guys: the enemy is using pleasure to nullify our peace and neutralize our purpose. It's genius. He's taking something that appears to be fulfilling to keep us from experiencing something that *is* fulfilling! We are fighting a clever competitor. For many, the enemy has lured us with the objectifying fantasies of a woman's body. For others, he has told us that sexual relationships don't have to be within a marriage to be permissible. And for some, he has convinced us that romantic relationships with other men are completely okay. But rest assured – every attack on our sexual purity is accompanied by a universal message from the enemy: "Just do what feels good."

Men – the enemy is feeding us a bunch of bull! And it's time to stand up and confront his lies! It's time to realize that it is *our* responsibility to lead this generation of men and to set the example of *complete* purity when the rest of the world is embracing hedonism! It's time to realize that as our sexual purity deteriorates, *everything else* follows suit! I'm tired and even a little ticked, because we've made a foolish trade deal by exchanging supernatural authority for sexual amusement. We've *voluntarily* declined the supernatural peace, purpose, and power that accompany sexual purity, and we've exchanged God's best for some insubstantial, momentary sexual sensation that leaves us depressingly empty and full of regret. Guys – sexual impurity is crippling us. And it's time for the Warriors to wake up and stop living to satisfy our privates and start living to gratify our Savior! The question is – are we ready to do *whatever is necessary* to win the battle for sexual purity so that we can receive God's best and reach our fullest potential? It begins with knowing God's perfect plan and perspective of sex.

Stand firm on God's perspective of marriage and sex.

Genesis 2:24 "Therefore a man shall leave his father and his mother and hold fast to his wife, and they shall become one flesh." (ESV)

Knowing who we are and what we believe is the foundation for success in our battle against sexual immorality. And as Bible-believing men of God, we need to *know* God's perspective of marriage and sex.

Biblical marriage is between one man and one woman.

God's Word tells us in Genesis 1:27 that "God created human beings in His own image...male and female he created them." And it doesn't leave much room for interpretation later in Genesis 2:24 when it says, "A *man* shall leave his father and his mother and hold fast to his *wife*." Even Jesus Himself refers back to these passages in the New Testament in Mark 10 and Matthew 19 bringing attention to God's plan for marriage and sex, which involves one *man* and one *woman*.

Now it seems like the world changes its view of sex and marriage daily, continually redefining its regulations in order to flatter the feelings of the masses. After all, it's much easier to live by a relative standard that conforms to our cravings than to live by an absolute standard that constrains our cravings! An unchanging standard leaves no flexibility for our evolution as a society, so it's much easier to abandon the standard altogether! It is a tremendous inconvenience for culture, but God's standard of marriage and sex doesn't change. It is between one *man* and one *woman*. And it always will be.

But God's Word condones love, so what's wrong with a relationship between two men? Well, Romans 1:27 paints a pretty clear picture of how homosexuality is plain wrong in God's eyes describing it as unnatural and "shameful." Sure, culture can change its stance, but God's stance on homosexuality is crystal clear, guys. Now I don't doubt for a second that there are men whose feelings naturally gravitate romantically toward other men. In fact, I've had conversations with men confirming this exact sentiment. But predisposition doesn't justify participation. And if it *did*, we would *all* have an excuse for some type of dependency stemming from a natural tendency!

Guys – we're *all* born with a susceptibility to certain types of sin. And while those areas may differ from man to man, there is one universal commonality: sin is sin even when it feels good and even when it comes natural to us right out of the womb! God didn't "make us" to lust after women, nor did He "make us" to lust after men. That's simply the desire of the flesh trying to pull us away from God's purpose for our lives! Homosexuality is no exception. Natural or not, it is a sinful tendency that can only be suppressed with the power of the Holy Spirit – just like dozens of other tendencies that men face. God doesn't see sin in categories, nor does He make exceptions. God sees *every* sin as sin! And homosexuality doesn't get a "pass" just because pop culture or our government decides to empathize with an "oppressed" segment of society.

Homosexuality is just another sinful tendency on the target list for our enemy. It is no different than any other sinful tendency. We all have our tendencies, and every one of them demands spiritual confrontation to control. I'll be the first to admit that I have to monitor and pray about temptations stemming from heterosexual tendencies every day to make sure that if they aren't in line with the Word, the Holy Spirit would strengthen me to abstain from them! And the same should be true for any man battling temptations stemming from homosexual tendencies.

Warriors – let's stop listening to the theories of people because they're unequivocally irrelevant. And let's not be deceived into believing that God is okay with men being with men or men simultaneously having multiple wives. God's original intent for marriage is clear: one man clinging to one wife. Let's stand firm on God's Truth that He designed sex and marriage to be a monogamous experience between a male and a female. No matter what *feels* right to the world or even what our legal system labels as permissible, God's Truth trumps man's opinion. God's standard doesn't change, and His views don't evolve.

Sex is for marriage.

God's plan for marriage is best. So is His plan for sex. And no matter how our culture paints the portrait of sex as a mere physical union, it is *so* much more than that. Sex is a huge deal, guys. And it involves a supernatural spiritual and emotional union that carries immeasurable consequences! That's probably why God intended sex to happen within the confines of a committed, covenant relationship between one woman and one man.

But where does God's Word tell us that sex is for marriage? And how do we know that sex is wrong outside of marriage but permissible within a marriage? Well, 1 Corinthians 7:2 (NIV) draws that line perfectly: "Since sexual immorality is occurring, each man should have sexual relations with his own wife, and each woman with her own husband." The first half of this verse clearly condemns sexual activity outside of marriage calling it "sexual immorality." But the second half of the verse condones sexual activity within marriage endorsing each man having "sexual relations with his own wife," and each woman "with her own husband!"

The line is in the sand, guys. There's no argument. God intended sex for the confines of marriage. That's because He is trying to protect us from the brutal consequences of sexual immorality. God knows the emotional ramifications sex renders on our spirit. He knows that sex outside of marriage will likely eventually result in broken relationships, discouragement, depression, tears, worry, anger, bitterness, and often a permanent attachment to someone. And although Jesus can mend the scars of sexual intimacy outside of marriage, it's not a place that we want to go.

Young Warriors and unmarried Warriors – let's commit at all costs to sexual purity and to abstain from flirting with that line of disobedience. I'm speaking from the perspective of someone who waited for sexual intimacy until he got married. And I wouldn't change a thing about remaining a virgin until I married Brooke Gilleo! It is so evident to me now *why* God designed us to become one with only one woman. Now that I've experienced Mark 10:8 (NIV) – how we are "no longer *two*, but *one* flesh" – there is a new level of understanding regarding the spiritual, emotional, physical, and relational significance of that bond I share communally *with* my wife. It is unimaginable to me how painful the wounds would be if we ripped that one flesh apart now!

Young Warriors and unmarried Warriors – just wait for marriage for any type of physical intimacy. And *please* wait for the right woman. Wait for a woman who lives out the Word – a woman with a laser-sharp focus on doing things God's way and reflecting Jesus with her attitude, her conversation, and her career. Don't buy into Satan's lie to "settle" or to be "unequally yoked" with someone who doesn't love Jesus, because the right woman is totally out there, and God *will* provide in His timing (see 2 Corinthians 6:14, KJV). In the meantime, let's be sure to keep ourselves pure and prepared for our bride until God reveals her to us. It will be the most rewarding experience if we will patiently follow God's plan for marriage and sex.

Don't fall for the world's progressive perspective of sex.

Psalm 119:160 "The very essence of Your words is truth; all Your just regulations will stand forever."

God's Word was truth yesterday, today, and will be truth for eternity. So no matter *how* much the ideas and opinions of the world change on relationships and sex, they're frankly irrelevant. Psalm 119:160 tells us that the Word "will stand forever." And what God's Word says about sex and marriage is *far* from the lies that pop culture tells us. Pop culture tells us that sex is an extracurricular activity for momentary enjoyment. Pop culture tells us that sex is totally okay outside of wedlock as long as we "use protection" to avoid pregnancy or sexually transmitted diseases. Pop culture tells us that if we *do* participate in unprotected sexual intercourse outside of marriage, take a pill the next morning to avoid getting pregnant. And pop culture tells us that if we somehow *still* get pregnant after all of the precautionary measures, to just kill the baby while it's in the womb.

Our culture is sick. We're talking intensive care! And we can't buy into the ridiculous lies about sex outside of marriage. Guys – sex *isn't* harmless. And there is no such thing as "meaningless sex." If the TV, movie, and music industries highlighted the realities of sexual activity outside of marriage, those industries would cease to exist, because the content of those documentaries would be downright depressing! Every episode would feature unthinkable emotional issues, broken dysfunctional families, deadbeat absent fathers, overwhelmed single mothers, aborted and abandoned children. *These* are the realities of sex outside of marriage.

But this is about *so* much more than the act of having sex. Sex is the surface result of an underlying heart issue. God is more concerned about keeping our minds pure than our actions, because He knows actions are simply a result of our thoughts. When we get our thoughts right, our actions will follow suit. But in order to get our thoughts right, it begins with our *eyes*. Culture has told us that it's fine to "look" as long as we don't "touch," but there could not be a more delusional and dangerous fallacy! God's Word debunks that theory in Matthew 5:28 urging us not to even "*look* at a woman with lust" and that doing so means we've *already* committed adultery! God knows that if He can get our eyes, our thoughts and actions will fall right into purity!

But proper eye control isn't for the fair-weather Christian man. It is for Warriors who, like Psalm 101:3 says, "*Refuse* to look at anything vile and vulgar!" Warriors – we do anything and everything to keep this commitment. And it *is* possible. With Jesus' power, it is a feasible reality to entirely eliminate sexually immoral thoughts from our minds. I'm living proof. I could slip up five seconds from right now, but I can honestly say it has been almost five years as I write this since I have had entertained one sexually impure thought with my eyes or my mind. Tempted? Tons. Fallen? None. And that's because I've "refused" to look at "vile and vulgar" things, and I've remained connected to the victorious power of the Holy Spirit controlling one thought at a time. And this is coming from a guy who used to not be able to go 30 minutes without a sexually impure thought!

We are *all* going to have an occasional split-second visual that flashes in our minds. That's what a temptation is. But we've got to learn how to turn that visual off immediately, just like pressing the power button on a TV remote and seeing that visual instantaneously disappear to a blank screen! Men – it's time to start letting impure thoughts pass through our minds instead of giving them a guest room to stick around! We can do this together! And when we do, it is going to transform our culture!

Watch out for outlets and situations of sexual temptation.

Job 31:1 "I made a covenant with my eyes not to look with lust at a young woman."

If we want to win the battle with our eyes, we have to be aware of the potentially destructive outlets and situations that offer sexual temptation through photography, pornography, virtual relationships, premarital relationships, and extramarital relationships.

Television

Sadly, pretty much every channel on television now offers some type of sexual temptation. It's hard to even watch sports anymore without seeing girls prancing around with clothes covering 5% of their bodies. And in the rare occasion that we do find a program that is pure, the commercials will be sure to interrupt with a new set of sexual temptations – anything from a woman in her bra and panties trying to sell us a hamburger to some sexually aroused middle-aged lady essentially telling us to take a pill to "correct" our sexual appetites! Warriors – we need to be guarded, remote in hand, ready to flip to another channel immediately...or just shut the TV off completely if it is offering visuals that trigger sexual thoughts for us or for our children. And it should go without saying, but it's an absolute *must* to get rid of channels that offer *any* type of pornographic material. If there's a movie channel that we've been quietly and covertly watching while no one is around, and it's a secret outlet for porn, it's time to discontinue that cable package or block the channel with a code that even *we* don't know.

Movies

Unless they're PG-rated, we need to be extra careful with the movies we watch, rent, or let our children see in the theaters. From story lines, to visuals, to dialogues – the sheer number of sexual messages in movies is mind-blowing. Let's be sure we are attuned to the Holy Spirit's discretion and that we are sensitive to any content that could contaminate our thoughts, because even PG-13 movies are overwhelmingly saturated with inappropriate material. It's just proof of how off-kilter the world's moral compass has become, especially regarding sex.

Magazines
Print media might be on the decline, but until the day the shelves are empty, magazines will offer plenty of danger for men. Here's a reality check – it was the "Swimsuit" issue of a popular sports magazine shown to me by a friend in fifth grade that exposed me to my first sexual temptation. And to this day, I'm proof that a single 8.5" x 11" high-resolution photo of an attractive woman in a bikini can lead to internal destruction! Guys – we don't just need to flee pornography…we need to flee *any* magazine that sells the allure of sex and scantily clad women. It doesn't have to be a hard-core pornographic magazine to tip the first domino in a devastating series of steps toward sexual addictions. In fact, that preseason football publication showcasing cheerleaders in their two-piece uniforms on the coffee table can be as dangerous as anything! Men – let's be overly protective gatekeepers for ourselves, our sons, and our daughters by discarding all reading material that could even be considered questionable!

Web / Computers, Tablets, Phones
As wonderful as technology and the Internet can be, they are killing many men with their infinite access to sexually appealing content. It takes five seconds, two clicks, and zero money for us to be looking at sexually seductive photos, watching sexually explicit videos, and engaging in sexual affairs through online relationships. The web will inevitably entangle us in sexual filth if we aren't ready to fight every time we pick up our phones or look at our computers. Sexual temptation is flashing at us with every website we visit or application that we open. The persuasions never cease. And that's why, Warriors, we must be on guard against the constant barrage of seduction. Let's not walk into spiritual kill zones without having an intuitive battle strategy in place. Let's be armed and ready to execute our plan, avoiding the obvious hits that we know are coming our way!

Social Media
Social media outlets like Facebook and Instagram are hotbeds for sexual temptation. Think about it – they give us instantaneous access to an endlessly updating gallery of hundreds of millions of trending photos and videos! Talk about a recipe for being pulled off track in a split second! Even the strongest,

most committed Warriors, bent on obedience, can stumble with a single click of the wrong hashtag or profile picture!

But spectating isn't the only danger of social media. *Communicating* through social media can open unsafe doors to unfaithful relationships. And sadly, I know from experience! I'm not proud of this, but a couple of years into a dating relationship with my now wife, I used social media to send an innocent, friendly message to another girl without Brooke knowing it. Well, that "innocent" message turned into flirtatious conversation, and before I knew it, I was communicating with this girl regularly behind Brooke's back. Long story short – God revealed this deception to Brooke, and, praise Jesus, she forgave me! But guys – I was *wrong!* And I was led astray by my flesh's sexual and emotional whims!

Now looking back, I'm so thankful that God grew me through that situation. But, boy, was that a dark season in my life. It's frightening how poor our decisions become when we aren't spending enough time with God getting equipped with the supernatural defense of His Holy Spirit during certain days, weeks, and seasons. I was doing things my own way, and my choices on social media damaged my relationship, crushed Brooke's feelings, and stole my peace. Married Warriors – here's a perfect, practical preventative measure for all of us: Give the wife the login and password for every social media account, email account, bank account, electronic device – anything and everything that could provide an outlet of concealment. And if that isn't enough, let's *delete* the apps, browsers, or whatever outlet that's enabling our bad habits!

Dates

There's nothing like dating that girl who gives us butterflies in our stomach. When there is newness and chemistry, it's a thrilling experience to spend some one-on-one time with that special someone. But dates can become a petri dish for sexual sin if we aren't intentional about boundaries. And here's boundary number one for dating outside of marriage: *always* stay in public locations where other people are around. As unrealistic and undesirable as this might sound for us, there is never a time when we should be alone with a woman until we are actually *married!* Aloneness sets us up for guaranteed disobedience. Because let's be real – if we are passionate about a girl, attached to her emotionally, and attracted to her physically – we aren't going to turn down an opportunity to get touchy feely with her in a secluded situation! That's just the truth! And that's why it's best to just avoid the solitary settings!

Sure, we can take that special girl out on a one-on-one date night to the Italian restaurant downtown. But after that, it's probably a good idea to take her home and go our separate ways. And hey – chatting it up for a few hours with our girlfriend at the coffee shop is awesome, but it's not a good idea to go back to the house where mom and dad aren't coming in until later in the evening. We win the battle for sexual purity on dates by *never* being alone in private. Single men – let's *always* have someone around us during dates to serve as a safeguard for our sexual purity.

Engagement

The season between putting a ring on a woman's finger and our wedding night is the time when Satan hits hardest to convince us that it's okay to go ahead and experiment with the future wife. After all – it's pretty much a done deal, right? The enemy is masterful in destroying healthy relationships during engagement by convincing us of that lie! But guys – we've already talked about God's intent for sex, and it's tied to marriage. And marriage means marriage. Marriage doesn't mean engagement. In the same way we need to be careful in a dating relationship, the importance is heightened tenfold during engagement! Let's not plan a movie night alone, because we *know* that it's going to lead to trouble. Let's not go over to her place when we *know* her roommate is out of town, because that is going to land us in a situation where we will undoubtedly be tempted to think lustful thoughts. Guys – let's not play dumb when it comes to representing Jesus, leading a fiancée, and protecting her emotions during engagement.

And while we're on this topic...guys – let's not be living under the same roof as a girlfriend or fiancé. Yes, it may be monetarily beneficial to have one set of utilities and one rent payment. Yes, we may not be *technically* participating in sexual immorality. Yes, we may even be sleeping in different beds! But 1 Thessalonians 5:22 (KJV) urges us to "abstain from all *appearance* of evil," and that means protecting our testimony of holiness and purity to outsiders looking in! Besides, we all know what happens when we flirt with situations that could lead to sexual immorality: one day we'll cross the line.

Workplace

Wake up, men. Because whenever we spend 20, 30, 40-plus hours a week around others, the conditions are favorable for unhealthy relationships to develop if we aren't careful. That's why our workplace merits precautionary measures. Hey, guys – are we trustworthy at our workplace? Would our wives approve of the conversations we are having with the girl in the cubicle across from ours? Are we glancing and smiling at the beautiful young sales rep in the office? Are we justifying subtly flirting with that secretary in order to feed our confidence?

Our workplace has the potential to develop our testimony or destroy our testimony. And the way we interact with and think about the women around our work environment is an extension of that testimony. For some of us, it's time to cut off the "innocent" flirting with that coworker, because it is anything but innocent. And that daily conversation we have with the woman in accounting who is clearly attracted to us? That needs to stop because it is getting close to exchanging phone numbers and "grabbing coffee" during our lunch break. This is exactly how Satan infiltrates our sexual purity. He coaxes us curiously closer to some nonexistent, consequence-free fantasy until we step into his deceivingly devastating trap. Let's remind ourselves often in the workplace of what Pastor Chris Hodges says: "We're all one step away from stupid." And let's prepare accordingly!

School

It started in seventh grade for me, and it didn't stop until I graduated my last college course at Auburn University. It didn't matter what the class was – the first item on my agenda was to hunt for the hottest girls in the room and get a glimpse of whatever piqued my interest. I was just like most hormonal teenage and college guys, salivating to satisfy my sexual urges. I had a one-track mind as did about 99% of my buddies.

To this day, I still get a sick feeling in the pit of my stomach when I think back about what Friday night hangouts and sleepovers consisted of throughout those middle and high school years – pornography on the television or messing around with girlfriends in the basement of friends' homes even from the age of 13. I even recall "cheating" physically on a girlfriend during that sin-filled teenage season. It was no good. And I knew better. I had been taught better. But I was deliberately living in sexual sin because a sensation had become more important than my stance. And my relationship with Jesus had transitioned from being *experience-based* to being *knowledge-based* during that adolescent period. I lacked desire, and I lacked Jesus' power – mostly because my personal walk was void of the daily worship that would have kept me aligned with God's path.

Young Warriors – this generation needs young men who, unlike me, *refuse* to exchange spiritual purpose for sexual pleasure. This generation needs leaders at school standing strong for sexual purity and treating young ladies with dignity and respect. And this generation needs young men who are intentionally avoiding the situations that could result in impurity. It's up to the young Warriors to demonstrate 1 Thessalonians 4:3-4 for classmates and peers with their eyes and their conversations – to "stay away from all sexual sin" and "control [their bodies]!"

Business Trips

Going out of town for business can be hazardous if we don't plan properly. And while it might be inconvenient to forget toothpaste or deodorant when we travel, it can be *life-changing* if we forget accountability. Guys – when we travel away from our cities and stay overnight outside of our homes, the enemy *knows* we are without the type of accountability that accompanies our typical home environment. This makes us especially easy targets for sexual temptation. And whether it's watching a risqué free channel on the hotel television, ordering a pornographic Pay-Per-View movie, meeting a female coworker for late night drinks, or heading out with the guys to the club – the opportunity for covert infidelity on trips is endless!

When it's possible, it's wise to have another man of God to go and stay with us on trips, because their mere presence deters temptation. Sounds simple, but we aren't going to watch pornography or flirt with that dangerous relationship when our Christian buddy is there with us. But in the cases where we can't have someone physically present with us, that's where self-discipline kicks in! Warriors have a friend check in on us periodically and ask the right questions to ensure we aren't compromising with our eyes or actions while we are away. Warriors schedule a call with our wives before bed after we've turned off the television to go to sleep. And we decline the invites to head out to the bar or the club for the evening. Plain and simple – we consider the potential situations that we might face on trips *before* we face them. We plan accordingly, and we plan ahead of time to ensure victory in our purity when we're on the road.

Public

It's nearly impossible to go *anywhere* in public without being bombarded with sexual temptation. It truly is unavoidable. A simple run to the grocery store or a walk around the local shopping mall gives our eyes plenty of content to be lured into lustful thoughts. Advertisements, billboards, magazine covers... they're all positioned at eye level and designed to draw our eyes in. Then there are the actual *people* walking around in public providing its own set of temptations. Sexual temptation is not in short supply – no matter where we go!

We've all experienced that awkward moment when we glance to our right in the middle of a department store only to see a ten-foot-tall ad with a woman in lingerie looking seductively at us. Or how about that unexpected moment when an attractive woman catches our eye while walking through a mall or eating at a restaurant. These are the make or break moments that define a Warrior, and our first move is to *look away!* Warriors master the art of physically turning our necks away from the temptation as we live out Job 31:1. That's standard protocol because we "made a covenant with [our] eyes not to look with lust at a young woman."

Guys – a whole lot of us have a whiplash problem. We uncontrollably glance back at the object of our stimulation. And if you don't believe it, just watch how men behave out in public when there's a sexual stimulant in our proximity. I hate to say it, but we're pathetically predictable. And we've *got* to break this mold. There's *got* to be an upper echelon of Warriors who exercise discipline time after time by obeying Jesus with our necks because we *refuse* to compromise our calling as reflections of Jesus! There's *got* to be a top tier of leaders that identify the temptation and turn away immediately knowing that it just takes one snapshot for our eyes to pull our hearts into a sexual gutter. It's time we step up and *set* the example for the world instead of *joining* the example of the world. Warriors – we are the generals whose necks remain steadfast, our eyes resolute on representing the blood of Jesus in the heat of public sexual warfare!

Be prepared for the moment of temptation.

1 Corinthians 6:18 "Run from sexual sin! No other sin so clearly affects the body as this one does. For sexual immorality is a sin against your own body."

We discussed in detail in chapters two and three the absolute urgency of taking every thought of every day into captivity and comparing it with God's Word. And there's not a more applicable scenario in a man's life to practice this than in a moment of *sexual* temptation. But what does this process look like in regards to sexual temptation? What do we *do* when that attractive girl walks by? When that coworker starts flirting? When that seductive woman in a bikini flashes on our computer screen? When that cute cheerleader wants a one-on-one date after the football game? When that female friend starts messaging us on social media? Guys – the temptations *will* come. And they'll keep coming. And if we're not ready, we'll be devoured and rendered useless for the kingdom by the attacks of the enemy.

Identify the temptation. ("That just stimulated my sexual desires.")

The first step of defeating temptation is identifying it. And identifying a temptation as a temptation is an extension of knowing God's Word and being connected to His Holy Spirit. Men – the Holy Spirit will tell us what visuals and thoughts are dangerous to our purity. He absolutely will. But we have to stay in a conversation with Jesus to receive those notifications. The Holy Spirit will provide the conviction, but we have got to preserve the connection! When we're connected to Jesus, the Holy Spirit will prod us (sometimes through our own voices inside our heads) and tell us, "Hey – that's not what I want for you." 1 Corinthians 3:16 (ESV) tells us that "the Spirit of God dwells in [us]," meaning He is *literally* a part of our minds and bodies. So when we see that temptation and then hear a voice in our heads saying, "That's impure," or, "That's not right," let's pay attention! It's God in us helping us identify a potential purity killer! So we have this temptation waiting to be dealt with...but at least now we have taken the step of recognizing that it is a temptation!

Take the thought captive. ("God, I don't want this if it doesn't please You!")

Following the instruction of 2 Corinthians 10:5, our immediate response to the initial moment of sexual temptation is to activate that armed security checkpoint at the front gate of our minds. We pull out that spear and stick its sharp point right in the face of that temptation, placing it under the magnifying glass of God's Word so that the Holy Spirit can examine it for impurities. This is the moment when we pause our thoughts, envision Jesus' cross, and say in our minds, "Hey God – I don't want to chase *any* thought that is out of Your will, so here's this thought!" God asks us as Warriors to take every individual thought and temptation into a brief holding area...a waiting room...a judgment chamber. And that's where God gives us wisdom to flee and strength to overcome. This is where the rubber meets the road in our commitment to righteousness and purity. Because if we let just *one* thought go unfiltered by the Holy Spirit, James 1:14 (NIV) tells us that we will be "dragged away" and "enticed" by "[our] own evil desire."

Look away. ("I'm not looking back.")

One habit that is compromising our sexual purity is an inability (or unwillingness) to just look away! I'll say it again...we've got a serious neck control problem. We're addicted to turning our heads to get just one more glance at that object of our enjoyment. We are like squirrels, incessantly and nervously pivoting our heads to experience a brief sensation of sexual suspense – by capturing mental snapshots, exchanging flirtatious glances, or even entertaining physical advances. But like Psalm 101:3 says, we adamantly refuse to go there! We aren't going to look back at that picture just one last time. We aren't going to check out that ad for just one more second. And we aren't going to make eye contact with that girl for just one more moment.

Say Jesus' name out loud. ("In Jesus' name, get behind me.")

Paul demonstrates the power of Jesus' name in Acts 16:18 when he casts a demon out of a possessed woman by saying, "I command you in the name of Jesus Christ to come out of her." The simplicity and power of this story are a testament to how we should handle *every* type of opposition we face, especially sexual temptation. A Warrior audibly voices the name of Jesus to claim authority over temptation. Men – hear this! We deliver a brutal blow to the enemy's attack when we introduce a temptation to the name of Jesus! We're talking haymaker. A guaranteed knockout. Because there is *undefeatable* power in His name, and that name is the surefire solution to even the most insatiable sexual drive! So let's get in the habit of, if nothing else, simply whispering, "Jesus," in the moment of temptation! And let's confront Satan with devastating defeat: "In the powerful name of Jesus', get behind me!" Guys...I'm telling you – it *works!*

Voice a go-to verse from God's Word. ("God, Your Word tells me...")

If we don't know God's Truth, we *will* buy into the lies of sexual temptation. We have to be armed with verses to combat the enemy's tactics to lure us into sexual sin. And whether those verses recall our identity as representatives of Jesus, declare our victory through the resurrection of Jesus, or proclaim our authority over temptation in the name of Jesus – we need a verse or two that are our "go-to" verses in the heat of a temptation. I voice John 3:30 often in moments of sexual temptation, simply whispering, "Jesus – increase as I decrease." That's one of hundreds of verses that can help us combat the enemy whenever and wherever we're facing sexual temptation. Let's create an arsenal of poignant verses and pull them out in the heat of battle, because Scripture *slaughters* sexual temptation!

Pray for power and discipline to endure. ("God, give me strength, and the self-discipline to endure.")

It goes without saying that we need to pray in the moment of a sexual attack... but how many of us are in the habit of actually doing it? Guys – if we aren't connected to God in the midst of temptation, we're destined for defeat. Because only the Holy Spirit can give us the supernatural discipline to say, "No," and the tolerance to endure the moment when our flesh is *starving* for sexual pleasure. We all know "that" moment – when that sexual temptation feels hypnotically inescapable! This is the moment we've *got* to have the partnership of the Holy Spirit. The peak of a temptation's beckoning has a way of making us feel like *we* are the slaves, but 1 Corinthians 10:13 reminds us that "God is faithful" and "He will show [us] a way out so that [we] can endure!" Warriors – let's access that supernatural endurance from our Savior and remind sexual sin that it is *our* slave! It doesn't tell us what to do. We tell it what to do!

Run away and don't look back. ("It's time to physically run away.")

The mental and spiritual aspects of dealing with a sexual temptation happen at Mach speed. And they involve a series of split-second, circuit-board-like signals that are transmitted between our spirit and the Holy Spirit. But there's also a *physical* aspect of dealing with a sexual temptation, and it's simple: run away! 1 Corinthians 6:18 is pretty easy to translate when it says, "Run from sexual sin!" Hey – if the girl in the gym keeps grabbing our attention doing those squats, we should literally run away from her! Like, leave the gym. We can get the rest of our workout in later! It's not worth it to hang around and risk our purity! The same goes for the flirty business relationship, the pornographic website, the sexually explicit TV channel, and the date where we're about to be touching areas that we shouldn't be. The answer is simple – physically *run away* from the temptations! Like...get up...stick one foot in front of the other...and physically move away from the temptation!

Practice it, one temptation at a time.

Seven steps though? There are *that* many steps to defeating *one* temptation? Yes, but it's like driving a car. When we drive down the road, we are simultaneously accounting for probably a dozen factors. But it's like second nature once we've been doing it for long enough. Yes – it will always require focus. But we don't have to run down the checklist...we just *do* the checklist! These seven steps are collectively a part of a Warrior's instantaneous reflex to sexual temptation. And after enough practice, it becomes a piece of cake to execute them all within literally two or three seconds!

But even if it *is* a tedious process to adapt, isn't it worth it? It baffles me how we are so strategic and tactical in our sports, hunting, fishing, careers, and financial future – just to ensure success. Why aren't we willing to invest the same effort into gaining an advantage in the battle for our spiritual purity?

It's time to get meticulous with these principles and practice them. Memorize them. Study them. Practice them. And finally – master them! We can eventually *master* sexual temptation through the power of the Holy Spirit and the truth of the Word of God. We can eventually get to our target destination of Galatians 5:16 when we instinctively "let the Holy Spirit guide [our] lives" so we don't "[do] what [our] sinful nature craves." And if these steps seem overwhelming, let's start small! Next time we are tempted, let's at least voice the name of Jesus! Just say, "Jesus," out loud next time we're tempted... and give God a chance to show us that He *will* provide a way out!

Obliterate existing pornography.

James 1:21 "So get rid of all the filth and evil in your lives, and humbly accept the word God has planted in your hearts, for it has the power to save your souls."

Pornography is killing us, guys. And Satan is destroying us with the ridiculous lie that women are mere objects for our sexual fantasies. Pornography's aesthetics promise pleasure, but its substance delivers destruction. And if any of us has even a *trace* of sexually seductive or pornographic content on our phones, on our computers, on our tablets, in our nightstands, under our beds, in our closets, on our DVRs, on Pay-Per-View channels...it's time to step up, man up, and burn it up. It's time to rip up that one picture that we've got hidden somewhere as an enabler of our sexual addiction. It's time to sign up for an Internet filter that automatically sends our search results to a Christian brother. It's time to burn up every magazine stacked in the attic. We're talking a publication purification *bonfire!* Warriors – it's time to "get rid of all the filth" as James 1:21 tells us, and *obliterate* existing pornography.

Get accountability for sexual and relational purity.

Proverbs 28:13 "People who conceal their sins will not prosper, but if they confess and turn from them, they will receive mercy."

Overcoming sinful habits requires transparency and accountability. We know that. It doesn't matter *how* much I desire to defeat my addiction to pornography or sexual immorality if I don't have someone that is looking me in the eyes on a regular basis asking, "Hey, how's your purity been lately?" But it is up to *us* to initiate that relationship, and it is up to *us* to be honest with someone. If we want to defeat sexual sin, let's take the uncomfortable step of exposing our weakness to a brother who can keep us in check!

A perfect example: if there's a relationship with a woman at work that we know deep down we're tempted by, it is up to us to tell someone immediately and set up the correct preventative measures to avoid disaster. There is no way for you to know that I am struggling with a potential affair with the friend at work unless *I* expose it! A true Warrior knows how dumb he can be and that the safeguard from his dumbness is identifying weakness, exposing potentially dangerous outlets and relationships, and enlightening another Warrior to fight alongside him through the battle!

Invest only in our wives.

Ecclesiastes 9:9 "Enjoy life with your wife, whom you love." (NIV)

Married men – it's time for us to make a deliberate choice that we are going to, as Ecclesiastes 9:9 (NIV) says, "enjoy life" with the wife God has blessed us with. No other woman deserves our enjoyment. No other woman deserves our investment. No other woman deserves our encouragement. No – this isn't referring to thinking *lustfully* about another woman. We're talking about the simple act of placing value on another female!

We all know what this looks like. We admire another woman's attraction. We meditate on the intrigue of another girl's face or body. We voice a compliment to another woman about her personality, talents, or successes. Sometimes it is simply our *mind's* investment into other women, but often it extends to our *mouth's* investment through compliments and conversation. Either way – these are stealing more than we realize from the abundance of our marriages.

Men – every thought is a transaction. And a Warrior reserves every positive transaction for his wife and his wife only! We don't make deposits into another woman's account with our flattering words, aesthetic admiration, and expressions of impression, because we are stealing from our spouses' accounts! And with every silent, emotional thought or subtle, enthusiastic effort we distribute to another woman, we are depriving our spouses of something that belonged to them!

Warriors – it's time for us to get on our knees and ask the Holy Spirit to shed light on even the subtlest thoughts and emotions that we invest momentarily in other women, and pray for a supernatural appreciation of our wives! True Warriors give thanks to Jesus for every feature and characteristic of our wives, because we know that a wife is a sign of "favor from the Lord" according to Proverbs 18:22. Although comparing our wives to other women might disguise itself as innocent, it is an insult to our Creator's unique gift to us! And I refuse to find any flaw in the gift that God wrapped just for me. Brooke Ingram will *always* remain the sole object of my fantasies and affections!

Stay away from married women.

Most of us at some point in our lives *will* face a temptation involving a woman who is married to another man. It might be our child's teacher, a small group friend, a business colleague, a neighborhood acquaintance. And we need to be on guard – single men, too – of the adventurous, flirty, needy, naughty, irresponsible gestures that literally every woman is capable of exuding. And *Christian* women are *no* exception! *Every* woman is a human being, and *all* human beings are capable of falling into sexual sin, especially when they are in need of comfort, advice, validation, and security.

Guys – this might seem like an insultingly obvious caution flag, but if there's a married female that is seeking our support or advice during a vulnerable time in her life, we need to flee immediately! Or even if there's a casual friendship with a married woman that keeps producing regular conversation and obvious chemistry – get away! Tell her, "I'm praying for you, but I think it's best for you to find someone else for counsel." It's time to apply Hebrews 13:4 and "give honor to marriage!" Warriors respect the sanctity of wedlock and get as far away as possible from situations where we could be lured into interfering with anyone's marriage. There is no excuse...let's quit the flirting, the compliments, and the empathy, and cut off relationships with other married women.

Get away from any woman outside of our wives if we are married.

In the same way that every man should stay away from married women, married men should stay away from *any* woman outside of our wives! Genesis 2 tells us clearly that God made women to be our complement because it was "not good for us to be alone." Literally, God's purpose for making a woman was to give us a mate, and that's why we're not wired the right way to be "just friends" with women.

God's design for men and women is for them to be together, help each other, and reproduce with one another. And as married men, there is not *one* relationship with a woman outside of our wives that doesn't pose potential problems for us. We aren't made to be "friends" with women. We are wired to be companions. So let's keep in mind that even that relationship with the girl who we've been friends with for twenty years can lead to mental, emotional, and physical connections that detract from our marriages. Married men – let's cut the communication off with other women, because whether we realize it or not, we are one step away from lifelong consequences when we cultivate any relationship with any woman but our wives.

Celebrate our wives' value by having sex.

Proverbs 5:18 "Let your wife be a fountain of blessing for you. Rejoice in the wife of your youth."

The pleasure that we experience from the physical act of sex was God's plan from the beginning, and when we enjoy it within God's parameters, there is nothing like it. Proverbs 5:18-19 *encourages* us to enjoy sex saying, "Rejoice in the wife of your youth. She is a loving deer, a graceful doe. Let her breasts satisfy you always. May you always be captivated by her love." Sexual intimacy is God-inspired! And sexual intimacy is an essential part of a healthy marriage because it is what makes the relationship with our wives different from any other relationship! God designed sex to serve as a delicate spiritual, physical, and emotional bond shared uniquely and exclusively between a man and his wife. And as romance and sexual intimacy fade in a marriage so will the uniqueness, and thus the *specialness* of the relationship.

Warriors – we cannot lose the romance in our marriages, because it's what keeps spouses excited, secure, and passionate with one another. Sex is a celebration of the worth of our wives, and if we aren't celebrating their worth, the relationship will inevitably lose its significance! It's up to us to invest in regular celebrations! Yes – the frequency of sex might differ from marriage to marriage, but the *necessity* of sex exists in every marriage!

While it's not difficult to convince most men of this, let's make sure we are having sex with our wives or at least pursuing it frequently, because sex is the lifeline of security and exclusivity of the marriage relationship. And even if we are getting rejected regularly, let's make sure our wives feel like they're worth being pursued.

Honor our wives in sex.

1 Peter 3:7 "...You husbands must give honor to your wives. Treat your wife with understanding as you live together."

Sex is a perfectly designed gift from God. And when we follow *His* plan (one woman, one man) and *His* timing (in marriage) for it, we will experience an ecstasy of body, spirit, and emotions like no other. This is totally Biblical! God *wants* us to enjoy the benefits of sex as evidenced in Proverbs 5. But He also wants us to *honor* our wives as we pursue them. God urges us in 1 Peter 3:7 to be considerate in how we view them, speak to them, and treat them...because sex is more than just a physical connection with our wives. It is a connection of spirits, emotions, and bodies.

God's desire is for us to always make our wives the origin of our sexual pleasure and for them to exclusively be the source of our sexual arousal. But let's be careful not to treat our wives as if they are merely sex objects. When we objectify something, we treat it as if it has no meaningful depth and deserves no intentional appreciation. We view it as something to be *used*, not something to be *cherished*. And while God may have partly purposed our wives to be used for enjoyment, they possess depth and a desire to be first and foremost appreciated! They desire to be intentionally understood and gently cherished, not just employed for our pleasure!

So let's honor our wives by treating sex as more than a street to our satisfaction. Let's appreciate them for who they are, not just what they look like. And let's make them feel comfortable and secure as we seek sexual intimacy. Warrior husbands make sex more about commemorating our wives' value than experiencing our own pleasure.

SUMMARY

+ A Warrior stands firm on God's perspective of marriage and sex knowing that God intended marriage to be between one woman and one man and that sex was designed to take place in the confines of marriage.

+ A Warrior doesn't fall for the world's progressive, evolving perspective of sex, because he knows that God's Truth is the same yesterday, today, and forever.

+ A Warrior is aware of the outlets and situations of sexual temptation and is on guard against potential threats to his purity.

+ A Warrior is prepared for the moment of temptation. His instantaneous response is identifying the temptation, taking the thought captive, looking away immediately, saying Jesus' name out loud, voicing a verse from God's Word, praying for power and discipline to endure, and physically running away from the source of temptation.

+ A Warrior obliterates every trace of existing pornography.

+ A Warrior gets accountability for sexual and relational purity knowing that he will inevitably remain a slave to sexual sin if he doesn't expose his weaknesses to someone.

+ A Warrior invests positive thoughts only in his wife and appreciates his unique gift from God. A Warrior also protects his wife from comparison staying away from potentially dangerous relationships with other women.

+ A Warrior celebrates his wife's value by having sex understanding that sexual intimacy is the lifeline of passion, excitement, and exclusivity in the marriage relationship.

+ A Warrior honors his wife in sex by intentionally cherishing her, not just selfishly using her.

RESPONSE

God, I want to be grounded in Your Word when it comes to sex and marriage. I want to do things Your way and in Your timing. That's why I'm willing to wait to get Your best! Lord, give me the strength to remain sexually pure until marriage, and then keep my eyes on my wife only once I am married.

Don't let me fall for the lies, evolving theories, and opinions of pop culture. Instead, let me embrace the Warrior mindset of not allowing even one thought to look at a woman in lust. God, I know that's who You've called me to be! And that's why I really, really need Your help, especially when it comes to guarding my purity from TV, Internet, dating, engagement, work, school, business trips, and even walking around in public. From thoughts to relationships, I want to align my life with Your Word!

Jesus, I need Your Holy Spirit to prepare me for the moment of temptations so that I can identify them and squash them immediately with Jesus' name, God's Word, and self-discipline! Keep my eyes pure, and forgive me for the times when my eyes have looked lustfully at women.

God, I give You my stronghold of pornography and ask that You would provide the strength to flee and the accountability to ensure victory in my struggle against the enemy's lies. Lord, give me the maturity to run away from temptation, and give me the boldness to be transparent with someone.

Lord, give me a supernatural passion for my wife right now and let me invest positive thoughts only in her. Protect my wife from comparison in my mind, and give me the discernment and desire to stay away from other women.

Jesus, bless the sex between my wife and me. Let it become a relaxing, fulfilling celebration that increases passion, excitement, and exclusivity in our marriage. I pray that my wife feels valuable and that You would allow me to take a selfless approach to sex understanding that it is more about valuing my wife than satisfying myself. God, just let me honor my wife in sex cherishing who she is rather than using her for what she does.

God, just make me sexually pure right now. Completely pure. And let Your Holy Spirit lead me to absolute, 100% purity each and every day so that I can be looked at as a Warrior example for the boys and men around me!

CHAPTER 8

MONEY, POSSESSIONS, AND PASSIONS

Winning the spiritual war requires having God's perspective of money, possessions, and passions.

It's the million-dollar question: what is it that motivates us? We all have *something* that gives us a spark of excitement, a ray of hope that drives us to roll out of bed in the morning. It prompts us to push. It inspires us to endure. It propels us to keep grinding. Our motivation tells the story of our priorities. It spotlights our feverish obsessions. It uncovers our deepest convictions. It discloses our primary purpose in life with pinpoint accuracy. Our motivation reveals our true identity – because it is a magnification of our heart's fixation.

Let's be honest. It is a tremendous struggle on some days and in some moments to keep our motivation rooted in our purpose of making Jesus famous. And it never fails – it's usually money, some thing, or some hobby that steals my ambition. It can happen to every one of us in an instant. There we are, resolutely focused on our eternal purpose, and out of nowhere – some stack of cash, shiny thing, or exciting hobby steals the top spot in our hearts. And just like that – an *immediate* motivational shift. Something that has potential for good instantaneously becomes god.

Here's the problem: Culture tells us that money, possessions, and passions are worldly rewards to reap pleasure. But the truth in God's Word tells us that they're eternal resources to reach people! Every *dollar* that we make, every *thing* that we have, and every *desire* that we experience – they were intended as vehicles, not destinations! Those dollars, things, and desires we possess are nothing but God-provided resources to accomplish a much more meaningful operation – reaching people! And hey – it is tough to maintain that perspective. It is downright demanding to keep our deepest motivation – those heartstrings – fixed on our eternal mission.

I'll be the first to admit that during some seasons, it has indeed been the pursuit of *money* and *possessions* that motivated my existence, and at times even my obedience! We obey God for what He's *going* to do for us instead of obeying God for what He's *already* done for us. Self-centered obedience motivated by stuff-centered inheritance.

I've also struggled with allowing *passions* to become my motivation for existence. We all have those activities and hobbies that we "enjoy," but men – we are the worst about letting enjoyment become worship. I mean, we'll take casual enjoyment and parlay it into complete obsession in a split second! And before you know it, that "hobby" is determining our attitudes, consuming our efforts, and dictating our schedules! It is interests becoming idols.

It's time to get intentional and specific in our prayers asking Jesus to give us *His* perspective of money, possessions, and passions. And I'm telling you – when we start utilizing them as eternal resources to reach people instead of using them as worldly rewards to reap pleasure – we are going to unlock a level of peace and purpose in our lives that we never thought possible!

Stop trusting money, and start obeying God.

Matthew 6:24 "No one can serve two masters. For you will hate one and love the other; you will be devoted to one and despise the other. You cannot serve both God and money."

I'm just gonna say it like it is – money is a beautiful thing. It just makes life easier. And the sheer power of money gives it god-like characteristics. Think about it. Outside of physical health, money is the answer to any *worldly* need or want we have. Money is the ticket – the ticket to necessities, non-necessities, and fulfilled dreams. We could even argue that money is freedom! After all, it provides peace of mind and a sense of security. Anyone who has experienced low funds in the bank account, even for a brief season, can attest to the fact that financial stress feels like a 15,000-pound elephant standing on your back. It's heavy, and it's overwhelming. And honestly – you'll do just about *anything* to relieve the pressure. Ironically, what does the world tell us is the solution to that pressure? Money of course!

That's because in our culture, cash is king. It is the king we live for...the master we serve. We'll do just about anything for it. And sadly, we'll compromise just about anything for it. It is no coincidence that God's Word confronts this pseudo-god, this false master that promises to bridge the gap between where we are and where we'd like to be. Matthew 6:24 draws a line in the sand and says, "You cannot serve both God and money." It's simple, guys. Either we trust in God, or we trust in money. We either go after God, or we go after money. Which is it? Do we rely on the Provider or the provision?

First response from most of us? "Money isn't my god." But a snapshot of our lifestyle and our countenance would beg to differ. For many of us, money dictates our entire demeanor. If we don't have *enough* money, we are consumed with worry. Conversely, if we have *plenty* of money, we are completely at ease. Ridiculous as it sounds, a number in our bank account has become our god and our peace of mind. That's why our first response to unexpected financial challenges is not to look up to God, but to look over at our checking account! The supernatural being bypassed for the literal.

But God's Word urges us to focus less of our pursuit on the provision and more of our pursuit on the Provider! Proverbs 11:28 says, "Trust in your money and down you go! But the Godly flourish like leaves in spring." Look at the two parts of this verse: God redirects our focus from *attaining money* to *obeying Him!* He shifts our priority from *receiving the provision* to *pleasing the Provider!* And He reassures us in Proverbs 10:3 that our obedience *guarantees* the provision telling us that He "will not let the Godly go hungry!"

Sure, the allure of money is seductive. But it will *never* provide true peace or security for us nor will it ever provide true satisfaction. Our flesh constantly demands more of everything we attain no matter how much of it we attain. That's why greed and a love for money lead to emptiness and unhappiness. God warns us of this in 1 Timothy 6:9 telling us "people who long to be rich fall into temptation and are trapped by many foolish and harmful desires that plunge them into ruin and destruction." We can look at Hollywood for evidence of that truth – the place where absurd affluence and desperate dissatisfaction coexist.

And speaking of dissatisfaction...Warriors – the most transformational principle that we can practice in regards to money is found in Hebrews 13:5, which tells us to "be satisfied with what [we] have," and to know that God will "never fail [us]" or "abandon [us]!" If we could just get this *one* command right, we would find ourselves living in the present moment completely content with what God has provided. This is a choice to tell God that we trust His perfect provision and that we look to Him, not things, as our source of peace. And *that* is how we dethrone money as our god. Instead of looking to money for our peace, security, and satisfaction, we set our hearts on simply pleasing God because of what He did for us through His Son Jesus.

Manage God's money well.

Psalm 24:1 "The earth is the Lord's and everything in it..."

It's no coincidence that God talks more about money in His Word than even Heaven and Hell. Almost a third of the parables that Jesus tells address our finances perhaps because God understands the power of money – both positive and negative! Money has the power to advance God's eternal purpose here on Earth, but it also has the power to distract us from God's eternal purpose here on Earth! The question is: are we using God's money for *our* purposes or *His?* The reality is that most of us are so focused on building *our* kingdom on Earth that *God's* kingdom doesn't even cross our minds when we receive our paycheck each month! That's our money to pay our bills and build our houses, buy our presents, and purchase our food. Everything in our minds is ours! Or at least we think it is! Truth be told though – it's not ours. In fact, Psalm 24:1 gives us a wakeup call that the money we attain isn't ours at all saying, "The earth is the Lord's and *everything* in it."

Hey, guys – our money isn't ours. It's God's, and He is allowing us to use it. And for us to take credit for "making" that money or claim that it was our effort that earned it – it's arrogant and it's inaccurate. Job 1:21 reminds us that the Lord gives and the Lord takes away! God is the governor that regulates every resource. He has entrusted us with His resources, and He's counting on us to steward them wisely. Warriors – God cares about how we manage money, and we should too.

Tithe first.

From a practical standpoint, there are countless plans, strategies, and programs that will set us up for freedom with our finances. But one tried-and-true budget plan that offers a great framework for success is the 10-10-80 budget, which is based around tithing the first 10% of our income, saving the next 10%, and living on the remaining 80%. And the foundational principle of this model – placing priority on our Provider before our provision – is *the* surefire solution for financial success.

Tithing is paramount, men. And you better believe it is the most crucial component of a Warrior's financial obedience. Tithing is evidence that we sincerely believe God is in control of everything, including our financial provision! And tithing is confidence that if we honor God with our first, He will bless the rest! Hey, guys – if we believe that God will always supply our needs, then we will bring Him one tenth of our earnings as He asks us to do! God is very clear in His Word in Malachi 3:10 (NLV) when He says, "'Bring the tenth part into the store-house, so that there may be food in my house. Test me in this,' says the Lord of All. 'See if I will not then open the windows of heaven and pour out good things for you until there is no more need.'"

Men – the Lord promises us that He's going to "open the windows of heaven" for us when we obey Him financially! What a relief to hear that our Provider *wants* us to test Him just so He can prove His faithfulness to us by pouring out more blessing than we can fathom! And all He asks is for us to obey Him and trust Him! He assures us of supernatural favor when our efforts are focused on pleasing Him rather than providing for ourselves. We might as well take advantage of this offer because no matter how hard we work to earn more money, we can't possibly outdo God's divine favor. It's just not gonna happen. The best thing we can do for our financial situation is simply give God what He asks and watch His incomparable power overwhelm us with provision! Let's not buy into the insanely foolish lie of the enemy – that tight-fistedly holding on to 10% for ourselves could yield greater gains than open-handedly welcoming Jesus' supernatural favor on our finances!

It's a signature Satan move to deceive us with the literal to make us forget the supernatural. He will whisper in our ears, "You can't *afford* to tithe!" He will cleverly use both fear and greed – from unpaid bills, rent payments, and credit card debts to planned vacations, holiday gifts, and selfish luxuries – to convince us that we have to have that 10% to make ends meet. Meanwhile, God's sitting on His throne in control of *everything* saying, "I'm ready to pour out good things for you until there is no more need," if we just obey Him. The truth is we're trusting way too much in the provision and not enough in the Provider. God's ready to release His abundance on our lives, but His abundance is activated by our obedience! Guys – we have the ability to unleash God's favor not only on our finances, but also on our health, our safety, our marriages, our children, our jobs. Fill in the blank! Insurmountable blessings are on the other side of simply doing what God has asked us to do!

But just as important as giving what God asked is giving in the *order* that God asked. God doesn't just want us to give Him money. He wants the *best* of our money, which in His eyes is the *first* of our money. Proverbs 3:9 says, "Honor the Lord with your wealth, and with the *best* part of everything you produce." The NIV translation describes this as our "*first* fruits." God doesn't want us to pay the mortgage, budget for utilities, buy the groceries, set aside gas money, fix the car, and *then* see if we'll have enough to give Him 10%... that's making choices based on what we see rather than Who we know! And it's essentially treating money as the supreme answer instead of trusting God as the supreme answer. Warriors – when we take 10% immediately off the top and tell God, "I trust You to help me pay for the rest of my expenses," *that* is putting our faith in Him, not money.

Save some.

When we look at the 10-10-80 budget plan, the second principle tells us to save 10%. And while there's nothing Biblical about saving the amount of 10% specifically, it's the concept of margin that not only safeguards us with cushion for the dry seasons, but also prepares us with possibilities for the future. Simple concept, right? To have more than we need so that when we do need it, it's there. You think we'd all have the sense to implement this fundamental of margin! But the truth is most of us have very little to fall back on if times get tough because we don't have the discipline to say "no" to impulse buys when unassigned dollars are lingering in our wallets. We consider it "extra" money, and it'll burn a hole in our pockets if we don't spend it quickly!

But 1 Corinthians 16:2 defines a Warrior's saving habits saying, "On the first day of each week, you should each put aside a portion of the money you have earned." This is a critical precautionary measure because we can't foresee the unexpected expenses that will inevitably arise down the road. And it's unwise – even ignorant – not to prepare for the possibility of a flat tire, a broken refrigerator, or a lost job. No, we don't enjoy thinking about these scenarios, but they are realities that happen! And some of us need to start immediately developing a small contingency fund for the unpredictable situations that may be coming around the corner. Warriors – let's be wise and take steps to have at least a couple of months' worth of expenses tucked away in the event of an emergency. Or if you err on the cautious side like my wife and me, aim for accumulating nine months to a year's worth of expenditures to fall back on after an unforeseen financial setback.

Disciplined saving doesn't necessarily require dramatic cutbacks either. Saving small can generate a substantial reserve over time. It may sound silly, but take for example simply saving $5 a week on our power bill all because we just turned that chandelier off and moved the thermostat to 76 degrees while we were away. Not a huge deal, right? Well, that smidge of awareness would save us over $2,500 in the next 10 years! And who wouldn't want to take advantage of that kind of cash? Warriors – let's be men who are resourceful, exhibiting excellence and prudence in our financial stewardship. And let's see beyond here and now by saving for our future. Let's be frugal with God's provision and be economical in our management of each penny. It's on us to be prepared for our families' future. Let's all consider how we can start saving *today* so that debt doesn't become our solution to the surprising setbacks *tomorrow*.

Spend less.

Spending money is tons of fun. If you don't believe it, just look at the debt that our nation is in collectively and individually. It's outlandish. The allure of purchasing more and receiving immediately has landed us in highly stressful, depressingly dark financial bondage. Immediate satisfaction and the thrill of the next purchase have spawned a reckless spending mindset. And it has done nothing but leave us in shackles!

Is there anything sinful about spending? Absolutely not. It is an inevitable, essential part of survival. But Proverbs 21:20 provides some painstakingly elementary advice to prevent us from the distress of monetary mismanagement saying, "The wise have wealth and luxury, but fools spend whatever they get." It's no fun to say this, but there are too many of us with "foolish" spending habits! There are too many of us that habitually "spend whatever [we] get," and it's resulting in frustration, stagnancy, and stress! We feel like we're not going anywhere, we're not getting closer to reaching our goals, and we're not able to dream simply because instant gratification has dictated our spending habits leaving us with incessantly empty pockets!

The only way to safeguard from spontaneous spending is by having a budget and *sticking* to a budget. If we are following the 10-10-80 budget, we have 80% of our paycheck to spend. Period! And when that's gone, it's gone! That said, if we want to successfully stick to a plan, we have got to *detail* a plan! And from a practical standpoint, this starts with drafting a spreadsheet of precise expenses and allowances. It's time to pull out a pen, paper, and calculator, and exhaustively line item every expense that we have throughout a month and throughout a year. From rent, to utilities, to insurance, to gas, to food...even expenses like pets, haircuts, yard maintenance, birthday presents, holiday gifts, family trips, and entertainment allowances. By detailing estimates on the front end, we can take our actual, documented expenses on the back end and compare the two. This system of checks and balances serves as the perfect monetary GPS for our spending habits, and it gives us visual red flags in areas where we need to cut back. When we as men actually *see* that we spent $550 on food when only $450 was budgeted, it's likely to initiate changes in our choices!

There is no doubt that financial responsibility takes effort and planning, but that's what we do. And by planning we might find that a simple change to take our lunch instead of eating out every day could save our family $175 a month. Or we might discover that saying "no" to those monthly fashion purchases could save us $1,000 a year, which would prevent us from having to open a new credit card to pay for Christmas presents. When we map it out, we might just be surprised at how a subtle tweak in the routine could pay big dividends! There are countless scenarios where we can spend less and build momentum for our future rather than spend quickly and settle for stress and stagnation. Now this doesn't mean that our *wives* make the sacrifices on their shopping trips, but we still get to buy our hunting gear or music equipment! That's *not* how it works! And even if we provide the only income for the family, that money belongs to our wives as much as it does to us! Every asset is collectively owned, and that's why we refer to it as "our" money, not "my" money! Nonetheless, spending less is a team effort, and men – *we* lead by making the sacrifices *first!*

Eliminate debt.

Give credit where credit is due, no pun intended, because our commercialized culture has done a fabulous job promoting debt as the glamorous gateway to watching far-fetched dreams become immediate realities. And we've all bought in. That's no pun either. But why is it that the clever credit card campaigns and loan commercials can't be honest with us and include the nasty realities that accompany their products? It's because distress, depression, and devastation make for the ideal "before" snapshot of a product, but they don't quite fit the profile for the picture-perfect "after." The realities of debt just aren't marketable. That instant ticket to enjoyment can render lifelong consequences, and that's exactly why Romans 13:8 speaks so directly against debt urging us to "owe *nothing* to anyone." That's because debt controls us, cripples us, and eventually crushes us if we don't plan properly and eliminate it quickly.

Avoiding debt altogether is obviously the quintessential approach to financial peace and freedom. But let's be real – while zero debt is an admirable goal, it's also an impractical one for nearly all of us. There are definitely situations where one might argue that debt is necessary, and even advantageous – like financing a house, a car, or a college degree. But the key in these scenarios is to make choices that adhere to affordable necessity, not unaffordable luxury. If that new car with the V8 engine and leather interior is going to cost half of our paycheck every month for the next five years, it's probably wiser to get the used car with the V6 engine and cloth interior for a quarter of the cost. And if that all-brick house with hardwoods, granite countertops, and an in-ground pool is going to drain our savings on the down payment and consume more than a third of our income on our monthly mortgage, then maybe it's smarter to hold off on that purchase or go with the property without a pool that is $18,000 less.

When debt is absolutely necessary, Warriors make choices based on meeting a need at the minimal cost, not satisfying a want despite the cost. And this is a discipline that relies heavily on controlling emotional impulses – an area where we could all use some restraint. Most of our debt is just a reflection of impatient, unsuppressed urges to attain some thing, enjoy some place, or experience some sensation. We weren't financially ready, but we pulled the trigger anyways because we needed to medicate that dissatisfaction with a quick pick-me-up.

Warriors – deep debt is a symptom of desperate discontent. It's when "I've got to have that," "I want to go there," or "I deserve to enjoy this" dismisses the rational reality of "I can't afford this right now." It's an abandonment of wisdom to instantaneously end a low or manufacture a high. And accumulating debt from whims is like telling Jesus that we aren't thankful for what He's given us and don't trust in His timing. We take things into our own hands, do things our way, and ultimately dig our own financial grave. Proverbs 22:7 (NIV) describes this exact process saying we become a "slave to the lender," and little by little, we find ourselves in this gaping hole with no way out. But guys – it's time for us to stop digging and start climbing out!

So some of us have made momentous money mishaps. But it's going to be okay! Yes – it may require *years* of discipline and planning to conquer, but it's time to stop cowering down and actually do something about it! It absolutely must be a priority to start clawing our way back to ground zero. Let's get strategic about paying off credit cards, paying down loans, and paying off lenders to destroy the debt that has been destroying us!

Starting today, let's find someone who can tailor a financial plan to make a dent in the debts with the highest interest rates first. And while we're knocking out the outstanding balance, let's keep tithing 10% from our paycheck, paying for necessities out of the remaining 90%, and putting every extra cent toward paying off that mound of debt no matter how massive it may be! It all boils down to this: Are we man enough to put enjoyment on the back burner until the debt is erased? Do we have what it takes to endure now and enjoy later? That's what you call financial discipline, and it's just not fun.

Eliminating today's debt is pivotal, but so is avoiding tomorrow's debt! Warriors – if we don't have enough money to comfortably pay for something in full, we need to be big boys and just wait! It's time to stop jumping the gun on God's plan to fulfill our own. Contrary to our culture's perspective, we are not entitled to enjoy things that we haven't already earned. We don't deserve to indulge in pleasures now that we can't afford until later!

Give often.

Acts 20:35 quotes the words of Jesus saying, "It is more blessed to give than to receive." Anyone who has voluntarily given his efforts or resources to those in need will inevitably vouch for the reality of this truth! Guys, there is *nothing* more invigorating than blessing someone who has very little or giving to a person who is struggling to make ends meet. Proverbs 11:25 describes this experience saying, "Those who refresh others will themselves be refreshed." Giving is indeed a refreshing experience. And there is a supernatural anointing that descends on us when we generously pour into others without compulsion or obligation.

Sadly, this phenomenon of radical generosity has become a rarity in our culture because we're self-obsessed and oblivious of how rich we actually are! Think about this: If our family income is $50,000 or more a year, we make more money than 99% of the world! That means most of our families are among the richest segment on planet Earth! Yet, when was the last time we gave radically to someone and shared Jesus' love with them? When was the last time we left an unexplainably large tip on the table for our waitress and invited them to church? When was the last time we used some of our money to bless a family living in poverty with some Christmas gifts and reflect the generosity of our Heavenly Father?

God loves when we give to others and tie it back to Him – when we meet a practical need and magnify a perfect Father. In fact, He loves it so much that He promises in Luke 6:38 that "[our] gift will return to [us] in full!" But that's not all! He says that our gift will be "pressed down, shaken together to make room for more, running over, and poured into [our] lap!" What a beautiful trait of our Provider – that He delights so much in our generosity that He fills our pockets back up with even more so that we can keep blessing others! When God sees that we are using resources for His purpose, it inspires Him to multiply His blessings! In fact, Proverbs 11:24 guarantees this saying, "Give freely and become more wealthy; be stingy and lose everything."

Guys – let's be marked by thoughtfulness and consideration for the needs of others. Let's measure success by how much we can give away, not how much we can hold onto. Stinginess is lazy and self-centric, and, frankly, we have plenty of that in our culture. But what we don't have enough of is strong leaders who are willing to be inconvenienced to exhibit the gentleness and generosity of Jesus. Generosity is the cure to our boredom, our tiredness, our frustration, and our search for purpose. That was God's intent – that refreshing others would refresh *us!* Let's target a recipient, meet a need, brag on Jesus in the process, and experience God's refreshment *today.*

Plan ahead.

Finally, the ultimate financial goal of a Warrior is to prepare *so* meticulously that future generations benefit from his thriftiness. God's Word tells us in Proverbs 13:22 (ESV) that "a good man leaves an inheritance to his children's children." But this kind of legacy doesn't just happen. It requires purposeful planning, sustained sacrifice, and careful consideration of every detail of the future – well in advance of its arrival.

From providing children with financial assistance for college to investing in retirement funds to leaving kids and grandkids an inheritance – there are plenty of considerations to be made for our families' future. Luke 14:28 (ESV) encourages us to plan ahead asking, "Which of you, desiring to build a tower, does not first sit down and count the cost, whether he has enough to complete it?" Let's be the wise man that puts in the effort to "sit down" and "count the cost" of future needs. Sure, it requires some intentionality, but I want to be the father, uncle, grandfather, and great grandfather that our children, nieces, nephews, grandchildren, and great grandchildren talk about for decades to come, because of how we considered them, planned for them, and sacrificed for them.

Use our possessions to connect people to Jesus.

Luke 16:9 "I tell you, use worldly wealth to gain friends for yourselves..." (NIV)

Why is it that we love *things* so much? Why do we wake up each morning motivated by what item we are closer to attaining? It's a baffling phenomenon, but reality is most of us spend our entire lives pursuing something – a house, a gun, a car, a boat, a wardrobe, a TV, or a gadget. And the irony is – the pursuit is a complete waste of time and energy, because we are never satisfied once we actually attain those things! It's always *something*...yet that *something* always leaves us wanting something else. And this will never change.

All throughout the Word, we are warned that life isn't about accumulating possessions. In Luke 12:15 (NIV), Jesus says, "Watch out! Be on guard against all kinds of greed; life does not consist in an abundance of possessions." Then there's Ecclesiastes 5:10, which reiterates the inevitable emptiness of looking to the attainment of some *thing* to give us contentment: "He who loves money will never have enough money to make him happy. It is the same for the one who loves to get many things. This is for nothing." Men – most of us *know* what the Bible says about possessions and how they won't satisfy. We *know* that no amount of any thing will ever fill us up. Yet, we continue striving for the thrills they provide convincing ourselves that the possession itself is the payoff.

But the possession itself never brings peace. The Ingram house is the perfect example. A couple of years into our marriage, my wife and I were fortunate enough to build a beautiful custom home, complete with high-end finishes and features – stone exterior, wood-burning fireplace, granite countertops, solid hardwood floors – all the works. And with every step of progress, my excitement grew, as did my expectations of how much fulfillment this house was going to provide. I painted a mental picture of how ideal every day would be in this house. And in my mind, there was no way in the world I could ever want anything else once this house was completed! Go figure – it took less than six months to begin a checklist for our *next* custom home. My flesh wanted something. My flesh got it. My flesh wanted more. My flesh wanted different.

No way. A possession can't provide peace. But...a possession can be *purposed* to provide peace! See, guys – there have been a handful of moments when our home *has* been a source of peace. And those moments all have one thing in common: the home was being used as a tool to influence people and connect them to Jesus! Peace didn't come from the possession, but peace did come from activating the possession's purpose! A possession's purpose is not rooted in our enjoyment, but others' eternity! So what does this mean? We prompt peace over possessions by purposing them to imprint people's eternity.

Just like Luke 16:9 tells us – God wires us with the purpose of impacting people with our possessions: "I tell you, use worldly wealth to gain friends for yourselves." It's the concept of using possessions to get to people, not people to get to possessions! See, guys – no matter how much luxury we live in or how nice the things are that we enjoy, they'll never bring us true peace; however, we unleash a supernatural satisfaction over our resources when we utilize them to bless others. So instead of looking where the rest of the world looks – to the possession itself – let's look *past* the possession to its eternal purpose, because it's in the eternal purposing of a possession that we find peace in that possession. The house won't satisfy us even if it has a massive TV, a deafening surround sound, and a comfy leather couch, but if I use that house to bring 25 men together to eat some food and talk about Jesus, suddenly a possession becomes a source of peace! *That's* the moment when God gives us perspective on why He provides possessions...and it's all for His purpose!

There's nothing wrong with enjoying things *while* we're here as long as we remember *why* we're here. Enjoying those things isn't the end goal. And it's time to take inventory and prayerfully ask the Holy Spirit whether any *thing* has disguised itself as our motivation, as our priority, as our god! Let's pray specifically that God transforms any idols into instruments that connect others to Jesus!

Houses

A living environment is so much more than concrete, lumber, sheetrock, paint, floors, fixtures, and furniture. Houses are powerful forces that can influence emotions and attitudes in a profound way. Our surroundings can truly be agents of transformation. We all know how being in our parents' home can put us in an entirely different mood during the holidays than being elsewhere. We've all experienced how going over to a certain friend's home can be more relaxing or rewarding because of the way it looks, feels, and functions. And chances are we've all seen a house in a magazine or on a TV show that has piqued our interest because of its features and furnishings.

These experiences leave us vulnerable to buying into the romanticized lie that attaining a particular house or living situation is the avenue to satisfaction. We become convinced that having the perfect setup with tailored features and furnishings for our family, or having a different living situation than our current home, will finally quench our appetites. It's just another example of how we hop around like frogs from lily pad to lily pad trying to appease our spirit with fleshly possessions, and it just *never* works. In fact, my wife and I still joke about how the hot chocolate in front of the stone fireplace of our cozy, custom home is no sweeter than it was at the kitchen table of our crusty, cramped apartment!

Vehicles

They are empowering. They are substantial. They are sexy. And they are aggressive. They are controllable but reckless, predictable but dangerous. And with their horsepower and speed, it's no mystery that vehicles rev every man's engine. We love having an outlet for our testosterone-driven desires, and there's nothing better than releasing that pent-up masculinity through a uniquely accessorized transportable territory that no other man can touch! I mean, what could be better than a customizable collection of steel, chrome, and electricity? It doesn't matter *what* the vehicle is – cars, trucks, motorcycles, off-road vehicles, boats, planes – you name it, and we can love it.

Ever since we were little boys, we've been itching for the adrenaline-pumping thrills and oohs and aahs of rubbernecking spectators. And for some of us, vehicles have become idols. They're items of worship. We get more excited about time with our cars than time with our wives. We are more enthusiastic about getting to the garage than we are about getting to church. We are more passionate about telling people about a restored vehicle than a resurrected Savior! Real talk – we need to move our worship service away from the driveway.

Is there anything sinful about being passionate about vehicles or dreaming of that car, boat, or Harley? Is it a problem that we want that dual exhaust and lift kit for our truck and those chrome rims for our car? No way! But time in the Word, in worship, and with our families is *far* more important than our latest restoration project. And it's time to start investing the effort into repairing our walk with Jesus as we do into repairing our 1967 Corvette!

Fashion

It seems comical to think that we would ever bow down and praise something as silly as cotton, wool, or some kind of fabric. But isn't that essentially what we are doing when we spend 20 minutes on Monday morning picking out our outfit but don't give God even one second of thought? Are we not worshipping clothing when we spend $250 at our favorite outfitter but don't tithe a dollar? And are we not idolizing garments when we get more excited about what we're wearing to church rather than Who we're worshipping at church? For some of us, our apparel is our calling card. We're more meticulous about our outfit than our obedience. We aren't concerned about being a representative of God's Word as long as we are a representative of culture's trends. We don't want people to notice us because we look like Jesus; we'd rather people notice us because we look like the cover of a fashion magazine. We live for the glances and the compliments, and our validation is deeply rooted in the perception that our style is remarkable and relevant.

Fashion becomes a god when the prettiness of our attire becomes more important than the purity of our hearts. And when it becomes more about drawing attention to *us* than drawing attention to *Jesus*, there's a high probability that we have a heart issue. And typically that heart issue is either vanity or insecurity. Vanity uses fashion to *display* while insecurity uses fashion to *distract*. Vain men use fashion as an accessory to showcase their bodies as artwork to be admired while insecure men utilize fashion as a diversion to conceal their bodies as mediocrity to be ignored. But in both cases, it's rooting our identity and value in our appearance. And as 1 Samuel 16:7 tells us – "People judge by outward appearance, but the Lord looks at the heart." Warriors – if we were brutally honest, are we more passionate about the outward or the inward?

Technology

I have a love-hate relationship with technology. I love it because, well, it's technology! And what guy doesn't like shiny new toys? But I hate technology because its lightning-fast-paced industry ceaselessly highlights what we *don't* have. It is impossible to remain satisfied with what we bought today because there's a newer, bigger, better, faster version coming out tomorrow! From televisions, to phones, to computers, to tablets, to gaming systems – the perpetual list of gadgets is persistently baiting our entertainment-enticed eyes. And whether it's the emotional rush that accompanies a new purchase, the entertainment that ensues after the purchase, or the attention we receive from others by making that purchase – we are infamous for having an infinite infatuation with the trendiest technologies. We get the 70-inch TV today. Tomorrow we begin drooling over the 80-inch one. It never stops.

Guys – we all need to say this together: "There *is* no such thing as sustained satisfaction with technology." We *want* sustenance, but it's not gonna happen in an industry where businesses become obsolete within hours if they are not advancing and innovating. The inevitability of technology is this: what's *in* today will be *out* tomorrow. So instead of obsessively trying to attain the latest and greatest, let's consider how we can utilize technology to connect others to the life-saving message of Jesus! And hey - it'll be okay if we don't have the newest gadget...we will survive.

Physical Appearance

Contrary to popular belief, women aren't the only ones who battle with body image insecurities. Satan's lie about not being good enough or attractive enough doesn't consider gender. And the enemy whispers in the ears of plenty of men that we're ugly, we're chubby, we're flimsy, we're short, we're awkward...the list could go on. He starts by whispering false flaws, but he continues by whispering false fixes! And once we buy into the lie about a physical imperfection, he will tell us that *adjusting* that aesthetic feature or *fixing* that glaring defect in our design will finally alleviate those feelings of inferiority and discontentment. If we can just possess that physical characteristic, we'll finally experience peace of mind. We'll finally discover confidence. We'll finally get the girl. We'll finally be the alpha of the bunch. Life will be perfect once we look perfect...because finally we'll *feel* perfect!

We're self-focused. And the focus isn't on our reflection of Jesus, it's on our reflection in the mirror! Sometimes it even plays out in our attitudes. Like when we're feeling unattractive or haven't received a compliment on our aesthetic appeal in a while, it depresses us. Or, when we see a photo of ourselves that we don't like, it can ruin our day. It sounds crazy, but reality is there are situations where some of us get into an emotional funk based on nothing more than physical covetous! And this obsession over physical appearance is usually a *silent* struggle. We could be battling hundreds of thoughts from both vanity or insecurity throughout the course of a day, but absolutely no one would know it because men are really good at masking the screams of superiority and inferiority that litter the ongoing, internal conversation about our identity!

Let's remember, guys – our identity isn't rooted in attaining the sculpted abs, the 3% body fat, the beautiful smile, or the trendy haircut. Let's get rid of those unbiblical thoughts – both the "You *wish* you looked like me" and the "I wish I looked like *him!*" We don't exist to look good. We exist to look like God!

Use our passions to connect people to Jesus.

1 Corinthians 10:31 "...Whatever you do, do it all for the glory of God."

God not only gives us possessions to reach others but also wires us with passions to reach others. Possessions are the things we have, and passions are the things we do. Each one of us has dynamic interests that inspire us and drive us to get out of bed every day. We all have those activities or hobbies that get us hyped – the ones that give us butterflies in our stomach and get our adrenaline pumping. *These* are our passions. And they aren't just happenstance. Passions are uniquely chosen, God-given directional arrows intentionally designed to lead us to the people He wants us to affect. The problem? Just like our possessions, we tend to misuse passions. We treat them as if they're for our pleasure rather than God's purpose. And when our passions become more about our enjoyment than others' eternity, we never experience God's peace in our passions. Warriors – our Creator intended passions to connect us to people, and then for us to connect people to His purpose. And only then will we find His peace in our passions.

God wired me with an intense passion for drumming, and from the age of three, I wanted to be on a drum set. But even though my level of excitement was through the roof any time I got behind a kit throughout my childhood and teenage years, I never experienced a lasting, internal fulfillment from playing them...until my passion connected me to God's purpose. Guys – the moment I sat behind a drum set and led others in worshipping Jesus, I finally felt an indescribable peace. And to this day, each and every time I use my God-given passion to connect people to His purpose at Church of the Highlands, I am overwhelmed with indescribable peace! I know from experience that when our passions connect us to people, and we connect people to God's purpose,

God connects us to His peace. I'm telling you right now – if we want peace in our passions, it is 100% found in utilizing them, not indulging in them.

Warriors – it's time for us to ask a simple question: are we using our passions for *us* or for *God?* If we were honest, most of us would have to admit that we rarely consider Jesus as centric in our passions. We compartmentalize our interests and hobbies leaving God out of the equation until Sundays. But 1 Corinthians 10:31 urges us to keep God's purpose as our motivation for every activity saying, "Whatever [we] do, do it all for the glory of God." It's time to welcome God to the center of our activities. It's time to start letting God's purpose infiltrate our passions and stop letting our passions ignore God's purpose! And it's time to acknowledge the epidemic we have among men – that our passions oftentimes become addictions that are distracting others from Jesus instead of activities that are attracting others to Jesus.

We can easily determine whether these activities and affiliations have become idols by examining how much they control our time, money, efforts, emotions, attitudes, and principles. Guys – if a "passion" has been dominating our schedules, consuming our finances, expending our efforts, determining our emotions, manipulating our attitudes, and altering our principles with no eternal purpose fueling its existence – then it has become our god.

Warriors – *we* should be managing our passions, but in a lot of cases, our passions are managing us! It's time to stop letting those passions control us and get back to letting Jesus control them. Let's stop blending in with a culture that obsesses over worldly, purposeless endeavors. Instead, let's stand out from the crowd by letting Jesus be the *"why"* of everything we do. Warriors don't let our passions determine our principles. Our *principles* drive our passions!

Sports

Whether it's football, basketball, baseball, golf, soccer, tennis, hockey, racing, wrestling, surfing, skateboarding, swimming, or anything in between, sports inject adrenaline into our blood and ignite our intrinsic desire for battle. As fans, they give us an excuse to get excited. As athletes, they provide a catalyst to compete. And as sportsmen, they offer us an outlet for relaxation and recreation. Sports not only provide the *motivation* for us to get through a day or to a weekend, but also the *escape* from a sometimes mundane and stressful routine of work and home responsibilities. Combine that with all of the thrills they bring, and it's no surprise that sports are a cultural centerpiece for men.

Fandom

If there is any confusion about what "worship" looks like, just go watch the way we as men respond to our favorite baseball team winning the World Series or our favorite NFL team winning the Super Bowl. Grown men literally weeping, screaming, and even praying for the ball to bounce in our team's favor! Undoubtedly, we see man's best worship when it comes to sports moments. And with all the gratifying effects of sports, it's easy to understand why many men, including myself, tend to struggle with allowing games, teams, and players to become gods.

We love seeing mortals become immortal for a moment. We relish watching the impossible achieved. We find comfort and camaraderie in identifying with the victories and defeats of athletic organizations. But for many of us – sports fandom has crossed the line of enjoyment into the area of obsession. Sports have become the annual anchor in our arrangements, the seasonal sultan of our schedules, the everyday emperor of our emotions. College football in the southeastern United States is a glaring example and one with which I can relate!

During the Fall, for countless men, it's a given where we are going to be on Saturdays – either on the couch watching the game or at the stadium pulling for our team. And real talk, men – if this is ever questioned or inconvenienced by our wives, our families, our friends, or even our Sunday plans – we will have a conniption! I mean, how *dare* someone interrupt my time with my true love! I will stand by its side, defend its honor, and declare my allegiance to my god!

This isn't a joke. We are quick to defend our stance that we love football. And it's obvious that we love football! We love it so much that it controls weekends and shoves our families' desires aside! We love it so much that it doesn't just take up several hours on Saturdays, but also manipulates our Friday night plans as well as our Sunday morning plans! But it doesn't stop there. It doesn't just control our time, but it controls our money! We will nonchalantly throw thousands of dollars towards trips, tickets, and traveling expenses to be a part of the fellowship and festivities weekend after weekend.

And we haven't even mentioned what the outcome of the games does to our attitudes if our teams win or lose! It's pathetic, but reality is we become unkind, even unapproachable, to others because of something that has zero effect on our lives. On the flip side, it's just as pathetic that we will treat others better because the team that we support had more points than the team that someone else supports. Yes, I know we are all desperate to find *something* that actually matters in this life, and we try *so* hard to treat silly sporting event outcomes like they are truly meaningful. But they aren't. They're meaningless. And it's preposterous to act as if our world revolves around the ebb and flow of a sports program.

Guys – enjoying sports is one thing, but the emotional toll that sports have on our psychological state is proof in itself that we have let them become god. We have a problem. A *major* problem. And it's time to open our eyes to the signs. If we aren't willing to be away from the television or the tailgate on Saturdays to invest in our families...if we passionately pump our fists and scream for our team on Saturdays but can't lift our hands and shout for Jesus on Sundays...if we regularly say, "We probably won't make it to church," because we based our weekend plans around worshipping football instead of worshipping Jesus...or if our post-game behavior is any different than our pre-game behavior toward others – we have a heart issue that we sincerely need to pray about!

It's worth taking a step back to look at our hearts. Are we truly more impressed with a 19-year-old kid who carried a leather ball for a touchdown than we are with the 33-year-old Man who carried a bloody cross for our salvation? The way I see it – since no team on the field has ever given its life for my eternity, I think I will save my best worship for the One who *did* on the *cross!* And I'll tell you this much: My legacy sure as heck better amount to more than the fact that I loved a certain sports team. At my funeral, I don't want them to talk about how much I loved Auburn football. I want them to talk about how much I loved Jesus Christ.

Competition

Being a fan of sports poses plenty of temptations for us in the spiritual realm, but so does being a participant. In our youth, especially, playing sports competitively can demand tremendous time and effort. Throughout elementary, middle, and high school, we can find ourselves worshipping a sport, enticed by the esteem, recognition, and even the monetary potential that it might bring. Those athletic aspirations can quickly dethrone Jesus from being the purpose of our participation! Before we know it, we're an athlete first and a man of God second! Life becomes about doing whatever we need to do to get ahead, to be the best, to land the endorsement, to get the medal, the ring, or the trophy. Yet even when the achievements come, they don't allow us to enjoy their company for long. The accomplishments do nothing but remind us that irrelevance awaits if we don't win again tomorrow! Then one day when we are forced to relinquish the title of elite athletes, we start asking, "If I'm not an athlete, then who am I?" In fact, research has shown that when participation in sport subsides, athletes can experience the psychological equivalent of grieving the loss of a loved one!

The progression is predictable, and it's predictably unfulfilling. Because there is no peace in medals, rings, or trophies. Cursory counterfeit happiness? Maybe. But it's far from enduring contentment. That isn't found on football fields, on tracks, or in swimming pools. It's found where Jesus bled and died for all of us – on a hill called Calvary! And until we use our athletic abilities to showcase that perfect Sacrifice, we're wasting our talents. Because no matter how much or how little athletic talent we possess – God gave us that talent to impact our teammates for *His* purpose!

If we can throw a baseball 100 miles per hour with pinpoint accuracy, that's a tool God placed in our arsenal to advance His Kingdom, not just to advance our career! If God blessed us with the ability to shoot a basketball better than 99% of players in our state, He wants us to use that talent not just to succeed *on* the court but also influence *off* the court. And for those of us who end up on the bench every game because we couldn't catch a punt after signaling for a fair catch – *my* greatest talent – even there on the sideline, God wants us to model the life of Jesus. Warriors – let's use our talents to alter eternity for others, not just to achieve success for ourselves!

Recreation

Men love sports for competition, but we also love sports for recreation. Nothing excites us more than that email from the boss telling us that Thursday's office will be on the back nine at the country club instead of the back seat in the conference room! We much prefer sports to the everyday work routine, and sadly, sometimes that same sentiment carries over to the everyday *family* routine. Let's be real for a second, guys. The truth is a lot of us would much rather spend an afternoon at the tennis courts than an afternoon at home with our wives. We would much rather spend Sunday on the golf course with our buddy than in God's House with our family. We live like recreation supersedes relationships.

The truth hurts, but our "casual" enjoyment of sports, golf in particular, is anything but casual. It's a god that we've nicknamed "hobby!" Men – when it's a staple of every Spring Saturday, a pillar in our post-workday pleasure, or a source of strife in our marriage – we might need to take a step back from the tee box and see if there's a hazard on the horizon! Sarcastic golf analogies aside, this is a serious issue! And it's time to reconsider where we're investing our time and energy, and remember that the only scorecard that matters is based on how well we obeyed, not how well we played. Warriors – it's time to man up and quit using the self-seeking pleasure of sports as an escape from the sometimes harsh realities of our Biblical responsibilities. Let's put the clubs in the car and go home! It's time to grow up.

Betting

As dangerous as the temptations of sports fandom, competitive participation, and recreational participation can be – *none* are as dangerous as the addiction that accompanies sports betting. It is a seriously frightening phenomenon when our emotions and finances get tied up in the uncontrollable result of an unpredictable game. I've experienced firsthand the overwhelming rush and stimulation that comes from putting just $20 on a football game's outcome, so I can only imagine the unbridled force behind higher stakes. Even with my relatively insignificant bet, the whole experience completely engulfed my attention and emotion. We are talking *glued* to the television and *antsy* with anticipation.

While some might argue that betting on sports is technically not a sin if it's done legally after we tithe and provide for our families, gambling is an inconceivably hazardous habit that almost always stems from a love or desperation for money. And while the Bible might not literally say, "Do not gamble," it directly warns us of the hazardous derivatives of obsessing over money. 1 Timothy 6:10 masterfully describes gambling's cause and effect warning us that "the love of money is the root of all kinds of evil. And some people, craving money, have wandered from the true faith and pierced themselves with many sorrows." Guys – a love for money can coax us into some terribly desperate attempts to attain that money instantly, and that's exactly what sports betting promises us. It promises us that we can eventually convert a small amount of cash into an abundance of wealth! But in the end, betting delivers nothing but disappointed expectations and, like 1 Timothy says, "many sorrows." That's a fact.

Even in the rare case that we did accumulate some type of wealth from gambling, the inevitable, ensuing addiction will eventually leave us bankrupt – both financially *and* spiritually. Just like every other thing that our flesh chases, gambling demands more until it depletes us. It will ultimately lead to monetary demise because everyone loses eventually if you bet enough. Everyone. It's a vicious cycle that inevitably consumes every person it engages. And it doesn't care who we are – it will relentlessly, ruthlessly chew us up and spit us out. So let's see betting for what it delivers, not for what it sells. Because in the end, it commands our attention, exhausts our emotions, and manipulates our attitudes, all while stealing the money it promised to produce.

Hunting / Fishing / Outdoors

There's a common theme when it comes to most of a man's passions – they serve as an escape for us to rest and recharge. And no escape is more perfectly tailored to meet that need for decompression than the great outdoors! Relaxation? Check. Adventure? Check. Nature? Check. Dominion? Checkmate.

It all makes perfect sense why hunting and fishing often become culprits that pull us away from Jesus and our families. They allow us to recoup while stimulating an inherent part of our design. Genesis 1:26 tells us that we were created to "reign over the fish in the sea, the birds in the sky...the wild animals on the earth." It makes sense why we come alive if you put us in the middle of the wilderness and assign us a low-stress supremacy mission that yields no repercussions if we fail!

There's nothing more serene than the solitude of that tree stand. There's nothing more refreshing than a ride over to our favorite spot on the lake to wait for the big ones to bite. And there's nothing more calming than basking in the vastness of God's creation. The therapy of the crisp air, the thrill of the kill, the exhilaration of the conquest – sometimes it feels like God created us with the *sole* purpose of uniting with nature!

And for some of us – we run with that feeling. We make our sole purpose doing just that – spending time with our terrestrial wife, Mother Nature! We long to get closer to nature than we do our Savior! We get adrenalized for the anticipation of a hunting season but apathetic for the approach of a worship service! Reality check: let's set our passion for pursuing a deer side-by-side with our passion for pursuing Jesus. Honestly, how does it stack up? Do we "look forward" to meeting with Christian brothers and worshipping Jesus as much as we "look forward" to hunting season or visiting our buddy's land over a Fall weekend?

The word "seasonal" sums it all up. I know for me, there are just certain times of the year when my flesh tries to make specific passions become idols. The temperature, the humidity, the color of the sky, the foliage of the trees – these *environmental* patterns affect my *spiritual* patterns. Plain and simple – seasons have the ability to push us away or pull us toward Jesus. So weird, but so true. And considering the deceptively powerful coercion of the seasons, could it be that we might need to pray about the Fall? Or the Summer? Or the Spring? We've all been there. And when a certain time of year rolls around, our schedules are suddenly *consumed* with what we enjoy. Before we know it, we've drifted from the church to the hunting club. We've gotten off our knees and onto our boats. And we've abandoned the friends who push us to be better spiritual fishermen to join the guys that make us better literal fishermen. The seasonal undertow prevails *every* year and without fail, our outdoor hobbies drag us and drown us!

Warriors – let's pinpoint these seasonal struggles and figure out how we can use the outdoors to be moved more by a living Savior than a dead animal!

Music

The cultural influence of music is mind-boggling. It can define so much about us: who we are, who we hang out with, where we go, how we act, and even what we believe. The music we listen to plays a monumental role in shaping our attitudes and perspectives about life. And we as Warriors absolutely have to be on guard against the evolving, secular values attempting to infiltrate our thinking through the guise of catchy choruses and untouchable vocals. Because whether we see it or not – our connectedness to secular influence directly determines the effectiveness of our spiritual influence. And it's time we start wrestling with the amount of pop culture that we're allowing into our minds and our homes.

Hey, Warriors – it wouldn't hurt for us to know a little less about pop culture these days. In fact, I'd go so far as to say it would be *beneficial* for us to be confused when today's entertainment topics are brought up. Many of us have become obsessed with contributing to conversations and mimicking the lifestyles surrounding the music and entertainment world. It has become an indispensable aspect of who we are! It's like we can't part ways with the world. One foot in. One foot out. It is the epitome of lukewarm.

A perfect example? Let's talk about the culture of living that's heralded in much of the genre of country music. Speaking of lukewarm! I know I'm going to ruffle some feathers with this stance, but country music is infamous for painting the picture of partying it up on Friday and praying it up on Sunday. It's a pathetic excuse for Christianity. No, guys – a Warrior doesn't have his Bible in his back pocket to pull out once a week! He doesn't wear Jesus under his cowboy hat as an occasional consultant after making out with the girls in bikinis and drinking too many beers! And he certainly doesn't endorse the pitifully casual "get a little bit of God, but a little bit of the world" approach that is largely painted on the canvas of country music and some other genres for that matter. No, this isn't some attack on country music, because there are plenty of wholesome artists in the country industry, but we need to be careful with *any* type of musical influence that flippantly couples God with godless living!

Another influence of music that we don't talk about enough is the culture of *being* a musician. Having been a drummer since the age of five, I can honestly say that there is an indescribable pull from every secular genre of music to live a certain way – from creative approaches, to fashion choices, to conversation styles, to social behaviors, to spiritual perspectives, to moral beliefs. Music culture isn't just a hobby...it's a *lifestyle!* And when we aren't firmly grounded in who we are, we'll be defined, or *re-defined*, by the ideals of a culture instead of God's Word.

Warriors don't let music determine our lifestyle habits, nor do we let it define our identity. No matter how much equity we build in our brand as a musician or singer, how much talent we develop, how many gigs we book, how many awards we receive, or how much respect we have among other musicians – they'll never satisfy us. That's because God wired us with the passion for music to accomplish His agenda, not ours. And if we go to the grave clinging to our musical notoriety and accomplishments, we will have missed the entire purpose of our God-given abilities. Let's excel at what we do so that we can use it as a platform to reach others and ultimately worship *Him* with our talents. I can say from my own story that I never experienced true fulfillment in my drumming until I used it to lead others in worshipping Jesus. That's *not* a coincidence, because true satisfaction comes from finding the eternal purpose in our passion.

Social Interaction

Jesus is the example we aspire to mimic in every area of life. And no matter *where* Jesus went, *what* He was doing, or *who* He was around – His Father's mission was always His first priority. When He interacted with others, He wasn't focused on being accepted, being popular, or being comfortable...He was focused on being obedient. From community gatherings, to dinners, to weddings – *God's Word* was Jesus' fixation, not the drink He had in His hands, the number of popular people around Him, or the indulgence of His social situation. His entire existence centered on His Father's assignment.

We could all take a few notes from His example, because every one of us has probably neglected God's purpose in pursuit of our own popularity or pleasure at one point or another. And for some of us, it's an addiction! If we were told to give up going to a certain place on Friday or Saturday night, we would be absolutely devastated. Or if someone told us to give up drinking and hanging out with a certain group of people, we would be offended and defensive in our stance. Simply said, our God-given passion for connecting with others has become more self-focused than others-focused. And our social life is about the external, not the eternal.

Guys – we are too immersed, even camouflaged, into social culture. And most folks don't notice a difference when they look at us because we walk, talk, dress, drink, and interact just like the rest of the world. Maybe it's time for us to take a step back and ask if we've exchanged our testimony for the cultural comfort of the social scene. And maybe it's time to stop *defending* why habits aren't wrong and start *questioning* how those habits are helping us bring people to Jesus. At the end of the day, our rights in social settings take a back seat to others' relationships with Jesus! It's up to us as Warriors not to get caught up in becoming a part of culture, but instead be set apart from culture.

Social interaction can pose its challenges to us in the virtual world as well. In fact, social media has created a monstrous addiction among so many of us. We spend entirely too much time monitoring what others think about us and gauging how popular we are in the cyber realm. We elect to spend time interacting with people we don't even know rather than investing that time into our wives, our children, and most of all – our Savior. It's absurd! But are we doing anything to starve these habits? Are we praying that Jesus changes the priority of our heart from what others think to what He thinks? Warriors – God wired us with a heart to connect with others, but the enemy is working overtime to pervert that divine desire and pollute it into a self-centric passion.

Politics

Political affiliations in and of themselves are some of the most divisive, destructive, disconcerting platforms that our culture deals with from day to day. Think about it – how much unneeded division and unmerited fear is churned out each day from the political factory? Each political party stands on its own egocentric agenda hypnotically luring us as citizens into this delusional, arrogant, stubborn, and most importantly, *unbiblical* stance. And wildly enough, some of us even look to these political affiliations and platforms to get our cues on what is and isn't important, what to and not to believe, and even how to and not to talk about certain subjects. It's hilariously sad.

Guys – politics can be dangerous. Because at the end of the day, they are human-contrived principles that try to dictate our stances and choices. And most of the time, these principles aren't based on God's Word, but rather an agenda to leave a mark in history books or retain a seat of power. Yes, laws are essential, but if we aren't careful, the political handbook can essentially become a substitute for God's handbook. And we need to make sure we aren't putting too much hope or identity in government, political parties, causes, laws, or politicians. Warriors don't trust in political entities to provide food for us to eat, and we definitely don't trust them to provide purpose for our lives. So when we passionately stand as activists behind any political movement or cause-related group, let's make sure it is their *Biblical* principles that we support – not meaningless, attention-seeking, self-serving agendas.

Another danger that our political culture has created is the god of "political correctness," which discourages us from believing in *anything* that would offend *anyone*. Political correctness tells us to shut up, back down, and dilute what we believe to protect the feelings of others, and it is essentially eroding our boldness to stand for God's Truth! It is a phenomenon growing momentum by the day, and it is manipulating many to curl up in the fetal position in fear of being persecuted.

But Warriors – we don't back down in the face of political politeness! We believe God's Word, not progressive thinking! God's Word remains our bedrock, and just as Hebrews 13:8 tells us, its principles are the same "*yesterday, today*, and *forever*." We don't need the Republican or Democrat parties to define our views because the Bible has already provided that foundation! Warriors don't let politics dictate what we will stand for because we know who we already stand for! And we stay out of the heated, surface-focused debates, *especially* on social media, that encourage division based on party affiliation, or race, or income level, or whatever other ridiculous division that the media tries to create! Warriors don't instigate division with our words; we initiate unity with our actions!

Guys – let's shut up, love people, and trust God with our country and our world, because contrary to the paranoia generated in political culture, Daniel 2:21 reminds us that *God* controls the landscape of political power: "He controls the course of world events; He removes kings and sets up other kings. He gives wisdom to the wise and knowledge to the scholars." We can relax because *He* determines when and where the chess pieces are moved. And hey – if we have an uncontrollable itch to speak up about politics, why don't we use our words to thank a military service man or woman for risking it all for our freedom. John 15:13 reminds us that "There is no greater love than to lay down one's life for one's friends." It's easy to *talk* about ultimate sacrifice, but I'm so thankful there are ineffably brave men and women who *live* it!

Stock Market

The stock market might be a collection of volatility and instability, but it's also an up-and-down thrill ride that offers the potential for big financial gains. That possibility for profit alone should explain why we dismiss the fragile realities of Wall Street to participate in its unpredictable conquest. After all, if we are strategic in our planning and wise with our investments, we can retire early, pay for our children's college education, and maybe even leave an inheritance for our grandchildren! These market-dependent dreams – the kind that live and die with the growth and decline of uncertain businesses – are precisely why we fall victim to obsessing over that ever-evolving dollar figure in our investment accounts. Our hope for the future is literally entangled in our financial portfolio, and it's easy to catch ourselves compulsively revisiting that number just to verify our aspirations still have a pulse! It's no wonder so many grown men have more passion for a nest egg than anything else in life.

Just like sports gambling, the stock market scratches that itch to experience a rush of adrenaline. And if we aren't careful, the deceptively enticing "hit-it-big" mentality can entrap us in questionable investments and irrational money management, sometimes even resulting in tremendous financial burden. But financials aside, the stock market can become an addiction that consumes our thoughts and our time. Some of us spend a ridiculous amount of time checking our stocks incessantly look at that ticker to see how our bulls and bears have performed, and it's *there* that we find our moments of euphoria, our sense of accomplishment, and our source of provision. Our god is the market.

Guys – there's no doubt the stock market can yield incredible blessings for us. God can most certainly use it as a vehicle to pour out His favor on us. But the stock market isn't our hope. It can't give us peace or eternal life, and it surely can't give us the consistency and dependability that Jesus supplies as our Provider, Jehovah Jireh. And as Warriors, we need to ask ourselves if we're a little addicted to the thrills of Wall Street. The love of money can manifest itself in a host of ways, and one of those is indeed through our financial portfolio.

TV / Movies / Video Games

There are few forces more persuasive than the entertainment world. From television, to movies, to video games – this ever-evolving melting pot of interests and ideas that we call "media" can both *consume* us and *define* us. And let's not be fooled. Satan loves watching entertainment shape our beliefs and behaviors.

The enemy wants us to be so enamored by celebrity culture that we spend our entire lives pursuing that lifestyle. The enemy wants us to take cues from movies to define our moral standard and social behavior. The enemy wants us to be more passionate about watching every episode of a television series than we are about reading God's Word. The enemy wants us to be so obsessed with a video game that we stay up all night playing it, neglecting our work responsibilities, and missing church as a result. Warriors – the enemy wants to direct our paths and consume our time with media because it simply distracts us from doing what God wants us to be doing!

We can't obsess over Jesus and obsess over media simultaneously. Believe me – I've tried. This is coming from a guy who used to play the NCAA Football video game for six, eight, even ten hours a day on occasion! I spent so much time hypnotically fixating on virtual accomplishments on the latest gaming console furiously competing online to the point where I would become angry at any disappointing cyber outcome. It was embarrassing and ridiculous. I would be in a foul mood the rest of the day based on the result of a stupid video game!

But I've struggled with more than video games. I remember in college treating the weekly episode of that new TV series as *the* staple in my schedule. And whether I was sick, tired, or busy, I would not miss that TV show. But church? Oh, rest assured, I'd "see how I felt" before deciding on whether to attend each week. To some, these habits might sound hilarious, but they're an epidemic among young men and grown men alike!

Real talk – many of us are more concerned about the fate of a character in some make-believe drama than we are about the eternal fate of our coworker in real life! We are more passionate about living vicariously through a celebrity on TV than we are about living obediently for our Savior in Heaven! We are more obsessed with shadowing the life of an athlete than we are about shadowing the life of Jesus! Warriors – it's time to put this childish, cultural norm aside! Let's stop worshipping consoles, celebrity lifestyles, movies, and TV shows. Instead, let's be grown, mature men who are *daily* realigning our hearts to be consumed with Jesus and His Word, not today's media and entertainment options!

Travel / Vacation

It's just hard to beat a relaxing vacation, is it not? I mean, who doesn't love getting out of the routine and abandoning the daily grind to recharge? Whether it's a secluded white-sand beach, a serene snow-capped mountain range, or a stunning skyscraper-filled cityscape – *any* break from the norm is refreshing! Plus – vacations are a glimpse of where we'd like to end up one day, right? Isn't life's ultimate destination a permanent vacation? That's what society sells us at least. Life is about creating Heaven on Earth.

Take for example the few weeks leading up to the vacation we've circled on the calendar. That pre-vacation period before our glorious departure becomes nothing but an annoying obstacle delaying our trip to paradise. We've all had that experience, when we mentally check out from work anxiously letting our hearts romanticize and fantasize about that picture-perfect moment on our upcoming trip – the one when *everything* will be perfect and we'll finally have it just like we like it! Like little children, we daydream of this unrealistic utopia, defaulting to autopilot until we can pack up the car and hit the road.

Men – this describes *way* too many us! We are motivated by the next sabbatical on our schedules! We don't just look forward to the next trip. We literally *live* for the next trip! We "get through" several workweeks to "get to" one vacation week! We expend all of our energy trying to generate that second in time where *every* variable is perfect. It's all about creating a few moments of Heaven on Earth. Yet, no matter how restful a vacation is or how beautiful a destination is – this Earth never provides the contentment that comes from Heaven.

Here's the depressing reality for our flesh that *so* many men aren't mature enough to face: this Earth will never be Heaven. Translation: even a *permanent* vacation won't ever satisfy our spirit. And the most liberating thing we can do for ourselves is to stop expecting Earth to meet Heavenly expectations. Sure, we can milk a vacation for all its worth, savoring every moment and squeezing every memory out of it that we can, but we are going to return home as empty as ever if our spirit hasn't been fed. That's because the blueprint for guaranteed refreshment on vacation is spending time connecting with Jesus, not just disconnecting from the chaos.

Men – even in the middle of a vacation, we can still be preparing for Heaven instead of trying to produce Heaven! Let's not fall for Satan's scheme to use Creation to distract us from the Creator. The enemy is crafty, and whether it's palm trees, yachts, deep-sea fishing, mountains, log cabins, or snow skiing – he will dangle these carrots of comfort in our faces to keep us from ever experiencing *true* contentment. He knows that it is only by connecting to the presence of Heaven here on Earth – the Holy Spirit – that we receive perfect peace. Isaiah 26:3 says – "[God] will keep in perfect peace all who trust in [Him] and all whose thoughts are fixed on [Him]!"

Warriors – let's be men who fix our thoughts on Jesus even in the middle of what our world considers "paradise." And just as importantly, let's be prayerfully pleased in our present moment, even when we are in a cubicle instead of a beach house! Philippians 4:11 says it best: "Learn how to be content with whatever [we] have."

Starve the things and activities that have become idols.

Titus 2:12 "...Say 'No' to ungodliness and worldly passions, and live self-controlled, upright and godly lives..." (NIV)

Our perspective of possessions and passions can be all about God's purpose one moment and *our pleasure* the next! I know for me, it is a daily, even *secondly*, battle to keep both *things* and *activities* from becoming recipients of my worship! It takes just a split second for our minds to transition from an obedient perspective of moderation to a sinful perspective of infatuation. And we desperately need the Holy Spirit to keep inventory of our heart's desires every day.

Warriors – we have to beg God for an eternal perspective toward things and activities on a daily basis. And it's a fight that takes maturity and self-awareness. A Warrior knows his weaknesses, and he does whatever is necessary to safeguard himself from himself! That first line of defense is initiating supernatural resistance through prayer. Whatever passions and possessions we love the most are typically the topics we need to pray about the most! Those areas that excite us are the areas where we have to fight to maintain balance. But it doesn't stop with prayer. The only way to establish victory and maintain victory over any deep-rooted addiction is to starve it! And whether it is a hobby or an item that has become our source of contentment – *every* addiction requires starvation. This is where we separate the Warriors from the boys.

Guys – whatever has taken God's place, it's time to take control, celebrate the discomfort in the flesh, and conquer it with the aid of the Holy Spirit! It's time to just say "no," tap into the supernatural empowerment of God's presence, and "live self-controlled" lives as Titus 2:12 (NIV) describes! Simply said – we have to quarantine our thoughts and our physical bodies from connecting with whatever our obsession is. If we're being controlled by our love for hunting, it's time to disconnect from it for a few weeks or weekends...and maybe even take the challenge during *peak season* just to stretch ourselves with the highest level of discipline. It wouldn't hurt us to remind our flesh occasionally that our *spirit* calls the shots! Maybe it's media, fashion, traveling, sports, or music. Regardless of *what* it is, perhaps it's time to for a starvation break!

Let's administer a brutally honest assessment and examine our unique struggles. And then let's challenge ourselves in a way that isn't the easy test but actually the toughest test we can devise for ourselves. Remember, guys – it's through fleshly discomfort that we develop spiritual toughness, so let's endure a 21-day fast from our addictions and ask the Holy Spirit to give us the supernatural power to say "no" to worshipping any passion or possession in both our thoughts and actions. Then let's watch the one-two punch of God's dominion and our discipline absolutely decimate these addictions! It's a guarantee: Jesus is going to see our deliberate recognition of gods before Him and deliberately bless us in response. And *no* addiction can stand up to the name of Jesus, men.

SUMMARY

+ A Warrior isn't focused on attaining money but obeying the Word of God. A Warrior knows that by pursuing Jesus, the supernatural Provider, He will always provide money, the literal provision.

+ A Warrior manages God's provision with meticulous attention knowing that our Biblical stewardship is critical to receiving God's best. Tithing first, saving some, spending less, eliminating debt, giving often, and planning ahead are principles that lead to God's greatest financial blessings.

+ A Warrior doesn't obsess over possessions but uses possessions as tools to influence people and connect them to Jesus.

+ A Warrior doesn't use his passions for his own pleasure; he uses them as tools to connect the people around him to Jesus. A Warrior doesn't allow his passions to alter his principles. Instead, God's principles define the purpose of his passions.

+ A Warrior starves the passions and possessions that have become sources of identity and contentment knowing that complete elimination of an addiction begins with complete starvation of that addiction.

RESPONSE

God, this world is enticing at times, and it's a daily temptation to be motivated by money, things, and activities. But I know that You are the supreme Provider and will supply all of my needs as long as I focus my life on knowing You and obeying You. Instead of pursuing money, let me pursue You. God, I know You will prove Yourself to be faithful. And as You provide, let me manage that money according to Your Word – tithing first, saving some, spending less, eliminating debt, giving often, and planning ahead for my family's future.

Jesus, I also declare right now that I want an eternal perspective when it comes to possessions and passions. Lord, let my things and my activities direct me and connect me to others who I can love and influence to be more like Jesus. Don't ever let my pleasure become the focus of my possessions and passions, but instead urge me to seek Your purpose for every provision.

Lastly – Holy Spirit, I need Your unexplainable power to fuel me to victory over any addiction that has developed, whether it be an obsession with money, a possession, or a passion. I need You to intervene and reveal to me where my thoughts and actions have created gods before You, and I need You to be my self-control and discipline as I starve my flesh from worldly pleasures to put our relationship back in its rightful place!

CHAPTER 9

SCHOOL AND WORK

Winning the spiritual war requires having God's perspective of school and work.

Second only to our families, there is no greater opportunity for us to have eternal impact than at our schools and workplaces. And let me tell you guys – there is also no greater *need* for the presence of Warriors than out in the real world! Our world is drowning in darkness and is desperate for light. But the sad reality is we are being influenced more by the darkness than the darkness is being influenced by us!

One of the greatest tragedies of educational and professional culture is our lack of *eternal* awareness. We aren't focused on the supernatural because we are daily distracted by the literal. We have gotten so wrapped up in the task lists, business strategies, final exams, homework assignments, client meetings, and success goals that we've forgotten *why* we are *where* we are! Warriors – God has placed us in each of our situations, both educationally and professionally, for the *relationships*. Plain and simple. And while excellence, success, and hard work all matter greatly – we cannot lose our perspective on *why* they matter...and that is to influence people and represent the excellence of our Savior to the best of our abilities. We've lost sight of this sole meaningful purpose of our career environments, and that is why we've become the *influenced* instead of the *influencers!* It is also why so many of us are miserable with where we are and what we are doing.

The enemy has distracted us with the trivial, tedious routine of the temporary. And as a result, we're ignoring the *divine* purpose of working in the accounting department, serving at the fast food register, studying in that marketing class, playing in the marching band, leading in that fraternity, or building at the construction site.

Guys – we are *where* we are to love people and to lead people to Jesus. That's it. Nothing more. Nothing less. And the moment this principle becomes a reality in our school and work routines, we will experience an unexplainable, supernatural satisfaction that defies logic. Suddenly those classrooms and cubicles become about something far greater than what we see. They become high-stakes battlefields for souls! Talk about giving some purpose to our workday! You know, there are plenty of men out there asking on a regular basis, "Is this really all that there is?" Indeed, there *is* something *so* much greater – and it's rooted in staying close to Jesus, day after day, and maintaining an unrelenting perspective of *His* agenda: loving people!

Men – God wired us with a purpose. And believe it or not – He also placed us with a purpose. Where we are is no accident, and it's time to examine whether we are carrying a Warrior mentality into our school and work environments!

Embrace our current place as our eternal platform.

Ephesians 2:10 "For we are God's handiwork, created in Christ Jesus to do good works, which God prepared in advance for us to do." (NIV)

God has each of us right where we are for a specific purpose. And it isn't an accident that we are in our present situations, whether pleasant or unpleasant. We are *exactly* where God wants us, and *none* of our circumstances can catch our all-knowing God off guard! Ephesians 2:10 (NIV) is confirmation that the opportunities in front of us were "prepared in advance" by God specifically for us! The enemy wants us to question whether we're in the right place or not, but we're *always* in the right place as long as we're using our surroundings as an opportunity to reflect Jesus. Far too often we agonize over the decision of *where* God wants us, but God just wants us serving His purpose where He's already got us! It's important that we as Warriors embrace our current place as our eternal platform! Otherwise we are wasting opportunities to be light to someone.

Guys – we might *hate* our current situation. We might despise that math class. We might loathe the idea of working in the food industry for another year. We might be miserable with the ridiculous hours that we're working for our law firm. We might hate painting houses every day. However – we *cannot* allow those literal, temporal frustrations deceive us and distract us from God's agenda. God indeed has work that He has "prepared in advance for us to do" right where we are, so let's stop complaining about hardships and start focusing on relationships!

For those of us who are middle school, high school, or college students – we have a massive platform in our schools to influence those around us. And as Warriors, it's time to carry the mission of 1 Timothy 4:12 into our institutions and "don't let *anyone* think less of [us] because [we] are young," but instead "be an example to all believers in what [we] say, in the way [we] live, in [our] love, [our] faith, and [our] purity!" The world might tell us that schools define who we are, but Warriors know that *we* define *them!* And even if we are "fresh meat" in high school or the newcomer at our middle school, the truth still remains that God designed us to be the influence, not the influenced! So let's not get sidetracked by the physics homework, difficult teacher, relationship drama, basketball tryouts, or midterm exams. Because at the end of the day, we have one mission: to "be an example" of God's Word. It's time to stop wasting the opportunities and get strategic about exemplifying who Jesus is.

Take a second and think about this. What if we are the only true example of Jesus' love in the lives of our classmates and teachers? It sounds awful, but what if a shooter came in and took the lives of every person in our third period class? Would those around us have seen a difference in how we lived each day? Would our teachers and classmates have seen us passionate about our Savior? Please, Jesus, let Your Holy Spirit keep us attuned to the eternal destiny that is at stake for those that we are around on a daily basis! Because the shy guy behind us in our journalism class, the fourth-string lineman on our team, and the president of our fraternity – they all need You, and we want them to experience the unfathomable peace that You've given us!

The same goes for our workplaces. They are in dire need of more substance and less surface, but they're not getting it. Most of us are so tired of the same old, monotonous routines that we leave the house in an almost sedated state. We are fed up with the cubicles, the suits, and the ties. We can't wait to take off the hard hat, get off of the backhoe, and get in a clean pair of pants. We are on autopilot. Cruise control. And *please* – don't bother us with all that

"Christian" talk concerning our coworker's eternal fate! We're already stressed out enough by the workload alone!

That describes us at times, guys! We are so focused on the literal that we just don't have the time or energy to even care about the eternal! Warriors – we've got to see past the exasperation of every day to the eternity of every one. We can't get distracted by white collars or blue collars, because we have a spiritual assignment that makes our neighbor's fate far more important than our feelings. Hey, men – Luke 10:2 reminds us that "the harvest is great, but the workers are few." God is looking for a few men to stand up and stand out! And that's us!

Exhibit excellence in our work ethic.

Colossians 3:17 "And whatever you do or say, do it as a representative of the Lord Jesus..."

Our work and study habits might seem spiritually irrelevant to us, but to God they're an extension of our representation of who *He* is! Just think about this – Colossians 3:17 tells us that *we* are demonstrating God's character to those in our schools and workplaces. What an incredible opportunity but overwhelming responsibility! We represent Jesus! That means we are essentially brand ambassadors for God showcasing to the world what He is like and why they should buy into doing things His way! That's some darn good motivation to be adamant about our daily routine of prayer, worship, and the Word – because without that supernatural fuel and empowerment, we can't possibly tackle that job description!

But what does it even look like to represent Jesus in our everyday career habits? Well, it begins with obsessing over excellence! Just like we discussed in the first part of this study – God wired us for excellence, not mediocrity! It's time to unpack some of the practical principles where we can exhibit this excellence in our schools and workplaces.

Hard Work

Excellence begins with hard work. Warriors don't complain about having to sweat, having to stay later than everyone else, or being exhausted after a long day at work. We *relish* the opportunity to push harder than everyone around us. We seek out ways to earn what we receive instead of looking for handouts as an entitled exchange for laziness. We embrace the pain that accompanies standing out from the crowd because we know it's part of the price of separating ourselves from the status quo. And we don't expect a participation trophy if we don't have what it takes to win the championship trophy! We aren't complainers, and when lazy tendencies creep in, we battle them with Colossians 3:23, which tells us to "work willingly at whatever [we] do, as though [we] were working for the Lord rather than for people." Men – first and foremost, let's work our butts off to impress our Heavenly Boss.

Skill

Warriors are marked by precision and skill in whatever we do, because it is our attention to the minutest details that enables us to impress and influence the largest number of people with God's purpose. The rare and remarkable skill of a Warrior causes people to take notice, and we maximize our reach by striving to be the elite in our classes and organizations. We build the sturdiest houses. We create the most polished presentations. We pull off the most flawlessly executed events. And we don't cut corners. We go all in regardless of what we're doing knowing that Proverbs 22:29 (ESV) tells us that a "skillful man" will have opportunities to work in places of great influence. Unprecedented skill creates uncommon opportunity to influence.

Drive / Initiative

Just how Jesus was a man driven by His Father's purpose, a Warrior is driven in the same way – disregarding distraction, motivated by a mission *far* more important than his own agenda. We possess a spiritual drive that perseveres through personal frustrations remembering that we exist for others in our classrooms and workplaces. But we also portray a professional drive that annihilates any hint of apathy. We are the go-getters in every environment and the archetypal initiators of task lists. We are the ones who find work to do when the majority is lazily avoiding assignment or complaining about workload. We act without having to be asked because we are standard setters, not standard seekers!

Cleanliness / Organization

Warriors exhibit cleanliness and organization in our work habits. From attire, to workspace, to computer desktop, to vehicles, to checklists – every outlet is an opportunity to exhibit the worship principle of 1 Corinthians 14:40, which reminds us to "be sure that everything is done properly and in order." Hey, guys – order and organization matter to God! And 1 Corinthians 14:33 tells us, "God is not a God of disorder but of peace!" That's why every impeccable detail is an opportunity to impress and attract others as we reflect the ordered, set apart nature of our God! Yes – that means a clean desk and an organized backpack can testify to the character of our Heavenly Father! Let's be men who manicure the messy details and keep our spaces pristinely organized as an extension of our testimony of excellence.

Punctuality / Dependability

Warriors are on time. It sounds simple in theory, but in our culture's fast-paced environment, we have gotten lackadaisical in our follow-through, guys. Commitments have become "optional" obligations. Deadlines have become formalities but rarely realities. We're quick to appease clients, bosses, and coworkers with convincing words but almost certain to disappoint them with unkept promises.

Procrastination and tardiness have become the norm instead of the exception, and it's inexcusable if we are trying to reach people. Warriors respect others' time by being on time – with meetings, projects, assignments, bosses, teachers, clients, classmates, and colleagues. Men – when we aren't on time, we disregard someone else's quality of life. And in doing so, we sacrifice our ability to influence by becoming their inconvenience. Matthew 5:37 reminds us that a Warrior's "yes" is "yes," and that his word is sufficient enough to bind him to his commitment. Guys – we've gotta get back to a place where "I'll have this assignment completed in three days" means that we *have* that assignment completed in three days! And we've gotta start doing whatever we have to do to make sure that what we *said* we'd do translates into what we *actually* do! Let's remember – we are representing the reliability of a perfectly dependable Savior.

Honesty / Integrity

Warriors don't compromise our integrity for anything or anyone. No amount of money, notoriety, or power can lure us into dishonesty. Because even if the world doesn't see lies and corruption, *God* does! And *He* is our standard. Warrior leaders operate with transparency, and we aren't afraid to take responsibility for our mistakes even when the consequences are severe. As CEO's and bag boys, we recall Proverbs 11:3 that says "*honesty* guides good people." We remember that balancing every penny of that budget honestly and accurately – *that* matters to Jesus. Fixing the crack in the wall that we noticed but the homeowner didn't – *that* matters to Jesus. Keeping our eyes on our own exam even though the smartest kid is basically showcasing his answers right beside us – *that* matters to Jesus. Approaching our boss to tell him that we received too much money for the amount of time we worked last month – *that* matters to Jesus. Purifying every situation with the filter of 100% truth matters to Jesus!

Warriors also own up to our mistakes even when we're ashamed and embarrassed, because public humiliation pales in comparison to supernatural retribution! And it's just not worth sacrificing the favor of our Father to remain popular with our culture! Proverbs 28:13 talks about the supernatural consequences of dishonesty: "People who conceal their sins will not prosper, but if they confess and turn from them, they will receive mercy!" Let's take ownership of our mistakes instead of blame shifting with excuses. Because admitting to that error that cost the company a substantial chunk of revenue – *that* matters to Jesus. And apologizing to that employee who we mistakenly placed the blame for our error – *that* matters to Jesus. Real leaders will have the awkward, uncomfortable conversations and endure the awful, unbearable consequences to remain pure in the eyes of our Heavenly Father!

Warriors can be trusted in school. We can be trusted at work. We can be trusted at the top of the totem pole. And we can be trusted at the bottom. Like 2 Corinthians 8:21 reminds us, "We are careful to be honorable before the Lord, but we also want everyone else to see that we are honorable." And whether our actions are being seen by many or seen by none, let's be "careful to be honorable" in all we do.

Serve the people around us.

Mark 10:44-45 "And whoever wants to be first among you must be the slave of everyone else. For even the Son of Man came not to be served but to serve others..."

There is only one entity we encounter in our daily routine that matters in the eternal scheme of things, and it's *people*. Luke 16:11 calls them "true riches" making them unequivocally our greatest assignment. And Jesus set the example of how we handle that assignment by serving the socks off every person He encountered! And whether people agree or disagree with our beliefs, it's our job to serve them so well that they can't possibly deny our love for them!

People are watching to see if there's a difference in us. And while they might be watching our work habits, they're *definitely* watching how we treat others. The question then becomes – are we blending in or are we standing out? When we are interacting with classmates, students, colleagues, contractors, bosses, supervisors, and clients – can we name even one way in which our lives stand out from the secular culture around us? The truth is – we either follow the culture, or we set the culture. Warriors are called by Mark 10:44-45 to set the culture by becoming a "slave of everyone" around us.

Wherever we are, we set a culture of servanthood, just like Jesus did. But practically, what does it even mean to become a "slave" to others in our schools and workplaces? It means we exist to lighten the burden of every person around us! Instead of looking out for our interests, we are constantly looking out for the interests of *others*. And there are plenty of ways to do this...

Prayer

The greatest thing we can do for our peers, whether in school or work, is pray for them. Because when we intercede on behalf of others and ask for the supernatural power of the Holy Spirit to be present in their lives, *it works!* They don't even have to know we are praying for them because it's not about getting credit for our piety; it's about building a covering over their path! Warriors know that prayer absolutely works, and even when it doesn't appear to be yielding immediate results, we stand on 1 John 5:14 – that "we are confident that [God] hears us whenever we ask for anything that pleases Him!" Men – even if it's just a few seconds here or there, let's be legitimate pray-ers in our career environments. Let's make sure that we are specifically praying for employees, employers, classmates, teachers, students, and bosses throughout the course of our days! And let's make sure that the temporary to-do list doesn't distract us from the eternal to-do list, because praying for our peers and their salvation is *always* a priority over the items on our work agenda.

Selflessness

With school and work assignments, it seems like everyone is out to receive recognition, achieve success, and add an accomplishment to their résumé. But Warriors work with a humble confidence that considers credit irrelevant! No matter who is credited with the recognition that accompanies success, we know that 1 Peter 5:6 says God has far greater ability to elevate our position than we do. It is simply our responsibility to "humble [ourselves] under the mighty power of God" exemplifying a humility that doesn't mind being behind the scenes! Yes, we might indeed be the genius behind the award-winning idea or the guru that came up with the solution, but we don't *need* the credit... because even if our classmates and colleagues don't ever sing our praises, God is watching. And He gets giddy about promoting that kind of atypical modesty!

Let's be all about forfeiting the acclaim, guys. Let's be willing to sacrifice the time, the effort, and even the credit in order to see others lifted up. And while our culture tells us to protect our position, let's be the guy whose goal is to promote others to our position! Instead of trying to defeat the guy under us, let's try to develop the guy under us! Philippians 2:3 is the perfect reminder to put others' success in front of our own: "Be humble, thinking of others as better than yourselves." Warriors – let's leave a legacy of being cheerleaders for our classmates and coworkers, not challengers. And let's exploit every opportunity to give *others* praise, even when *we* were the ones that deserved it! That's leadership.

Generosity

We all want practical, so here's a question: when was the last time we used one of our resources at school or work to bless someone in need? Come on, men. How 'bout that classmate working two jobs and paying his way through school – we could buy him a $5 meal after class and bless him beyond belief. Or that employee who just lost his dad to skin cancer and had to pay for burial expenses out of his own pocket – it would transform his entire demeanor to receive $50 and a word of encouragement. Guys – let's not miss opportunities to practically bless our peers! There's no better way to show Jesus' love than practical generosity. Let's always remember what Proverbs 11:25 tells us: "the generous will prosper," and "those who refresh others will themselves be refreshed!"

Positivity

Warriors set the tone of our school and work environments by keeping a relentlessly positive attitude. We know that a good attitude is non-negotiable if we want to represent the character of Jesus and attract people to who He is! We've all been around that coworker or classmate who complains about *everything* and finds the negative in every situation. It is defeating, exhausting, and repulsive. Seriously – a bad attitude *repels* people, eliminating any capacity to influence them. If no one wants to be around us, it sure makes it difficult to reach them!

If we want to maximize our reach potential, let's ask Jesus to give us the "cheerful heart" described in Proverbs 17:22, because it's the "good medicine" that *so* many people need, especially on their discouraging days. And let's embody Philippians 2:5 – even when we are overwhelmed with assignments and stressed to the max – remembering that our response to every situation should reflect "the same attitude that Christ Jesus had." Guys – it's a choice every day whether we will let our feelings or God's principles dictate our disposition.

Patience

Want to destroy a testimony in the blink of an eye? Let's just tell that annoying employee or classmate how we *really* feel. We all have that person that comes to mind who is just plain difficult. It's like they deliberately disrespect us and seem to even delight in the process of ticking us off! The enemy knows exactly who that person is, and you better believe he's going to test our patience with that little snide comment in the break room, that undeserved job promotion that should've been ours, or our rejected idea that was clearly better than theirs. Next time we're getting frustrated with "that" person who is undoubtedly out to wrong us, let's remind ourselves of Ephesians 6:12 and that we aren't frustrated with *them.* We are frustrated at the enemy at work *in* them! Let's look past the natural realm to the supernatural realm and remember that Jesus genuinely loves that difficult person, even when they appear to be a broomstick or pitchfork short of being trick-or-treat ready! Let's vent to God about the enemy instead of venting to people about people. And let's be unfazed by difficult associates no matter how often they get under our skin. Let's keep killing 'em with kindness, and as Ephesians 4:2 tells us, "Be patient with each other, making allowance for each other's faults."

Forgiveness

The world says "get even" with the subcontractor who wronged us, the coworker who betrayed our trust, the classmate who got us in trouble with the teacher, and the boss who treated us like we didn't even exist for two years. The world says it's our *right* to stand up for ourselves, and our retaliation is justified in giving them a taste of their own medicine! But, boy, does the world have it all wrong with that prideful approach. Matthew 18:22 provides us with some inconvenient accountability reminding us to forgive those who wronged us "seventy times seven!" Now I don't know about you, but I tend to dismiss forgiveness as an option if someone has wronged me even twice! Meanwhile, God's Word is asking us to forgive without limit! No matter how maliciously we've been wronged, we *never* stop forgiving. It is *the* defining trait of Christianity. We let people off the hook, and we let them off the hook fast! And we don't talk about their mistreatment *ever again*, because their slate has been wiped clean!

If *that's* not enough of a challenge, how about the radical ideology of Matthew 5:39? You're telling me I'm supposed to "offer the other cheek" if someone slapped me in the face? Absolutely. I mean, isn't that literally what Jesus demonstrated on the cross? Even if we don't ever receive a physical slap to the face, we most certainly will get slapped in the face metaphorically speaking. That fellow officer, that unhappy boss, that jealous classmate – they *will* deliberately try and hurt us on occasion. But...what if we were so well prepared for these occasions that we had already forgiven those who will wrong us? What if we decided *in advance* to let our boss off the hook for taking advantage of us? Maybe then we wouldn't be so aghast or rattled when the inevitable wrongdoing smacks us in the face!

As backwards as it sounds, let's embrace the situations when we are mistreated, because they're opportunities for us to exhibit just how deep our Savior's love is for us even when we are at our worst! Forgiveness is *the* greatest manifestation of Jesus' love!

Appreciation

Working *with* people and *for* people who appreciate you is just plain refreshing. But let's be real – it's as rare as a Bigfoot sighting! Sad but true. Most of us never get around to appreciating people because we aren't even appreciative of where God has us! We're so discontent with where we are that we hardly even consider who we are around! Appreciation comes from a foundation of contentment. And the very moment we become content with the quality of our day, we will be equipped to improve the quality of someone else's day! The bottom line? We can't be self-focused and others-focused simultaneously. It's one or the other. And a Warrior prepares himself to appreciate others daily by choosing contentment daily – even when nothing is going right! Living out 1 Thessalonians 5:18 – being "thankful" in every school and every workplace – ensures that we remain focused on encouraging others!

And that's what Warriors do. We voice an almost annoyingly grateful appreciation for the place God has us and for the people around us. We change the tone of conversations, the atmosphere of classrooms, and even the culture of entire organizations by establishing a precedent of appreciation. We are quick to give others credit, and we are vocal about it as well. We acknowledge both the efforts of those around us and the opportunities provided by those around us. Guys – let's err on the side of over-appreciation for people in our career paths. "Thank you so much," "I appreciate you more than you know," and "Wow, you did great job" are sentiments that we just can't use enough as we highlight the best in others!

Respect

As men, we *crave* respect. At the office, in the conference room, in the classroom, in a marriage, on the field, on the court – it doesn't matter where we are, we want to be perceived as legitimate, authoritative, and respectable. The desire to be held in high regard among peers, partners, teachers, classmates, employees, and employers is just a part of our DNA. And that's a universal trait for the male species.

But while *getting* respect is society's measuring stick for manliness, *giving* respect is our Savior's measuring stick for manliness! Romans 12:10 is proof telling us to "take delight in honoring each other." Notice how there is no qualifier at the end of that passage! It doesn't tell us to "honor those who are our bosses." It doesn't tell us to "honor those that you like in your class." And it doesn't say to "honor those who honor you!" We are called to honor the superior, the inferior, the talented, the untalented, the likable, the unlikable, the respectful, and the disrespectful. There is no prerequisite to becoming a recipient of a Warrior's respect! *Every* person qualifies!

We respect that coworker enough not to talk about her negatively behind her back even though she has been seriously slacking on her assignments. We respect that condescending boss and give him a humble smile, a firm handshake, and intentional eye contact even though it is obvious that he has abused his position of authority. And we respect that teacher the first time she tells us to stop goofing off during class, even if she seems to always pick on us instead of the other troublemakers. *We* set the example of respect even when we feel like the other person should be the example setter. Because spiritual purpose supersedes societal position as the determinant of who should set the example of respect in our schools and workplaces. Culture decides who sets the example based on a title: teachers lead students, employers lead employees, and superiors lead inferiors. But Warriors know culture is wrong, that testimony trumps title, and no matter what our badge says, it's always *our* responsibility to set the example.

We are respecters. We don't badmouth authority, and we don't gossip about our peers. We prototype humble posture, encouraging words, pure motives, and genuine consideration for others. And while cowards forcefully demand respect, Warriors freely deliver respect!

Use secular popularity, power, and position for spiritual influence.

Galatians 1:10 "Obviously, I'm not trying to win the approval of people, but of God. If pleasing people were my goal, I would not be Christ's servant."

Chances are most of us have experienced at least a moment or two in the limelight. Whether through hard work or happenstance, we've likely all had at least a brief stint in the spotlight that elevated our popularity, power, or position. And just like every other tool that enlarges our territory and increases our influence potential, there's a ferocious underlying spiritual battle for how it will be purposed! Guys – the enemy loves it when we gain notoriety. Why? Because he knows that the overwhelming majority of the time we'll get addicted to the trappings of being in the public eye. It's just more enjoyable for our flesh to absorb the attention than to avert it! But while the enemy is on one side encouraging us to build our earthly kingdom in that annexed territory, God is on the opposite side waiting for us to build His eternal kingdom! And the choice is ours – we can waste popularity, power, and position to draw attention to ourselves and boost our confidence, or we can utilize them to deflect attention to Jesus and boast His character!

Hey, Warriors – God is ready to extend our reach. He absolutely is. But we've gotta prove that we can manage our existing estate before God decides to expand it! Matthew 23:12 begs the critical question: Are we using secular popularity, power, and position as tools to "exalt [ourselves]" or "humble [ourselves]"?

At Work

True humility in the workplace means we operate under a Heavenly hierarchy where more power for us equates to more glory for God and others. It means that God's handbook takes precedent over the HR handbook. And it means that as both employers and employees, status takes a back seat to service! Easier said than done though. As employers, we all know it takes just a moment of praise from the peanut gallery to let the power go to our heads, and before we know it, even *we* are impressed with ourselves! And justifiably so! After all, we worked our butts off to achieve that status and notoriety! We deserve the power! We earned the popularity! Right?

Power intoxicates. And when we aren't adamant about forfeiting that glory to the name of Jesus, we nurture superiority based on what we did to achieve power, not inferiority based on what God did to afford power. It becomes "I'm great because of what I did" instead of "I'm less because of what God did." Job 1:21 clears up which of those two perspectives is truth poignantly reminding us that *the Lord* is the One who gives, and *the Lord* is the One who takes away. Hey, men – that popularity we've gained with the board of executives, that power we've accumulated in our organization, that position we've attained within our company – they didn't happen because of *our greatness*. They happened because of *God's grace!* Let's not fool ourselves into believing that it was our talent, our hard work, our intellect, and our effort that got us to a position of influence. It's God who provided both the abilities that got us there and the opportunities that have kept us there! And if God wants to take it all away tomorrow, He can do it in the blink of an eye.

We can't waste the influence potential God has granted us. And there is nothing more influential in the workplace than a man who is *powerful* serving those who are *powerless!* In fact, that's really what it's all about – turning heads by doing it God's way, which is backwards from the world's way. As power increases, so does our service to those under us on the totem pole. Warriors in the workplace are more concerned with considering those under us than we are with controlling those under us.

On the flip side, as employees, we don't mind being stepped on, disrespected, or overworked, because that's just a part of the package deal of being in a servant's position in an organization! However, we don't subscribe to the cultural cop out that as servants we are mere *followers* who do what we've been told. As employees we *are* worldly servants who submit to professional authority, but we are still spiritual headmen who lead with supernatu ral authority! And in the same way that a leader needs to be on guard against thinking too highly of himself, a servant needs to be on guard against thinking too lowly of himself! Because guys – just as powerful leaders still serve, powerless servants still lead!

But how do we lead from a servant's position? As an employee, how do we submit and lead simultaneously? The answer is we bust our tails to help people and complete tasks to the best of our abilities, but we never budge on our principles. *We* define our work environment and our work ethic! And no employer can alter our unwavering Biblical standard of excellence. Wherever we are in the pecking order of our companies, we are there to be a mirror of Jesus. And if our mirror is small or large, the *only* thing that matters is that we're using it to reflect Jesus. So whether we are the president of a billion-dollar international corporation or a burger flipper at the local fast food restaurant – let's humbly serve with our actions but confidently lead with our principles.

At School

These same principles of humbly serving with our actions while confidently leading with our principles can be applied at our schools as well. In leadership positions, we are still there to demonstrate what it looks like to serve others. And conversely, in servant positions, we are still there to lead with an unshakeable boldness in what we believe. God didn't allow us to be voted "most popular" at school so that we could increase our social media following and date the prettiest girl in the class. He didn't give us that leadership position in our fraternity so that we could plan the best band parties and sorority socials. And God surely didn't grant us the power to mentor those freshmen in science class so that we could become the most well-liked teacher at the school. Men – we have countless platforms to influence, so let's not squander them on immaterial agendas.

To the young Warriors in middle school, high school, and college – how are we using our popularity at school to set the example of Jesus? Are we the all-city player on the team who remains poised after the gut-wrenching loss in the championship game of the playoffs or the one who throws a tantrum? Are we the stud guitarist for the band that is singing about hedonistic things on Friday night or Heavenly things on Sunday morning? Are we the standout student who conducts himself in the classroom like a secure, mature young man or an immature, little boy? And are we the prom king who rebels against our parents' curfew or the one who respects it enough to value the protective guidelines? Remember, guys – when "much" has been given to us, "much" is expected (see Luke 12:48). God is watching in *every* situation to see if we're utilizing these pedestals to passionately proclaim and rightfully represent the name of Jesus to fellow students, peers, and faculty!

In the Public Eye

It was a silly blonde Ken doll wig, a hideous pair of non-prescription "Plano" glasses, a Notre Dame Fighting Irish ball cap, and an ability to impersonate former charismatic college football coach and ESPN commentator Lou Holtz. This was the recipe that unexpectedly pushed me in the spotlight. I had been impersonating this guy for *years*, but never in a million of them would I have guessed my "talent" (hardly a talent) would ever land me an invite to perform on a live radio show in Birmingham, Alabama. But that's exactly what happened. I still remember getting an email from producer Calvin "Speedy" Wilburn of the nationally syndicated *Rick and Bubba Show* saying they wanted me to join them during their prime segment at 7:35 a.m. on opening day of the 2010 college football season. And being that I loved their comedy show and loved college football even more, I was all in. And when I say I was "all in," I mean it! If I was gonna go, I was gonna go all out!

And I did. I went the whole nine yards suiting up with my oversized khaki pants pulled up to my chest like an old man, whistle dangling from my neck, a pre-scripted comedic monologue in tow to ensure I didn't flop on live radio! And much to my surprise on that Fall Friday morning, what started off as a complete joke turned out to be an instant hit. There I was just goofing off on the radio like I was at home with the family, decked out in a bleached blonde wig, fake spectacles, and a navy blue cap with a stitched gold "ND," bouncing my way through this mindless football humor with literally a million plus people listening! I was having the time of my life!

And that was about all I had expected...a one and done segment to add to the scrapbook of memories. Then Monday morning I get a message saying, "Lance – the video of your 'Coach Lou' segment is getting a lot of attention on one of the nation's most popular college football blogs!" Even more bizarre, within a week, it was being featured front and center on the "Extra Mustard" page of the *Sports Illustrated* website calling my impersonation "As Good as the Real Thing!"

That's when it happened, guys...I remember experiencing this sensational rush throughout my entire body. What a thrill to be publicized on a national level! I may not have had any true talent, but it did feel good to be recognized regardless! Was this brief phenomenon absolutely ridiculous? Of course it was. Was the praise for my foolish antics preposterous? Absolutely. Trust me – I recognized its silliness. But even so – that popularity was seductively addicting!

But the spotlight didn't subside there, and for almost a decade, this "Dr. Lou" segment has remained a seasonal staple, a recurring annual tradition during football season on the *Rick and Bubba Show*. My wife flatteringly refers to my character as "the Santa Claus of college football season!" Nonetheless, *every* time I enter that studio for a segment, I have to remind myself that my spiritual purpose is far more important than my secular popularity! And while adding in that off-color joke or that filthy word might get another laugh and a few more followers, I've learned it's totally not worth compromising the purity of my testimony!

The spotlight is *notorious* for coaxing us into spiritual compromise. We've all seen it happen...a man is projected into the public eye by the media and exposed to just a taste of popularity. Almost instantaneously he begins clinging to the newfound attention as his source of self-worth and identity. But one day, the attention dies down and without the applause, he struggles to find purpose and peace. So, what does he do? He does whatever is necessary to regenerate that validation. And suddenly, popularity *is* his purpose. Popularity becomes priority and principles become peripheral as he steps out onto this terribly slippery slope of moral justification and eventual deterioration. The story hardly ever ends well.

Warriors – popularity reveals our true convictions. And whether it's something as silly as a wig, glasses, and a hot microphone on the radio or as legitimate as a Super Bowl trophy as an NFL coach that propels us into the spotlight, let's declare in advance that we will *not* alter our principles for popularity! As Galatians 1:10 says, we are "not trying to win the approval of people, but of God!" And if standing up for what is Biblical makes us unpopular, then so be it! We won't compromise even on the most inconsequential issue, because little by little, we will be so far removed from God's principles that we won't even be able to distinguish Biblical truth from popular opinion.

Work to live. Don't live to work.

Matthew 16:26 "And what do you benefit if you gain the whole world but lose your own soul? Is anything worth more than your soul?"

For most men, we don't need to be told to work hard because that's just a part of our DNA. We are tough. We are driven. We are strong because we are *supposed* to be strong, because we are *men!* And you better believe we are going to work our tails off to achieve success and pay the bills. Because that's what men do. We do what we've got to do.

But where's the line? At what point does our life become more about working than our work is about living? Like Matthew 16:26 says, *so what* if we "gain the whole world" through our work? We have to know when enough is enough and when to shut down the computer, reschedule the meeting, forego the overtime, turn off the tractor, press pause on the film study, and *go home!* Like, stop working and go do something that's not work. Warriors work to live. We don't live to work! And whether our job is something that we love or it's just something that we do to pay the bills, our work is *what we do*, not *who we are!*

Of course work isn't who we are! We all know that! Right? Yet almost every one of us wears either the enjoyment of work or the frustration of our work on our sleeves. We may physically leave our work location, but our work never actually leaves us! Our attitudes, our energy, our time – they are all directly tied to the ebb and flow of what happened that day in the workplace.

On one end of the spectrum, there are those of us who enjoy our work so much that we don't want to put it down. Then on the other end are those of us who dread our work so much that we can't put it down fast enough! And these scenarios are exactly what the enemy wants. He works both ends of the spectrum trying to convince us that our jobs are either our greatest *motivation* or our greatest *frustration!* His strategy is to get us fixated on our work so that it consumes our entire existence and infiltrates our non-work lives! Satan knows that if he can coax us into an unbalanced perspective of our profession, we will either obsess over our success or obsess over our frustration. Both obsessions tend to seep into our homes.

Guys – let's not allow the enjoyment *or* the exasperation of our career to become the defining variable of our demeanor. It is just work. And at the end of every day, whether we are excited or disappointed about our work, Jesus, not a job, defines our demeanor when we head to the house.

Give Jesus some time.

So how do we know if we've lost that balanced perspective and are now living to work instead of working to live? One of the most obvious red flags is when Jesus gets no time or focus. I mean, if we are spending eight, nine, ten hours a day at work but can't find five or ten minutes to spend in prayer, worship, and the Word – that's an indicator that work is our priority. Period. We wonder why we're so drained and devoid of peace every day, and we wonder why there's this intense, indescribable dissatisfaction with our daily routine. But oftentimes the reason for our emptiness is insultingly obvious, guys! It's because the only thing that matters is missing! Let's be sure that time with Jesus is a staple in our daily school and work routines!

Disconnect from work. Connect with family.

Then there's family. And one thing's for certain: they eagerly await our homecoming every day. Yet we still apathetically arrive an hour late, monitor our email a dozen times throughout the evening, and regularly text on our phone to deal with "urgent," unresolved situations from the day's work! What a slap in the face to our families! The truth is we aren't disconnecting from work when we're home, and it is depriving our families of much needed attention. Men – it's a devastating problem! Because whether we like it or not, it's utterly impossible to invest in our work and our families at the same time! Whether these unhealthy work habits are by choice or requirement, it's time to set some boundaries to protect our families. Yes – there may be an occasional, unavoidable work issue that demands our attention when we are home, but this has to become the exception and not the norm. It's time to completely shut off all of the electronic devices and intentionally invest in the precious people in our families. Either we disconnect from our work or our work will disconnect us from our families!

Men – we *will* have workdays that exhaust us, frustrate us, excite us, or inspire us. But let's dig deep and spend that drive home praying for supernatural energy from the Holy Spirit to shut those work emotions down and enable us to be the husbands and fathers He has called us to be! It takes a true Warrior to leave work at work and focus on his *real* job when he walks through that front door, *especially* after those strenuous days.

Flee comparison.

Another telltale sign that our identity is stemming from our title and not our testimony is when we battle *comparison* in our work environment. Whether we're a house builder, firefighter, graphic artist, financial planner, or professional athlete – it's a given that we want to be better than the next guy. But the problem is there will *always* be someone out there with more talent, more notoriety, more accomplishments, and more money. So what's the antidote? Philippians 4:12 (NIV) urges us to "[learn] the secret of being content in any and every situation." Warriors make a disciplined choice to be content with our configuration! Otherwise, we will get stuck in this inescapable cycle of measuring *our* performance, *our* achievements, and *our* products with the next guy's, a certain recipe for discontentment. Let's refuse to hang our hats on a résumé, and instead embrace the skills, talent level, and location that God has uniquely composed for us.

Represent Jesus on the road.

1 Peter 1:14-15 "So you must live as God's obedient children. Don't slip back into your old ways of living to satisfy your own desires. You didn't know any better then. But now you must be holy in everything you do, just as God who chose you is holy."

If there's one place where men tend to struggle spiritually, it's on the road. From commutes, to business trips, to spring break adventures – we often dismiss our principles when we feel like others can't easily identify us! As strange as it sounds, when we are enclosed in a vehicle driving down the road or sightseeing on a road trip to an unfamiliar city, we relax spiritually because the accountability seems absent. We get comfortable because our identity seems concealed, and the repercussions for our indiscretions seem miles away. And it's time to address these hidden areas where the enemy is pulling us into even the *smallest* sinful habits. 1 Peter 1:15 tells us to "be holy in *everything* [we] do!" And the last time I checked, commutes and trips still fall under the "everything" category!

Commutes

Sometimes I feel like AC/DC wrote one of their songs just for me. Like, I will be mid-commute and become totally convinced that they composed their hit title – "Highway to Hell" – as some satirical tribute to the power of the highways to activate my most hellish behavior! Kidding aside, I have to remind myself often that my testimony *does* include my time behind the wheel of a vehicle. And it's not the easiest declaration because I struggle more on the road to represent Jesus than anywhere else. Surely I'm not alone.

There's just nothing more frustrating to me than a traffic jam, a preoccupied driver, or a texting commuter. And I'll admit I have trouble celebrating the occasion when Minivan Mom sits in my blind spot and ignores my blinker for 45 seconds! Public service announcement: if you get on the road to *drive*, please pay attention to *driving!* Lord, thank you for the countless testers and perfectors of our patience that inundate our interstates each day.

I joke, but in all seriousness – God is watching to see how we handle that guy who just gave us the middle finger because we were going the speed limit. He is watching to see how we respond to that reckless teenager riding two feet from our tail. And God is watching to see whether we will be the lone commuter to accommodate the elderly man who desperately needs to get over two lanes so he doesn't miss his exit. Guys – God wants our testimony to extend to the turnpike!

It's easy to throw our hands up, scream obscenities, and act like the rest of the world in our cars. But it's our responsibility to exhibit the same characteristics *inside* the car that we do *outside* the car! And just because it's dark outside, or we have tinted windows, or we are enclosed in metal and glass – that doesn't exempt us from glorifying Jesus. Let's never forget that there are *people* inside of each car, guys. And when we lose our temper on the road, we curse the very same people that we are aiming to reach off the road! Warriors – let's extend the grace of Colossians 3:13 by making allowance for people's faults even when they're a pain on the asphalt!

But enough about *other* drivers because a lot of us could stand to drive a little more responsibly ourselves! Hey, men – our driving is an extension of our consideration of others, and we need to lead by example in how we operate a vehicle. Let's not be distracted by our phones while we're driving. Let's buckle up to increase our chances of being around for our families if an accident happens. Let's obey the law by going the speed limit. Let's keep our eyes open to find that distressed driver who needs a courteous commuter to let him over! Let's give other drivers plenty of buffer space to maneuver so that the roads are as safe as possible. Plain and simple, let's *legitimately* put the interests of others ahead of our own when we get behind the wheel (see Philippians 2:4).

But how do we manage to keep an eternal perspective while we're driving? The answer is easy: pray and worship in the car! Use the commute to connect. We don't have to close our eyes or lift our hands to be connected to the Holy Spirit. We can have the worship music blasting, hands ten and two, with a simultaneous focus on the road and the resurrection! And it *sure* makes it difficult to cuss at the truck driver who almost ran us over if we're reflecting on the loving cross of our Savior!

Business Trips

Another glaring opportunity to evade accountability on the road is on business trips. And men – we are target practice for the enemy whenever we are physically distant from accountability. Isolation opens up a can of vulnerability, and those out-of-town work trips can quickly become breeding grounds for sin...sexual sin in particular. And even if no one in that city knows who we are during that secretive rendezvous, God is watching. Even though no one has a clue that we are watching a pornographic show on the free movie channel before turning in for the night, God is watching. There is no secret to God, and that's why it's best not to try and keep one!

Others are watching too, guys. Our business partners and coworkers are watching our habits to see if they're any different from the rest of the world. So let's not abandon what we stand for the other 99% of the time to "let loose" and "have some fun" with our coworkers because "we've earned it." Let's remember that the conversations we have, the jokes we tell, the drinks we consume, the places we go for entertainment – they're all extensions of our testimony. And sometimes we need to say "no" to late-night community if it compromises our character. Let's find another Warrior to hold us accountable or to accompany us on every road trip so that we don't do something dumb to damage our testimony or destroy our purity when we're away from home.

Spring Break

Speaking of trips, there are none more dangerously secular and grossly irresponsible than the one that pop culture has defined as "Spring Break." And I will admit right now that I probably looked forward to the glitz and glamour of that week as much as anyone when I was in my teens and twenties! Pop culture has brainwashed young people to believe that the answer to discontent is found in self-indulgence. And even scarier – they've convinced us that everybody's doin' it! From sex, to parties, to alcohol, to drugs – Spring Break has become a commemorative convergence of self-gratification.

I'm gonna call it like it is – we can't commingle in this type of sensationalized, hedonistic environment in any way, shape, or form! And we need to steer clear of these types of settings and find the *right* people and the *right* places instead. No one enjoys being left out of the get-togethers or missing out on the trips where friends appear to be having a good time. But let's not fall for the façade, guys. The countless posts, the smiling photos, and the spirited celebrations that portray ecstasy are a cover-up for an otherwise disappointing reality for so many! The truth is so many of those friends are being driven by discontent and insecurity to find something, *anything*, that will give them a temporary high.

Guys – let's be thankful we know the ultimate satisfaction, the satisfaction that is reliable *every* year, *every* season, *every* day of the week! 2 Corinthians 3:12 says, "Since this new way gives us such confidence, we can be very bold." Warriors – let's be bold in our new way of life! And let's be confident enough to go against the grain when God's Word urges us to do so!

Represent Jesus in the ridiculously frustrating moments.

Romans 12:12 "Rejoice in our confident hope. Be patient in trouble, and keep on praying."

It's easy to obey God's Word when everything is going our way. But what about those moments when we are clinching our fists because of how *livid* we are with someone or something? These moments might happen at school, they might happen at work, or they might happen suddenly and unexpectedly in the midst of our errands or while we're tackling our to-do lists. For me, it's usually on the phone with our Internet provider's customer service! But *wherever* they happen, these tests weed out the pretenders from the Warriors!

The last thing we want to do is pray when we're ticked off. We'd much rather punch a pillow or "vent" our anger by saying what we really think! Come on, guys, we are all familiar with these moments! Like when the cable company's customer service rep transfers us for the fifth time, or when we spend thirty minutes in the drive thru only to receive cold fries and a sandwich smothered in all of the wrong condiments, or when we find out that we've been incorrectly charged on our sewage bill but the company says they can't do anything about it, or when we are operating on three hours of sleep courtesy of a sick baby and ironically receive a phone call from a client telling us that they're displeased with our work.

We've all been there, guys. And it isn't coincidence that most of these painfully aggravating moments come when we're exhausted, hungry, overwhelmed, or stressed. That's because the enemy absolutely tailors his attacks for when we're at our most vulnerable. He knows that we're more likely to get impatient and snap on someone when we're already carrying the weight of other burdens! It's like shooting a wounded duck. Easy as pie.

But it's these insanely difficult moments when a Warrior becomes a Warrior, guys...the moments when it's literally impossible to obey without Jesus' supernatural strength. It's at that weakest moment when *nothing* is going right and we've reached our boiling point that we find out how "deep" our commitment is to Jesus. Warriors are unbreakable in the moments where 99% of the world justifies breaking. And unlike the majority of even so-called "Christians," we refuse to warrant a breaking point because *Jesus* didn't!

Guys – no matter how absurdly we have been inconvenienced, there is *never* a point in any situation where our temporary convenience should take precedent over our eternal testimony. Never. But do we actually have the discipline to remain calm and quiet when the rest of the world defends causing a scene? Are we able to maintain our composure and proceed slowly and softly instead of reacting quickly and harshly? Are we mature enough even in the midst of that nightmare scenario to take a deep breath, ask Jesus for supernatural patience, and proceed with unrelenting kindness?

It takes a rare Warrior to keep his teeth gritting from becoming a tongue lashing, because it sure isn't easy to nip our anger in the bud and give Jesus the reins in the heat of battle! But let's be the rare few that win these battles. Let's "be patient in trouble" and "keep on praying" like Romans 12:12 encourages us to do. And let's never allow Satan to use cable problems and cold fries to distract us from the eternity of the people we interact with in those annoying moments!

SUMMARY

+ A Warrior embraces his current place as a God-ordained platform for reaching the people around him both in school and at work.

+ A Warrior exhibits excellence in his work ethic – through effort, skill, drive, cleanliness, punctuality, and honesty – knowing that he is representing Jesus in everything he does in his school and workplace.

+ A Warrior serves the people around his school and workplace. Through prayer, selflessness, generosity, positivity, patience, forgiveness, appreciation, and respect for others, he lightens their load and sets the same example Jesus did by putting them first.

+ A Warrior uses secular popularity, power, and position for spiritual influence deflecting attention from his agenda to God's agenda and uses influence to demonstrate humility and service to others.

+ A Warrior works to live instead of living to work, and he disconnects from work when he is at home to invest in the relationships that matter most. He is defined by his testimony, not his title, and knows that a job defines what he does, but Jesus defines who he is.

+ A Warrior represents Jesus on the road. From commutes in the car to trips in another city, he knows that principles guide his decisions even when accountability seems absent.

+ A Warrior represents Jesus even in the ridiculously frustrating moments by disciplining himself to pray and remembering that his temporary convenience is secondary to his eternal testimony.

RESPONSE

God, remind me every day why You have me where You have me. I embrace my place right now, both at school and at work, as my divinely chosen battleground. And I ask right now that You would remind me daily that I'm in my specific place to do good works, which You prepared in advance for me to do. Let me exist to reach people!

Jesus, I want to represent You in all that I do. And even in my work habits, I want to obsessively pursue excellence because I might be the only representation of Your character that those around me ever see. Help me to work hard, to work with skill, to be driven, and to be clean and organized. And give me the discipline to be on time and to be honest as a student, an employee, and an employer.

God, give me the discipline and the desire to be a slave to others, because I exist to serve, not to be served. Let me be an obvious, shining example by praying for others around my class and office. Let my selflessness, generosity, positivity, patience, forgiveness, appreciation, and respect for others break down barriers so that relationships form and influence is enabled.

Lord, please don't let me be blinded or sidetracked by power and popularity or to compromise my principles to increase my influence. Any bit of added influence that You allow in my life is intended for Your agenda, not mine. God, use the spotlight to bring glory to Yourself, and let me deflect every bit of attention to Your goodness and the greatness of the cross of Jesus!

God, give me a balanced perspective of why I work and when I work. I don't exist for a job, and my job doesn't define who I am. Lord, don't ever let my title influence my testimony, but instead let my title be a vehicle to share my testimony! Jesus, give me the discipline to disconnect from work when I get home, and give me supernatural strength to invest my greatest effort into my relationship with You and my relationship with my family.

Protect me on the road from the temptations that I face while I'm in my car and out of town. Remind me during the moments where accountability feels far away that You are the only accountability that matters. And even if I'm the only one in the car or hotel room, You're still watching and wanting my attention and obedience.

God, when those frustrating moments arise in my daily routine, give me the discipline to pray and not react! Help me to remember that my character is more important than my convenience and that Satan simply wants to distract me from reaching the people that have inconvenienced me.

Make me a Warrior in my school and my workplace, because I might be the only extension of Jesus that my classmates and coworkers are exposed to on a daily basis. Jesus – let me represent You accurately and excellently!

CHAPTER 10

PHYSICAL HEALTH, INTERACTIVITY, AND INVOLVEMENT

Winning the spiritual war requires fighting for our physical health daily, interacting with other Christians regularly, and serving God's house consistently.

It's the elephant in the room that few men want to talk about. But we *need* to talk about it, so I'm gonna be *that* guy and go ahead and acknowledge the neglected pachyderm: physical fitness is a topic that isn't connected enough to spiritual fitness. You can thank me later. Or better yet, we can all thank God's Word for that mammoth introduction!

Sarcastic metaphors aside, we as men tend to dismiss our physical bodies as being irrelevant to our spiritual health when, in reality, the two cannot be torn apart. Whether we like it or not, our physical condition and spiritual condition go hand-in-hand. When *either* is neglected, the *other* will suffer. And it's time to stop sweeping this enormous issue under the rug!

We've bought into a dangerous lie, guys. We've adapted to a norm that God didn't intend. So many of us are unenergetic, unhealthy, unhappy, and unmotivated, and it is directly related the fact that our pace, exercise, and diet habits are grossly unbalanced! We've grown accustomed to physical lifestyles that are not alleviating, but rather causing, stress. And it's time to wake up and realize that our poor physical habits are *contributing* to our poor spiritual habits and vice versa! This vicious interdependent cycle is preventing us from living life to the fullest, because God intended that body and spirit work in harmony with one another.

Guys – there is a tangible supernatural satisfaction that comes from the Holy Spirit when we develop disciplines to nurture both our physical and spiritual health simultaneously! And there's just no way to explain the abundance that we experience when we are collectively conditioning both the physical and spiritual parts of our being. It's an indescribable contentment, and it's something that every one of us would prefer! But it comes at the price of pain and inconvenience! We revisit Hebrews 12:11, which describes both the price and the payoff saying, "No discipline is enjoyable while it is happening – it's painful! But afterward there will be a peaceful harvest of right living for those who are trained in this way."

Warriors – that "peaceful harvest" is our target destination *daily*. We fight through those "painful" moments to experience the peace of "right living." Discipline becomes the gateway to getting God's best and to being our best! And when we fight through discomfort to achieve balance in our physical habits – in our pace of life, exercise, and diet – we simultaneously cultivate restraint that fuels progress in our *spiritual* habits! It's in those physically unpleasant moments where we discover there are remarkable parallels between physical and spiritual disciplines.

We realize that the inconvenience we overcome by going for a late-night jog is the same inconvenience we overcome when we wake up 20 minutes early to pray, worship, and read the Word. We realize that the pain we endure while running up that monstrous hill is the same pain that we endure when we exit off of a website before we fall into sexual temptation. And we realize that the discipline it takes to say "no" to a double cheeseburger meal is the same discipline it takes to say "no" to flirting with the cute coworker.

There is an indisputable, symbiotic correlation between physical health and spiritual health and the disciplines that carry over from one to the other. But there is also an interconnectedness between physical health and spiritual *effectiveness!* And God knew this when He made us. That's why He clearly connects our physical bodies with our spiritual assignment in 1 Corinthians 6:19-20: "Honor God with [our bodies]" because [we] are "temple[s] of the Holy Spirit." God is urging us to protect our physical bodies because they serve a spiritual purpose! Our physical bodies are literal vehicles that carry His Spirit. The heart, muscles, bones, and skin – they are all tangible parts of the carrying mechanism of His presence. Now *that* is motivation to start caring about the food we eat and the exercise we get!

We are in dire need for more confrontation and accountability with our physical health because we're apathetically polluting the temples where the Holy Spirit Himself is hanging out. It's just *lazy!* Men – let's make a decision to be at our best physically so that God can use us most effectively. Let's stand united as pictures of physical health not ignorers of physical health. And let's be willing to go through some momentary pain to see just how peaceful the harvest can actually be! Worst case, we'll all reap the benefits of being more health-conscious. And there's not one of us who would refuse a boost in confidence, an increase in energy, and an improvement in how we feel.

God's ultimate goal is to make *us* our best so that we can give *others* our best. Satan's ultimate goal? It's to prevent us from ever getting there. But *please* hear this, guys – no matter *how* out of shape we are, *how* awful our habits have gotten, *how* old we are, or *how* apathetic we've become toward our physical health, we are *not* too far gone! That is a lie from the pit of hell! God is ready to renew our bodies and *shatter* our expectations! Jeremiah 30:17 is proof when God encourages us saying, "I will give you back your health and heal your wounds." We serve a God of restoration, and He wants to begin our transformations effective immediately! Let's get it going *today*, guys! Let's start taking practical steps to balance our pace, exercise routinely, and eat healthy so that we're at our most effective in our commitment to interact regularly with other Christians and serve God's house consistently.

Balance our pace.

Romans 12:1 "...Give your bodies to God because of all He has done for you...this is truly the way to worship Him."

We've all heard the saying "speed kills," but that phrase can be applied to more than just racetracks and football fields. The speed of our daily routine can kill both our spiritual *and* physical health if we aren't intentional about maintaining a balanced pace! It's entirely too easy to overcommit, overexert, and overextend our energies to the point where we have nothing left in the tank to invest in what actually matters. And for a lot of us, it's time to slow our pace and make a little room for both spiritual and physical nourishment.

Guys – why is it that we are involved in everything for everyone, yet we aren't making the time to take care of ourselves? From sun up to sun down, we are fixing lunches, attending meetings, coaching practices, cooking dinners, running errands, and prepping to do it all over again the next day. Except the *next* day, we start the routine even *more* exhausted and frustrated than the previous day. We are being run ragged because we're overcommitted and undernourished. But when are we going to make a change?

It's time to start taking Romans 12:1 seriously and remember that how we care for our physical bodies is an extension of our worship to God! Seriously guys – if "[giving our] bodies to God" is "truly the way to worship Him," then how are we doing in *that* area of worship? Yes – we might be well-intended by giving here, giving there, and giving everywhere. But we're ignoring the most important person of all – ourselves! It sounds selfish, but the truth is we can't nourish others if we aren't nourishing ourselves first! It's impossible to give *others* our best until *we* are at our best. And that begins with simplifying our schedules and making rest a top priority.

Simplify the schedule.

An unsustainable pace is always the by-product of a cluttered schedule. We have packed our schedules to the brim with too many activities, and it's a recipe for fatigue. We're drained because we're splitting our energy among too many outlets. And we're not reaping a worthwhile return on *any* of our investments because we're simply making too many of them.

Not only are we spreading ourselves thin with *too many* activities, but we're also filling our calendars with the wrong activities. Our busyness has become burdensome because it's a mere collection of eternally irrelevant efforts. We're pushing hard but seeing no relevant return on our investment, and this absent ROI is actually the underhanded culprit of our frustration. We're discontent because we're dedicating our energy to causes that aren't replenishing us spiritually. The bottom line is – we're not just suffering from too high a *quantity* of investments, but also from too low a *quality* of investments!

Warriors – it's time to get strategic with our schedules and begin trimming the fat off of our responsibilities. We will experience a new level of enthusiasm and efficiency when we consolidate our efforts in a unified direction with a meaningful purpose. It's critical to take control of the daily itinerary and set some boundaries in both our calendars and our families' calendars to utilize our spiritual assets most efficiently. It's time to take inventory on what's consuming our days and decide whether they are *allowing* us to sow seeds for eternity or *preventing* us from sowing seeds for eternity elsewhere.

But how do we do this? We start by reevaluating our responsibilities and restructuring our routines to minimize the number of activities that take from us physically but don't give back to us spiritually. Then we get better at saying the word "no" to frivolous engagements so we can progress more purposeful endeavors. We'll find out there are unparalleled freedom and refreshing that come from what we choose *not* to do!

Get enough rest.

Our spiritual enemy loves it when we are worn out, guys. Yes – he might find it extra enjoyable when we exhaust ourselves from meaningless pursuits. But let's not kid ourselves – he still celebrates when we exhaust ourselves on spiritual pursuits! To our opponent, exhaustion is exhaustion! And it matters not whether that fatigue is the result of flesh-driven efforts or spirit-driven efforts, because he knows we are most vulnerable when we're most exhausted.

Even Jesus knew the necessity of rest. In Mark 6:31, there He was with His disciples after an intense and demanding tour of ministry, and He demonstrates the importance of refreshing and refueling as He says to His disciples, "Let's go off by ourselves to a quiet place and rest awhile." I believe Jesus knew that without rest, His disciples' actions might become a contradiction to their words, and that His team's immunity to spiritual attacks was greatly dependent on adequate rest. Hey – if the disciples were anything like me, they were probably combative when they were tired! They probably had shorter fuses when they were tired! And they probably even struggled with keeping a positive perspective when they were tired!

A state of sustained tiredness is *such* a dangerous place for us to be, because it is nearly impossible to win the spiritual war without ample rest! The truth is when we're tired, we let our flesh call the shots. Rest protects us from that eternal negligence! And while prayer, worship, and the Word are our greatest *supernatural* defense against temptation, rest is our greatest *natural* defense against temptation. Guys – if we care most about our legacy as men of God, we'll see rest as a pivotal protector and preserver of right living. We'll be strategic, even *tactical*, about eliminating our tiredness so that conditions are most favorable for success in the spiritual war. But it all starts with planning.

Make sleep a top priority.

For me, being tired equates to feeling miserable, precisely the reason why a systematic approach to guarding sleep time is a necessity. And this starts with deliberate planning. Preparing early in the evening for the next day's activities is the first step to defending our sleep habits, because the earlier we're prepared for the following day, the earlier we're able to get in bed. Simple to understand but difficult to execute. Reality is, this requires the bags to be packed, lunches to be made, and clothes to be picked out for the day. And this is no easy task, especially when it involves children!

Declining late-night outings is another essential to developing healthy sleep patterns, especially for single guys and college guys. It's not easy to turn down an invite to do something fun with friends. But sometimes a "no" is necessary to prevent a lackluster performance at work, a below-average score on an exam, or a negative attitude toward the boss. These specific disciplines might seem nitpicky, but they're completely relevant to keeping our physical and spiritual bodies in optimal condition. And whatever it is that's costing us sleep, it's time to *do* something about it and begin treating sleep as an indispensable investment into our spiritual success. It will pay huge dividends!

Get to bed earlier and get up earlier.

It is no coincidence that many successful people in the world are early risers. We're talking bigwig CEOs, athletes, coaches, and presidents – most of them get out of bed incredibly early. From the outset, they have denied their bodies the luxury of calling the shots, taken control, and gotten a head start on focusing their priorities for the day. But realistically, rising early in the morning means getting to bed earlier the night before. And that's all about intentionality and planning in advance!

Warriors – we could all benefit from more restful nights and more productive mornings. The discipline to make these happen is yet another appendage of a self-controlled, spirit-accommodating lifestyle. We see it in

Mark 1:35 (NIV) where it says, "Very early in the morning, while it was still dark, Jesus got up, left the house and went off to a solitary place, where He prayed." Here is our Savior as a man intentionally getting up before it was light outside to focus His attention on what was most important. Yes – it was inconvenient for Jesus' flesh to get up at the crack of dawn just like it is for our flesh, but because Jesus knew His purpose was to be close to His Heavenly Father, He planned accordingly to make it happen. His preparation was proof of His priority!

Enjoy a Sabbath every week.

Enjoying a Sabbath each week is another crucial component to triumph in the spiritual war. And whether we are able to detect it or not, our bodies absolutely need that one day each and every week to just stop and rest. Exodus 20:9-10 tells us, "[We] have six days each week for [our] ordinary work, but the seventh day is a Sabbath day of rest dedicated to the Lord your God." A day of rejuvenation and reflection was so important to God that even *He* participated on the seventh day of this universe's existence! No, God didn't *need* rest. He wasn't tired from creating humanity. He didn't need a nap because He was in a bad mood after speaking the planets into orbit. He was doing a demo for us! The immortal Creator was giving us a tutorial on how to properly care for His mortal creation!

Working hard seven days a week seems more efficient than working six and resting one, but that's the paramount principle of Sabbath. God will bless the six more when we honor Him with the one! And it's a guarantee – we will be more productive in six days than we could have ever been in seven because His supernatural favor is fueling the six (see Ecclesiastes 10:10)! We can't fathom the importance of filling up our tanks and recalibrating our direction on a weekly basis!

Warriors – let's lead our families by taking them to worship Jesus with a community of believers! And afterward, let's have conversations with our spouses and children about how great God is, and utilize the free time to reestablish perspective and reinforce purpose within our families! Let's set aside time to discuss specific things that we're grateful for and reflect on the cross of Jesus and its magnitude. And let's treat our Sabbath Day as a weekly celebration of God's provision by doing something we enjoy.

God has *commanded* us to be lazy for 52 days a year and simply reflect on His goodness, so why wouldn't we take advantage of this immortal mandate to relax? That's like opting out of paid vacation days at work! It's a win-win scenario when Biblical obedience entails a sofa and some shuteye!

Plan occasional vacations.

Vacations are vital in recharging our batteries, guys. And while it's lazy to make vacationing a habitual lifestyle, it's *essential* to make vacationing an occasional priority. Taking a couple of days away from our normal surroundings and predictable routines to enjoy time with family or friends breaks the stress cycle and revives a healthier perspective on the blessings of life. And sometimes a view of the ocean and nothing but sand and sun in our periphery is the key to unlocking an accurate perspective on the trivial things that have been overwhelming us at home. Every now and then, we need to *force* ourselves to take a step back from the canvas and see how beautiful our picture really is! It doesn't have to be some extravagant, expensive, or exclusive destination, but let's set aside some funds to retreat and reenergize a couple of times a year if we can swing it!

Exercise routinely.

1 Corinthians 9:27 "I discipline my body like an athlete, training it to do what it should."

A sustainable pace is just the first piece of the puzzle when it comes to conditioning our bodies for maximum performance. Another monumental component to our physical and spiritual health is routine exercise – an area where we've become inexcusably lazy buying into this notion that physical activity is a non-essential of Christian manhood. We're comfortable! And we don't want anything or anyone to invade our space or disrupt our comfort! We have grown accustomed to stagnancy and have bought into the lie that fitness is an *interest*, not a *discipline*...that if we aren't "passionate" about fitness, or we don't "enjoy" physical activity, then we're exempt from participating! The result? Utter idleness. Plain and simple, there are too many of us doing no physical activity whatsoever on a daily basis, and it's handicapping us both physically and spiritually. From physical ailments to spiritual apathy, sedentary lifestyles are minimizing our impact and undermining our purpose!

It's time to make 1 Corinthians 9:27 a reality as we "discipline [our bodies]" by "training [them] to do what [they] should!" Hey, Warriors – we get one body each. One! And it's our single opportunity to demonstrate to other men just how valuable the carrying mechanism for the Holy Spirit really is! Besides, we're more energized when we're physically active. We're more motivated when we're physically active. We're more relaxed when we're physically active. We're more pleasant to be around when we're physically active. The list of lifestyle benefits is endless! But we can't experience this dramatic difference until we actually get off our tails and do something!

Do the best we can with the situation we're in.

Before discussing the specifics of improving our exercise habits, it's worth mentioning that every suggestion might not apply to every man. Some of us might be medically unable to participate because of circumstances that have handicapped our bodies. And these unique limitations each of us face should absolutely be considered before moving forward with physical activity. Look – not everyone can go out and implement drastic changes due to unfortunate impairments, and that's okay!

Having said that, no matter *what* our situation is – let's all go into this with an optimistic mindset! Let's approach this in a way that says, "I'm going to find *something* that I can do to improve my body" instead of sulking in self-pity and having a "woe is me" attitude! Hey, guys – if 16-year-old Iowan Kayla Wheeler, with no legs and one arm, can become a world champion Paralympic swimmer in high school, then most of us should be able to do *something!* I mean, if a young lady with one limb can find a way to not only be active, but *excel* physically, then what's our excuse? She didn't let her dynamic disability become an enabler for self-empathy and physical neglect, but instead she used it as a motivator to persevere!

Warriors – it's time to stop playing the "victim" card and straight up do the best we can with the situation we're in! The world has enough wimpy men who complain about their lot in life. When there's a glass that the world labels as 99% empty, true Warriors see a glass that is still 1% full!

Do something challenging for 15 minutes at least 4 days a week.

Taking care of our bodies through exercise doesn't mean we are prepping to be on the cover of a men's fitness magazine, but it *does* mean that we are putting forth effort to make workouts a priority. And contrary to fitness cynics, it only takes 15 minutes to complete even the most challenging workouts. We are talking 15 minutes, guys – something that is doable for every one of us! Let's take some initiative and make these 15 minutes a non-negotiable, rain-or-shine discipline at least four days a week. That's an hour a week of physical activity. And I'm telling you, men – if we'll give enough effort during those 60 minutes, we'll be blown away at how they can transform both our minds and bodies. This isn't difficult, guys. It's effort-grade stuff! So let's commit to doing something physically challenging for 15 minutes, four days a week, and see what happens! It's time for a lot of us to go do something we haven't intentionally done in a long time – break a sweat!

Start with a practical, practicable challenge.

So if we're going to allot 15 minutes, four days a week, to condition our physical bodies, then what are some practical steps we can take to improve our fitness? Most would suggest finding some sport or outdoor activity that we love doing, joining a fitness community, or hiring a personal trainer. The problem? These are not practical or implementable for all of us with regards to time and money. So what *is* a sustainable exercise routine for all of us? Well, there are three physical activities that can be executed anywhere, anytime, by almost anyone: running, push-ups, and sit-ups. They require *no* extra purchases, *no* travel time, and *no* membership. And I've personally *never* been in better physical shape than a season in which my regimen consisted *solely* of these three exercises! I didn't touch a weight or visit a gym. I simply *ran*, did *push-ups* and *sit-ups*, and then developed discipline to push my limits using only these three tools several times a week.

Run a mile.

For those looking for a place to begin, let's start with running one mile. It doesn't have to be a fast mile or meet a certain pace. Let's simply *run* one mile. And let's *finish* that one mile! *One* single mile, guys. And hey – if that one mile consists of jogging for 30 seconds, walking for 30 seconds, and then repeating that sequence, then let's do it! Or if we want to sprint for 20 seconds and then jog for a couple of minutes, then let's *do* it! It doesn't really matter *how* we do it; it just matters *that* we do it. Yes, that first attempt may be exhaustingly miserable, but it *will* get easier if we can just finish it! Let's honor Jesus with a little effort and like 1 Corinthians 9:26 tells us, let's "run with purpose in every step."

We'll find that the ensuing physiological impact of activating those God-given chemicals called endorphins is palpable and that few things are more rewarding than the moments *after* getting our heart rates up and pushing our cardiovascular limits. Real talk – I run not because I enjoy running. In fact, I don't like running at all! I run because I enjoy the *results* of running! Just give it a try and initiate some unwanted resistance. You'll find that the decompression and relaxation after some strenuous cardio brings unrivaled freshness and unimaginable clarity!

Do some push-ups and sit-ups.

Another practical step we can take is to supplement our running with push-ups and sit-ups. The crazy thing is push-ups and sit-ups alone can completely *transform* our bodies if we actually do them. Don't believe it? Just look up college football legend and renowned athlete Herschel Walker for living proof of how bodyweight exercises alone are enough to build even an athletic specimen! It's just a matter of actually *doing* the exercises.

So here's a practical challenge: let's do 100 push-ups and 100 sit-ups throughout the course of a day (and if regular push-ups are too difficult, then try them with your knees on the ground). This might mean doing five sets of 20 push-ups and sit-ups all at once. Or it might mean knocking out 50 reps of each in the morning, 25 more at lunch, and the last 25 in the evening. It doesn't matter *when* they happen or *how many* of them happen during each set as long as the 100 reps of each are completed. Whatever works for *your* routine is perfect. As for my routine, it involves push-ups and sit-ups on alternating days, and it's extremely effective!

Start with 100 reps a day. Then, if a total of 100 becomes too easy, let's bump it up to 150 reps of each. Then 200, 300, 400, 500, 1,000 or even 1,500! It sounds insane, but Herschel Walker does it! In all seriousness, let's *push* ourselves to get stronger each day! I mean, we're talking 30 seconds to one minute per set, so in all it might take five to ten minutes to complete a seriously practical, noticeably profitable workout!

This combination of running, push-ups, and sit-ups is about as practical as it gets because it can be accomplished by almost *any* man at *any* point in his life. It's feasible and it's versatile with no prerequisites attached. However, this isn't the be-all and end-all of workouts. And as the saying goes, "there's more than one way to skin a cat." Some guys might rather break a sweat and get the heart rate up by playing basketball, or swimming laps, or competing in ultimate Frisbee. But whatever the activity is, let's be intentional about *challenging* our bodies. Let's push them to a place where they are tired, sweaty, and even sore! It's through the discomfort that we develop both physical and spiritual discipline.

Celebrate discomfort and develop toughness.

Our perspective of pain is an integral part of physical and spiritual victory. Unfortunately, most of us view pain as this *dreaded* sensation, avoiding it at all costs. But we recall Hebrews 12:11 again, which *celebrates* pain as the price of progress, reminding us, "No discipline is enjoyable while it is happening – it's *painful!*"

Warriors – discipline stinks while it's happening, but we don't focus on the discomfort during, we focus on the advantages after! We willfully shift our perspective from the present pain to the future fruit! Let's be real – *no one* enjoys the pain during the process of getting and staying healthy. No one. And anyone who says they love pain is really saying they love the *results* that come from pain. That's exactly where the Bible tells us to fix our eyes – on the "afterward."

Men – we've got to get better at resisting and recovering, pushing forward through the present pain knowing that soon we will be able to pull back and enjoy the future fruit! We need to put Hebrews 12:12 into action and "take a new grip with [our] tired hands and strengthen [our] weak knees" pushing past that weak voice in our head saying "this hurts," or "I can't make it up that hill," or "I can't do 10 more push-ups!" Resist. Recover. Repeat.

Let's approach this with backwards thinking. Let's attempt a physical activity that we would usually avoid because of the challenge it poses, and let's reach a level of physical exertion that makes us uncomfortable! And let's push the envelope a little on what we can endure physically. Warriors choose the path of most resistance in training so that it's a breeze on the battlefield!

Too many of us stop the first moment we feel anything remotely unpleasant. Even our *definition* of pain is hilariously off-kilter. But whether we realize it or not, we have a whole lot more left in our reserve tank than we think. This mentality is what makes the Navy SEALS *the* toughest individuals in the world! These guys undergo the most brutal, unbearable training to prepare for battle, and they develop an exceptional grit to withstand the most gruesome mental and physical strain. And one of their secrets for uncommon toughness? The "40% rule," which basically says that when our minds are telling us we're done, we're only 40% done! That means we haven't even utilized *half* our potential at the moment we think we're incapable of continuing!

No, we may not be Navy SEALS, but every one of us is capable of doing far more than we believe we can do! Warriors – we need to start audibly telling ourselves in the middle of that run or workout that we stand on Philippians 4:13 and that we can do "everything through Christ, who gives [us] strength!" We need to keep moving when we are drenched in sweat, out of energy, struggling for air, and hurting in every muscle! Because guys – pushing through those oppressive moments when we can feel our heartbeats in our heads is where a Warrior is made! And enduring that discomfort several times a week is how we tame our flesh into complete submission!

Be careful.

Being tough doesn't mean being ignorant. And this call to physical action isn't a call to be stupid. If we've lived a completely sedentary lifestyle for years or decades, it would be *idiotic* to go and try to run sprints outside in 100-degree sweltering heat! A more sensible approach might be getting in a controlled environment with a personal trainer or medical expert to monitor heart rate and other variables. The bottom line is – let's not dare jump into physical activity without using common sense! Developing toughness doesn't mean we just abandon wisdom, so let's pay attention to the red flags that our bodies are giving us. Ignoring excruciating pain, medical conditions, or alarming symptoms isn't what this is about at all! Taking it super slow and easing into an active lifestyle is certainly the approach to take as we begin the journey to physical health.

Be persistent and consistent.

Consistency is always a Warrior's aim, and consistency is what sets us apart from the majority. It's easy to be physically active for a day, a week, a month, or even a year. In fact, almost every one of us achieves this at some point during our lives. We get that "fever" to get in shape for a season, or we find some short-lived inspiration to drive us toward improving our health for a brief stint. But it takes a resolutely unwavering determination to maintain a long-term habit of physical activity.

Achieving consistency in our exercise habits means being dead set on getting that workout in, especially when our routine has been thrown off by tragedies, transitions, holidays, vacations, and other inconveniences that life throws at us. Those times when exercise takes a back seat are typically the times when it needs to be in the driver's seat! When we're on that vacation at the beach for a week eating horribly, it would benefit us immensely to be getting 15 minutes of a physical challenge each day. Or when that family member dies and we're dealing with serious emotional exhaustion amidst the schedule shuffling, it would alleviate our stress by moving around for a bit.

Consistency means doing *something* regardless of the season or circumstance, but consistency also means not doing *too much!* Maintaining a long-term exercise habit requires *balance* in our frequency and intensity, and for a rare few of us, we're overdoing it. We're working out too much, working out too hard, and we're *punishing* our bodies with unsustainable, high-impact activities. It might be time to adjust our aim toward longevity so that years and decades down the road we're not suffering the consequences of pushing too intensely.

Quit making excuses.

If we want to evade physical activity, we can. In fact, there are enough employable excuses to write a novel if we want to go that route. Schedules, seasons, babies, families, feelings, weather, age – the list of reasons to *not* be physically active is endless. Proverbs 22:13 demonstrates the never-ceasing nature of our excuses saying, "The lazy person claims, 'There's a lion out there! If I go outside, I might be killed!'" Not only are our excuses *abundant*, they're also oftentimes *absurd!*

Can we just *stop* with the same ol', worn-out complaints, guys? We aren't going to be killed by a lion if we go outside for a run! It takes a real man to just shut up and go *do* something! Warriors don't abstain from exercise due to inconvenience; we adjust accordingly to keep exercise an immovable priority! Guys – our priorities should constantly reorder our activities, but activities should *never* reorder our priorities! This means we develop flexibility and adaptability through the ever-changing, ever-evolving conditions. We figure out a way to make physical activity happen during relaxing times and during chaotic times.

Counteract dietary mistakes with exercise.

Poor dietary decisions can kill our exercise routines. We're talking total termination. And chances are, we've all finished that unhealthy meal or series of meals that left us dreading the thought of getting up and doing anything physically challenging. That's why it is crucial to *quickly* follow up questionable meal choices with intentional exercise challenges. We *will* have bad days where we regret eating that greasy fast food meal or that piece of pie. But hear this, guys: it's how we follow those days up that matters most!

Men – there has to be a system of checks and balances with our diet and exercise. If we are going to enjoy a delicious meal, then we are going to take responsibility for that meal by working it off! And if our meal was really bad, our follow-up run needs to be really hard. Indulgence absolutely needs inconvenience as a governor.

Surround ourselves with men who challenge us to get better.

We become like the friends we are around, guys. And if we want to do better with our exercise habits, we need to associate with men who challenge us to push harder, endure longer, and stretch further. It's time to stop backing down from challenges that make us momentarily uncomfortable, and instead *seek out* men who issue those challenges! We need to be around men who can whip our tails athletically and press us physically, because those are the men who not only motivate us to achieve excellence, but also administer the inconvenient accountability to ensure we get there!

Honor God with our daily hygiene.

Like it or not, our daily hygiene is an extension of our testimony. It is just another opportunity to honor God with our bodies like 1 Corinthians 6:20 urges us to do. It might seem trivial to some, but all throughout the Bible we see references to cleanliness and personal hygiene. In John 13:10, Jesus ties physical cleanliness and bathing into His teachings of spiritual cleanliness. In Matthew 6:17, we see face washing connected to looking kempt. Then in Ruth 3:3, we see Naomi encourage her daughter-in-law Ruth to "take a bath and put on perfume and dress in [her] nicest clothes" to make an impression. And if those references aren't enough, we revisit 1 Peter 1:15 that simply says, "Be holy in *everything*...just as God who chose [us] is holy." Being holy means we are "set apart" in all that we do, guys. Let's not misrepresent Jesus with apathy and a flippant approach to our appearance, but instead be intent on presenting the best version of us possible. We never know when impressing someone physically might actually increase our chances to impact him or her spiritually!

Declare God's authority over sickness.

It's hard to care about our physical health when sickness, cancer, disease, and other ailments are standing in the way. These sometimes devastating obstacles not only handicap us physically, but they can also leave us powerless and confused both mentally and spiritually. But even though we may *never* understand the "why" of ominous medical circumstances, Warriors still declare the "Who" over them. We shove our flesh's frustrations aside, and we voice our faith in a God who can heal us in an instant! Warriors believe the truth even when we don't *feel* like believing the truth. And the truth is God is *the* preeminent power who controls everything, and He can heal whomever, whenever, and however He wants! Both big and small, God can cure any ailment that He sees fit. And while doctors and medicine are sometimes the conduits for healing, the promise in the hands of Jesus is far greater than the promise in the hands of medical experts!

Even when we've prayed ad nauseam and that second report from the doctor comes back even worse than the first, let's be the men who stand on 1 Peter 2:24 and declare that, "*By Jesus' wounds* we are healed!" Even after that grim diagnosis from top "experts" in the field, we pour the powerful blood of Jesus on those circumstances knowing that just one drop can create a medical miracle! And whether or not we experience physical healing in our earthly bodies, let's remember that 2 Corinthians 5 promises us that we will all have perfectly-restored eternal bodies the moment we leave this Earth! It sure is comforting to know that our earthly bodies are only "tents" we will leave to inhabit our "eternal [bodies] made by God Himself!"

Eat healthy.

1 Corinthians 10:31 "So whether you eat or drink...do it all for the glory of God."

A balanced pace and routine exercise alone will bring dramatic improvement to our physical health. But if we want a *complete* transformation, it involves paying attention to a third, equally important component – healthy eating! Guys – tightening the reins on our diet and being purposeful about the food and drink we consume is a biggie! And just like exercise, diet affects our mood, our energy, our confidence, our mobility, our productivity. The resulting consequences of our eating are *directly* connected to our spiritual effectiveness. It's time to get serious about applying 1 Corinthians 10:31, because "whether [we] eat or drink," we are called to "do it all for the glory of God!"

Eat to live. Don't live to eat.

I may be a skinny guy, but I know exactly what it feels like to live for the next meal. I've idolized food with the best of the best, even holding off on eating throughout the day just so I could indulge more in the experience of that big meal at night! Most of us can identify with this kind of scenario where we looked to food and drink to respond to emotions, medicate boredom, or relish an experience! It's essentially using food for satisfaction instead of using it for sustenance! And while there's absolutely nothing wrong with enjoying food, we've got to be careful that it doesn't become our motivation for existence. This is a legitimate issue with some of us. We live to eat instead of eating to live, and our days ebb, flow, climax, and decline based merely on the food we consume. The result? We've become accustomed to ingesting junk that our bodies can barely digest, and we've adapted to a culture where asinine, over-the-top, Americanized portions are expected. It's no surprise that so many of us are overweight, out-of-shape, depressed, tired, frustrated, and apathetic. Dietary wisdom and moderation have long been abandoned!

Men – we've got to wake up! A lot of us are not only going to die early physical deaths, but much more importantly, squash our spiritual influence if we don't fight against the gluttonous habits that have become a part of our norm! Warriors – we weren't put on this planet to eat; we were put here to do God's business! And it's time to realign our dietary habits to enhance our spiritual efficiency, not our physical enjoyment. Let's make this declaration: "I'm not here to eat. I'm here to impact."

Eat enough.

Junk food and overeating might be the most pervasive struggles we as men have when it comes to our diet, but under-eating cripples a contingency as well. No – it might not involve the majority, but there are still many men who fight against anorexia or bulimia on a daily basis, and it can be a devastating struggle when Satan deceives us into having an inaccurate and insecure view of ourselves! The enemy knows that. That's why he usually targets vanity as the vehicle to convince us that we're not good enough and that our aesthetic appeal is dependent on the amount of food we consume!

Indeed, malnourishment is a symptom of a much deeper issue. Anorexia and bulimia are conditions rooted more in spiritual sickness than physical, mental, or even emotional sickness! They are a result of letting an artful adversary skew our view of self and persuade us to starve our bodies to meet a worldly standard. It's a disgusting distraction from God's Truth, and that truth is embedded in Psalm 139:14 saying that we are "wonderfully complex" and God's "marvelous workmanship!"

Warriors – when the Holy Spirit opens our eyes to the fact that the ultimate Artist uniquely, intentionally, and skillfully crafted each one of us with the bodies that we have, it changes our perspective on how we care for them. The second we realize that we are the *only one* like us in the Artist's collection, preserved as dynamic masterpieces, we'll take scrupulous care of our physical bodies! And that means disciplining ourselves to eat the right foods and the right amounts. Let's not vandalize God's work of art just because we momentarily don't recognize its value! *No one* alters a masterpiece!

Make some practical changes.

The first thing God ever gave to man was food, and that's confirmation right there that it is a gift from God that He intended for us to enjoy (see Genesis 1:29). But enjoyment becomes excess when we are not cognizant of moderation of both quality and quantity in our food choices. We know that being our best spiritually requires being our best physically, but being our best *physically* begins with the dozens of daily dietary decisions we make. Every choice alters the complexion of our spiritual potency! And with every culinary choice we make, it yields yet another set of emotions that cannot only alter our attitudes, but can also dictate our *next* dietary decisions! It's an unstoppable cycle that either gains positive momentum from healthy choices or negative momentum from unhealthy choices. Let's start building some positive momentum, one minuscule choice at a time! Over time, we're going to be blown away by the dramatic results.

Take a daily multivitamin.

One simple, beneficial daily habit that every one of us can do is to simply take a men's multivitamin. Seriously. It might sound hilarious to some, but why wouldn't we take three seconds every day to go ahead and give our bodies a substantial dose of the nutrients and vitamins that they need? It's a no-brainer. Let's go spend a few dollars, get a couple months' worth of a multivitamin from the grocery store, and start taking one every day. It can't hurt!

Aim for 1800 - 2200 calories a day.

One approach to a healthier diet is simply watching the number of calories we consume. I know most men aren't "calorie counters," but plain and simple, there has got to be some kind of awareness in this arena. Yes, the quality of our food is crucial, but so is the quantity! And when we stay between the 1800 - 2200-calorie range, we'll experience firsthand that it is not only plenty of calories for survival, but also the perfect safeguard from both over-indulgence and starvation. And while some athletes and blue-collar workers need more than this amount, it's an ideal median for men of most ages and professions.

Eliminate something unhealthy for a month.
Most of us could use some correcting in the *quality* of products we're consuming as well. And one extremely effective way to cleanse our physical bodies and see improvements in our medical examinations is to simply *eliminate* something unwholesome from our diet. It might be fried foods. It might be sugar. It might be fast food. It might be desserts. Whatever the case – we all have something that we love eating or drinking that we just couldn't imagine doing without. More times than not, those dependencies are the culprits of our poor health. So if we want to take it up a notch with an even more multi-faceted challenge, let's combine this dietary omission with the 1800 - 2200 calorie total. We'll realize that a multi-level, coordinated strategy delivers eye-opening transformations.

Choose the healthier options.
For most men, the notion of substituting our entire menu for organic alternatives is just ludicrous. And while taking a holistic approach to our diet is admirable in theory, it's just *not* realistic in the context of our everyday lives. What *is* feasible is taking some of the items that we eat on a daily basis and choosing their healthiest versions instead.

The two simplest examples are bread and peanut butter. White bread is not necessarily unhealthy for us, but whole wheat bread is the healthier option. Our bodies take longer to process the complex carbs in whole wheat bread, causing us to feel full and satisfied longer. The end result? We eat less. And what about *natural* peanut butter? Because it doesn't contain added sugars and artificial fats, our digestive systems can break it down more efficiently than its more popular counterpart on the shelves.

We can apply this principle of going with the healthier alternative at the restaurant as well. Getting chips instead of fries, water instead of sweet tea, and grilled chicken instead of fried. Let's pay attention to the choices we are making and just try to do a little better, decision by decision! Each choice might not *seem* like a big deal in its own right, but combine enough peanut butter sandwiches over the course of a year and we'll find that it allowed us to maintain our weight instead of gaining ten pounds.

Drink only water.

It wouldn't hurt for us to get smarter about what we're drinking, too! And it is life-changing to eliminate all liquids except water from our diet. Various studies have shown that the average person drinks around 400 calories in a day, which totals up to nearly 3,000 calories a week! It's baffling to think that just by drinking water instead of the soft drinks, sweet teas, coffees, and fruit drinks, we will eliminate nearly 3,000 calories from our weekly caloric intake! Not to mention, water also assists in suppressing our appetites and purifying our systems. Now personally, I'm not a huge fan of plain water, but I've found that mixing it up with a zero-calorie flavor packet makes it more desirable. And after switching to this "water-only" drinking habit, my energy level increased in an obvious way. Now, I don't know about anyone else, but when I'm more energized, I'm more pleasant to be around!

Replace one meal a day with a low-calorie, high-protein option.

In the same way that drinking water instead of all the other liquids can tally up impressive calorie savings, so can replacing one meal a day with a low-calorie, protein-rich alternative. There are plenty of quick, practical options – from shakes, to smoothies, to snack bars – and while it might not be our most delicious meal of the day, a high-protein breakfast or lunch in the 250-calorie range will not only keep us energized, but it will leave some margin for error during our other meals. Besides, our bodies could use some portion control and a break from the typical 1000-plus calorie meals! Let's be okay with eating occasionally for sustenance, not satisfaction.

Fast for a day or for a meal.

Hands down, the best way to tame our appetites is to abstain from eating for a period of time. Whether it's an entire day or just one meal, fasting is the preeminent test of developing self-control and tolerance for the discomfort that accompanies denying our flesh what it desires! It's that discipline of becoming comfortable in our spirit with being uncomfortable in our flesh. We're not going to die from missing a meal or even a day's worth of calories, guys! Most of us could go *weeks* without eating and be just fine, so a brief reprieve from eating would be more beneficial for our health than it would be dangerous! Let's embrace this challenge and get a gauge on our self-discipline. If we can't prayerfully reject our cravings for food for a few hours, then how are we going to survive the intense spiritual attacks on our sexual purity, our marriages, our families, and our careers for decades?

Take lunch to work.

Another no-nonsense, easily implementable step for us is to take lunch to work instead of settling for the convenient option in the food court, the shopping center, or the restaurant down the street. Yes, it may break up the workday nicely to go with colleagues or friends to grab a bite to eat somewhere, but this can be costly in more than one way when we're too lazy to plan in advance! Financially speaking, spending $10 every day on lunch will put a dent in our bank accounts. But physically speaking, scarfing down that heavy midday meal on a daily basis will put a dent in our health! Let's start saving some money in our wallets and adding some years to our lives by bringing leftovers from home or simply preparing a sandwich, some soup, or some snacks from the pantry instead!

Stop eating out.

Convenience is king when it comes to our food choices, and it's usually to blame for our physical neglect. The proof is in the number of meals that we eat outside of our homes! We're too busy to prepare home cooked meals so we settle for the easy option to save time and effort. And it's completely understandable, especially when the chaotic dynamic of children is a part of the mix! But if we want a challenge that will yield immediate health benefits, it is to just stop eating out and do whatever it takes to figure out some simple meals to start cooking at home. Yes, it might take an hour to fix spaghetti, make some sub sandwiches, or grill some vegetables or chicken, but it's worth the small inconvenience to stay healthier and develop a healthier dietary culture in our families. Let's limit the frequency of meals around restaurant tables and plan ahead to create more meals around kitchen tables!

Plan ahead. Prepare ahead.

Smart eating begins with smart planning. But smart planning begins with smart *shopping!* The most pivotal battle we face in our diet is in the pre-battle preparation! The aisles of the grocery store are where we win the fight for healthy eating, and that checkout line is where we make the investment into who we are going to be tomorrow!

Go to the grocery store.

We can predetermine a better us tomorrow by shopping smart today. But the first step is to actually *go* to the grocery store! This is painstakingly elementary in theory, but if we don't have a full pantry of food, we *will* settle for eating out! Yes, it might be inconvenient to spend a couple of hours scouring the aisles in the supermarket, but it's the safeguard we need to keep us out of the drive-thru lines. We absolutely must have healthier go-to meals and snacks in our pantries, or we will assuredly end up hopping in the car and driving around until we find something to satisfy our hunger. Guaranteed.

Grocery shopping not only deters us from eating out; it also motivates us to eat in. Warriors – when we spend our hard-earned money on something, we'll want to justify our investment by putting it to use. Food is no exception. No one wants to spend $400 in the grocery store and then watch it go to waste, all while spending another $400 eating at restaurants! Grocery shopping is that inconvenient, self-instituted boundary that adds incentive to make the right choices. Let's start breaking the cycle of convenience-led eating by equipping our homes with options that *keep* us at home! It will pay dividends on our bodies *and* our wallets!

Get the right items.

Getting groceries is an admirable first step, but if we want results, it's all about getting the *right* groceries when we go shopping. That grocery run is our opportunity to intentionally invest in healthy options instead of racking up on comfort foods. It's a business trip, and those shelves are where we mandate that our *bodies* come first, not our appetites.

Reality is we all gravitate toward convenience in our daily decisions, and convenience is largely rooted in proximity. So we need to make sure the proximal option is a healthy option! When we have that craving before bed, we need the most accessible answer to be a can of peanuts or almonds instead of three different types of chocolate cookies! We need to look in our refrigerators and find water and yogurt instead of soft drinks and candy bars. Let's pay attention at the store so that we're adequately prepared to deal with the chaos and cravings of daily life in a healthy manner.

Celebrate discomfort and develop discipline.

It's a recurring theme, but the idea of celebrating discomfort applies as much, if not more, to our diet than it does to any other fleshly craving. Guys – it's extremely uncomfortable for our flesh when we deny giving it what it wants, especially the first few times. But practice makes perfect, and it gets easier with every piece of strawberry cake we refuse from mom and every buttery biscuit we decline at the breakfast buffet!

We can enjoy food, but we need to learn when and how to cut it off. Let's hang in there and withstand the pressure to "eat some more" because the end result will be a self-controlled Warrior whose spirit calls the dietary shots. Proverbs 25:28 says, "A person without self-control is like a city with broken-down walls." What a precise picture of us when we don't care about our dietary habits! We are vulnerable to every intruder, every flesh-led whim that attempts to advance into our jurisdiction! And eventually we will raise the white flag if we can't show some mental toughness with our appetites!

Adjust our diet accordingly if we miss days of exercise.

We've discussed the necessity of counteracting dietary mistakes with extra exercise, but the principle of maintaining equilibrium can also be applied to days when we miss exercise. If we know we aren't going to get any exercise for the next day or two, we absolutely need to compensate by eating less food and eating healthier food! It's important for us to look at each individual day as its own test to maintain balance between calories in and calories out. That involves making tweaks based on every day's unique schedule to ensure the scales stay steady! If there are days when we can't pardon our calories on the pavement, let's make the adjustments on our plates. Or if we've got several consecutive days when there's just no way in the world we can exercise, let's be adamant to counterbalance our diet. It will not only help us feel better during those days, but will also prevent scale shock after those days!

Set measurable, short-term goals and get daily accountability for long-term success.

Dramatic physical change doesn't come overnight, guys. And long-term goals can become daunting if we don't set achievable, measurable short-term goals.

Some of us might aspire to accomplish the unthinkable over time, but those long-term dreams are contingent on short-term goals and daily accountability. Maybe it's losing 50 pounds in the next 6 months. Maybe it's running a marathon next year. Maybe it's competing in a triathlon in the next two years. Whatever that long-term dream is or how radical it may be, it is totally attainable, guys. That's a fact. I've personally witnessed a friend accomplish the unimaginable, losing 108 pounds in one year and cutting his mile time in more than half from 15 minutes to seven minutes!

Guys – that 108-pound weight loss and eye-opening physical transformation happened to Drew Wright because of intentionality! Intentionality to spend time with Jesus. Intentionality to set the 4:30 a.m. alarm to run before work. Intentionality to stock his pantry with the right foods and deplete it of the wrong ones. Intentionality to prepare his meals in advance to avoid being pigeonholed into eating the convenient, unhealthy option. And it was intentionality to set measurable, achievable, short-term goals and to tell someone the metrics of his weight loss, body fat percentage, caloric intake, running distance, and pace *every day* that kept Drew focused on the final destination! Ultimately it was the two- and three-pound victories along the way that fueled the fire to cross the finish line, and it was the accountability that squashed any notion of quitting before the finish line! I know because I *was* his accountability!

Warriors – if no one knows about our efforts to do something difficult, we will quietly quit the very moment it becomes uncomfortable or inconvenient. That's just human nature. So whatever that extraordinary 108-pound dream may be, let's engage that annoying accountability to ask us every day how we're progressing! And let's set the 4- and 5-pound ordinary milestones to propel us to reach our extraordinary destination!

Combat cravings with prayer, worship, and the Word.

No matter *how* motivated we are to do better in our diet, we are going to have moments where the cravings are unbearable. But just like our struggles with any other appetite of the flesh, we must fight it with prayer, worship, and the Word. It might sound hilarious, but the answer to resisting that cheese pizza and a molten lava cake is in an immediate declaration that we need Jesus' supernatural power! And the answer to denying that craving for a cigarette is as simple as turning on worship music and feeding our spirit instead of feeding our flesh! Sure, we can try self-help books, therapy sessions, rehab facilities, recovery programs...but *nothing...NOTHING* is more effective and trustworthy than the power that comes through Jesus' name when we call on it! We are reminded in Philippians 2:9 that God gave Jesus the "name above all other names," and that the name of *every* struggle we face will bow down! Other tactics may help temporarily, but only one solution will permanently empower us to do what we can't do ourselves, and that's when we utter the name of Jesus in the middle of that overwhelming moment of temptation!

Starve dependencies.

In our product-obsessed society, it's a nonstop fight to keep dependencies from becoming realities. Whether it's soft drinks, sweets, fried foods, beer, liquor, nicotine, caffeine, over-the-counter pain medication, or drugs, we are programmed to look on the shelf or in the cabinet to convert our needs to actualities. And if we're not careful, that reach into the pantry, refrigerator, or medicine drawer can become a second-nature addiction where our flesh just expects routine consumption.

The question is – do we have something, anything, that we consume regularly that has become an inseparable staple? It might not even necessarily be a "sinful" habit, but if our bodies can't do without that cup of coffee, that ibuprofen, that glass of wine, or that energy drink, then maybe it's time for us to cut it off for a while just to rid ourselves of *any* dependency aside from the Holy Spirit! Jesus demonstrated this principle in Luke 4:2, where we see how He fasted 40 days without *any* sustenance for His physical body except God's supernatural power. Jesus exemplified the minimalist mindset that we need to adapt as Warriors: how little can we depend on anything outside of Jesus? Let's always be men who ask, "How little do we need?" instead of "How much can we have?"

Don't get distracted by alcohol.

The "A" word. It's sad how much division and dissension come from mentioning the word "alcohol" among Christians and non-Christians alike. What's even sadder is how combative so many of us get if someone dares to introduce the idea of staying away from it. We're protective of our bottle, guys. And when it comes to accountability regarding alcohol, we get quickly offended and highly sensitive, two surefire signs that something might just be an idol. Could it be that we are dependent on using alcohol as a substitute for the Holy Spirit? I mean, aren't we essentially trying to mimic the contentment and relaxation that the Holy Spirit brings by pulling out that whiskey drink or that case of beer? In many cases, it's obvious that we employ alcohol to do a job that only the Holy Spirit can do – bring peace!

Ephesians 5:18 actually addresses this issue saying, "Don't be drunk with wine, because that will ruin your life. Instead, be filled with the Holy Spirit." Now our tendency is to key in on the *first* half of this verse interpreting it as a mere rule or legality from God or some ambiguous Biblical measuring stick for intoxication. And that's precisely how the enemy wants us to interpret it. He wants us more focused on the controversial metric of what is and isn't "drunk" instead of looking at the principle of the verse as a whole. He wants us more focused on the technicality of the behavior rather than the condition of the heart. Warriors – I believe the point of this passage isn't to provide debatable fodder to fuel our discussions on how much alcohol we can consume without breaking the rules. It is *so* much bigger than that. Ephesians 5:18 isn't about legality; it's about priority! God is essentially saying, "Hey, guys – quit getting distracted with the world and trying to find a substitute for me, because it will end up messing you up! Just come experience me instead." That's the Lance Ingram Version (LIV) translation!

Kidding aside, we need to adjust our perspective on alcohol, guys. I totally get the cultural comfort and community that it brings, but what benefit does alcohol provide in advancing God's agenda? Real talk – when was the last time that a six-pack of tall boys assisted us in leading another person into a relationship with Jesus Christ? Maybe I'm missing something, but the only spiritual side effects I've seen that are synonymous with Christians and alcohol tend to involve damaged testimonies and dysfunctional families. So why even bother, guys?

This isn't even about whether alcohol is spiritually permissible. This is about whether alcohol is spiritually beneficial. 1 Corinthians 10:23 (NLV) sums it up perfectly: "We are allowed to do anything, but not everything is good for us to do. We are allowed to do anything, but not all things help us grow strong as Christians." It begs the question – how is alcohol helping us "grow strong as

Christians" and reach other people? Maybe our perspective on alcohol needs to be less focused on defending our freedom and more focused on helping others discover theirs! Let's not get distracted by culture and what's permissible, men! Instead, let's get near Jesus and ask Him what's beneficial! The stakes are too high to be selfishly focused on our freedoms.

Interact with other Christians regularly.

Hebrews 10:25 "And let us not neglect our meeting together, as some people do, but encourage one another, especially now that the day of His return is drawing near."

The ultimate goal of physical health isn't physical health; it is spiritual impact! And a balanced pace, routine exercise, and healthy eating – they are simply stepping stones to becoming our most physically efficient so we can emerge on the battlefield being our most spiritually effective. We sharpen ourselves so we can then sharpen others. Warriors get active so we can get interactive!

Interaction with other Christians is not only a reason to *be* our sharpest; it's also a necessity to *remain* our sharpest! Our spiritual effectiveness is contingent upon our connectivity. It doesn't matter how strong we are individually or how much we desire to be like Jesus...we will get destroyed by a cunning, calculated enemy if we try to fight the battle alone! 1 Peter 5:8 reminds us that the enemy is "prowl[ing] around like a roaring lion" patiently waiting for the moment when we get separated from the herd so he can devour us.

Translation? The enemy is waiting on us to be too lazy to commit to a church. He's waiting on us to put the lake house first on Sundays. He's waiting on us to let the weather dictate our decision on church attendance. He's waiting on us to accumulate so many extracurricular activities that we stop meeting with our accountability group. Men – Satan is waiting on us to get apathetic in the fight to be close to God and the fight to be close to other believers! And when we do, he attacks. And if you've ever seen a lion at the zoo around feeding time, it's not a pretty sight for the prey!

The enemy is extraordinarily intelligent, and he'll use anything, even pleasures, to isolate us from other Christians! He knows that once we're away from the worship, the accountability, the encouragement, and the unity with other Warriors, we're literally helpless! Isolation leads to annihilation. And we avoid annihilation by sticking close to the pack through every season. Just how it takes intentional effort to be physically active, it takes intentional effort to be spiritually interactive! Warriors – it's time to stop with the laziness, man up, and commit to a church and a small group of men who will have our backs. God's Word underlines the importance of remaining interactive with other Christians in Hebrews 10:25 urging us to "not neglect our meeting together." Now it's time to put this into practice!

Be at church every week.

If the notion of being committed to a church evokes feelings of frustration, exhaustion, annoyance, or inconvenience, then we haven't experienced church the way God intended it. When we read the description of Psalm 150 and the energy and excitement that accompany Biblical worship in God's house, it's perplexing to comprehend how church has evolved into the somber, ritualistic experience to which so many of us are accustomed. Tambourines, dancing, strings, and loud clashing cymbals...that describes the atmosphere of a rock concert or a prime-time sporting event, not some lamentable memorial service! God deserves reverence, but He doesn't desire staleness!

If a church community is truly passionate about Jesus, there will be a genuine eagerness and an unbridled enthusiasm in how we celebrate the Man who died in our place! We need weekly experiences that look like a Super Bowl, not a funeral! We need a place defined by authentic joy and genuine transparency. We need a place where we feel more accepted when we've messed up than when we've got it all together. And we need a place where we're challenged, not comfortable!

Warriors – it's time to lead our families by committing to a Bible-believing, Jesus-worshipping, people-loving church. No matter what age or season of life we're in, it's time to set the example that church is a non-negotiable priority in our schedules. Week in, week out, Warriors are there, visibly and vocally leading our generation with our presence, prayer, and worship!

Commit to a small group of Christian men.

We can't possibly survive without each other, guys, When we've had a rough week, we need someone to guard us in prayer. When we've made a regretful decision, we need someone to give us a gut check and then pick us up off the ground. When we've experienced a victory, we need someone to celebrate with us. We must have other Warriors that know the good, the bad, the pretty, the ugly, the embarrassing, the exciting...every bit of it! Because even the wisest, most seasoned Warriors need other men of God fighting beside them. It only takes *one* weak moment during that lazy season when we've disconnected from our pack for the enemy to destroy a decades-long testimony!

Men – when we don't physically get off our tails and commit to a small group, it opens the door to devastation in every area of our lives. So let's get active and *stay* interactive! Even when we aren't fired up about sacrificing those two hours on a Tuesday night, those two hours always leave us refreshed and refocused! We may arrive lethargically, but we inevitably leave energetically! It's proof, as Pastor Chris Hodges says, that "life change happens in the context of relationships!"

Serve God's house consistently.

James 2:17 "In the same way, faith by itself, if it is not accompanied by action, is dead." (NIV)

We can claim all day that we love Jesus and want to make an impact for Him, but words are worth nothing if we don't back them up with action! That's what God's Word says, in James 2:17 (NIV), that faith is "dead" if it doesn't result in "action!" Men – God is looking for Warriors to go and *do* something for His purpose! It's time to get off the sidelines, get on the front lines, and deploy our earthly lives to rescue others' eternal lives! That rescue mission is the essence of our existence. It's why God created us, and it's why God created us *uniquely!* 1 Peter 4:10 says, "God has given each of [us] a gift from His great variety of spiritual gifts" so that we can "use them well to serve one another!" We are armed with dynamic skills to render a dynamic service!

It could be leading a men's Bible study. It could be assisting widowed women around the community. It could be mentoring young men in a student ministry. There's an endless list of talents that God can provide from His "great variety" of gifts, but all of them require us to get up, get involved, and get busy! And it's a guarantee – the moment we start utilizing that gifting for God's purpose is the moment we discover our purpose. It's the instant when internal peace is perfected, because serving God satisfies our soul! And when we expend our unique, God-engineered talents to push people to the peace that is found in Jesus, the search for contentment concludes.

Men – it doesn't really matter what it is as long as we are giving our energies to do something good in someone else's life while attaching it to the saving name of Jesus. True love for Jesus simply means we'll "feed [His] sheep" as He told Peter directly in John 21:17! That's who we are, guys – we are leaders, and we are feeders! Let's get busy *today!*

CONCLUSION

Leave a legacy.

Life is *so* short, guys. James 4:14 tells us that our lives are like a "morning fog – [they're] here a little while, then [they're] gone!" Yet we're dillydallying around chasing one selfish agenda to the next like we've got plenty of time to kill! Meanwhile, whether we see it or not, we're losing in a violent spiritual war to a frighteningly opportunistic opponent! Men – this *entire* study has been about specific, simple, practical steps that will help us turn the tables against the enemy to win this war, but shame on us if it all culminates with mere education! This will have all been a monumental waste of time if that proves to be the case. Because education is worthless without execution!

Knowing and doing are light years apart from one another. James 1:22 sums it up perfectly: "But don't just *listen* to God's word. You must *do* what it says. Otherwise, you are only fooling yourselves." Men – head knowledge is useless without application! So the question then becomes "when?" When are we going to do something about it? When are we going to buy in completely to God's way? When are we going to give our unrelenting effort to fight in every area? I mean, how many more cleverly packaged quotes do we need to hear about God's Word before we start actually *living* it out?

The truth is – we're *all* looking to be known for *something*, so why not be known for being obsessed with living exactly how Jesus did! When people think of us, why wouldn't we want their first thought to be, "*Goodness gracious*, they sure are serious about fighting to please Jesus!" Now *that* is a worthwhile calling card! And I don't know about anyone else, but *that* is the kind of calling card I want! I want to leave a footprint on this Earth that simply guided people to Jesus' footprint! That is true legacy!

Legacy isn't rooted in how much people remember us when we are gone. Legacy is rooted in how much people remember *Jesus* when we are gone! And if we want people to remember Jesus when they think of us, it takes a heck of a lot of consistency and longevity. Guys – any of us can live for Jesus for a day, a season, a year, or even a few years. But who's ready to go fight to be near Jesus for the rest of our lives? Who's ready to fight for obedience day after day, year after year, decade after decade?

Warriors – we need less flash and more follow through. And we need our encounters with God to culminate with our execution of God's plan! Yes, those goose bumps in the worship service may be sensational, but they've got to translate into Godly behavior out in the real world! The hype on the mountaintop is great, but the substance of a Warrior is proven by the obedience in the valley.

Perfection, both on the mountaintops *and* in the valleys, is our quintessential pursuit. As Matthew 5:48 says, "[We] are to be perfect, even as [our] Father in Heaven is perfect!" But how in the world do we achieve perfection? The answer is – by staying close to the One who is perfect! Because guys – perfection might be an impossibility for us, but it is an inevitability for Jesus! And if we will just remain empty of everything but Jesus, we will become perfect because only perfection is in us! 2 Corinthians 12:9 says it best: we can "boast about [our] weaknesses, so that the power of Christ can work through [us]!"

Jesus – be *so* solely present *in* us that *You* live a perfect life *through* us! And let *Your* power work through us to turn our weakness into greatness! Make us careful. Make us intentional. Make us tough. Make us fighters. God – make us Warriors.

SUMMARY

+ A Warrior understands that his physical health is interconnected with his spiritual health, and that physical fitness begins with a balanced pace. By simplifying his schedule, getting enough rest, prioritizing sleep, enjoying a weekly Sabbath, and planning occasional vacations, a Warrior sets the foundation for sustainable spiritual success.

+ A Warrior exercises routinely developing disciplines that maximize his health both physically and spiritually. Through practical exercises like running, sit-ups, and push-ups, a Warrior conditions his body to be its most effective and influential in the spiritual war.

+ A Warrior is self-controlled with what and how much he eats and drinks knowing that what he consumes can greatly impact his mood, his mobility, and his motivation. By planning ahead and starving dependencies, a Warrior sets himself up for dietary success and spiritual success by taming the cravings of his flesh.

+ A Warrior is connected to other Christians on a regular basis because without consistent interaction, he is susceptible to the attacks of the enemy. A Warrior is not only at a vibrant, Jesus-centric church every week leading and learning, but he's also committed to a small group where other Warriors are keeping him focused and holding him accountable.

+ A Warrior puts his faith into action by serving God's house consistently, utilizing his uniquely God-given abilities to guide others to the peace of knowing Jesus.

+ A Warrior is obsessed with leaving a legacy that reminds people not of himself, but of Jesus. Through obedience marked by consistency and longevity, a Warrior wins the spiritual war by meticulously aligning his daily habits with the Word of God.

RESPONSE

God, I'm tired of being lazy. And ironically, I'm exhausted from being lazy. My physical and spiritual laziness are rendering me useless for Your purpose, and I'm ready to change that, one practical step at a time.

Holy Spirit, allow me to see the connection between my physical health and my spiritual health, and give me a supernatural urgency to get my physical body in better condition for Your purpose. It all starts with balancing my pace and allowing my body to rest and recharge for the daily spiritual battles I face.

Lord, motivate me to be more intentional in my exercise and dietary habits carefully considering how they affect the health of the only body You gave me. Give me discipline as I condition my body to excellence, and let me develop physical toughness that translates to spiritual toughness.

Jesus, I need a supernatural catalyst to push me to be more active spiritually as well. Don't let me be a spectator on the sidelines. Instead, let me be a participator on the battlefield. Show me that energized, excited church where You want me to be involved, and empower me to lead there every week. Provide more Warriors around me who desire to do things Your way, Jesus. And never allow me to isolate myself, because that's the moment when I get devoured by an enemy who is waiting on an opportunity to rip me to pieces.

Jesus, I need You. I need You to be in my heart, in my mind, and in my body. I need You to go before me in everything that I do, and watch behind me in everything that I do. Don't dare allow me to live a life that served no eternal purpose! Instead, let my legacy be eclipsed by You living in me. God, make me an authentic Warrior and let my life be remembered for fighting wholeheartedly every day to be close to Your Son and to be like Your Son.

AUTHOR

ACKNOWLEDGMENTS

This wouldn't have been possible without the support of so many.

There are far too many people to acknowledge for their encouragement, prayer, and support, but I owe a special thanks to:

Brooke: You're my favorite person in the world. There's no way God could have provided me with a more supportive wife, and Crew and Oakland with a more sacrificial mother. You were my rock through every up and down of writing this book, and you assured me that you were willing to do whatever it took to help me finish it. Thank you for being my biggest fan and for praying me through the whole journey. You're basically the co-author, and I owe you more than I can put in writing. I love you.

Crew and Oakland: One day I hope you'll read this book and connect the dots between what your daddy wrote and how your daddy lived. I wrote this for you, buddies. Always remember this: *the* only thing that matters in this life is whether we live it for Jesus.

Burr Ingram: Your example inspired this book. You are a true Warrior, and it is an honor to be your son. Thank you for showing Rob, Mack, and me how to live a steady, consistent, Jesus-centered life decade after decade. Well done.

Jan Ingram: You are the definition of joy, generosity, and sacrifice. Rob, Mack, and I don't take for granted how you encourage us every day to "shine for Jesus." Love you, mama.

Rob Ingram: I've got the best big brother. Thank you for having my back in prayer and pushing me past the tough days with your sincere encouragement. I could always count on a wise word to keep me focused on Jesus when I wanted to quit. Not to mention, incredible job on capturing the poignant cover photo.

Mack Ingram: I've also got the best little brother (or younger, I guess). I can't tell you how much I counted on you every day to propel me forward with your joyful attitude and passion for this project. Thank you for praying for me and injecting Biblical sunshine into every challenging day.

Drew Wright: You are the best of friends. It was your spiritual and physical change that confirmed to me this project might actually help someone. Thank you for not letting me give up...hundreds of times.

Rick Burgess: You believed in this project before anyone else did, and I don't know if I owe anyone more than you for bringing this to reality. Thank you for using your platform to pave the way for so many men to advance the Gospel, and for letting me share your airwaves during the college football season.

Chris Hodges: Not sure what to say except "thank you." As I've told you many times, you just look like Jesus, and your decision to come to Birmingham and plant Church of the Highlands has been life-altering for the Ingram family. We love you and Mrs. Tammy. Thank y'all for leading us to the cross of Jesus and for believing in me and this project. So much of its DNA is a reflection of your teaching and your example.

Kristi and Gus Malzahn: I'm so grateful for your immediate support and enthusiasm upon hearing about this project. You two are my heroes. War Eagle.

Karol Hobbs: You are the best. I can't communicate how grateful I am for your assistance in turning my vision into a reality.

Justin Bradshaw: You might not know it, but our conversation around a peanut-butter-covered table sparked the initial vision for this project. I appreciate your leadership and the way you and Sommer have poured into Brooke and me.

Kristie Garner: You're the best editor ever. This book may have never become a reality without the patience and resilience of a wordsmith like you.

"Remember, boys...shine for Jesus."
- Jan Ingram